ALSO BY JOHN BIERMAN
RIGHTEOUS GENTILE:
*The Story of Raoul Wallenberg, Missing Hero of
the Holocaust*

Odyssey

John Bierman

SIMON AND SCHUSTER   New York

1 3 5 7 9 10 8 6 4 2
LIBRARY OF CONGRESS CATALOGING IN PUBLICATION DATA

BIERMAN, JOHN.
ODYSSEY
1. WORLD WAR, 1939-1945—JEWS.   2. REFUGEES, JEWISH—
ITALY.   I. TITLE.
D810.J4B485   1984   940.53′15′03924   84-13868

ISBN: 0-671-50156-9

FOR HILARY

Naught is more wretched in a humane Race
Than Countrie's want and shift from place
to place.

(*The Odyssey*, Chapman's Homer, Book XV)

Prologue

The Ides of March brought winter back to Prague. With it came fifteen divisions of the Wehrmacht.

There was no resistance. To make sure of a bloodless victory, and to indulge his taste for bullying, Hitler and his cronies had browbeaten the timorous Czech head of state, Emil Hacha, into signing his own country's death warrant.

Brandishing pen and surrender document, Goering and Ribbentrop had literally pursued the hapless Hacha around a conference table at the Chancellery in Berlin until Hacha fainted and Goering bellowed for Hitler's personal physician to revive him with a hypodermic injection.

The sinister farce continued when Hacha came to, until at last—after another injection and repeated threats by Goering to bomb Prague to rubble—the Czech President could resist no longer. His signature on a declaration that placed "the destiny of the Czech people and country with confidence in the hands of the Fuhrer of the German Reich" provided a denouement remarkable even by the brutal norms of Hitlerian diplomacy.

Two hours after Hacha's surrender, the field-gray tide of invasion began to roll across the Bohemian Plain toward Prague, impeded by nothing more formidable than unseasonal snow flurries, driven by a fierce east wind. At five-minute intervals a radio warning went out to the bewildered Czech Army and people in the name of Hacha and his Defense Minister: ". . . The advance must not be resisted. The slightest resistance will bring grave consequences. . . . All commands must obey the order. . . ."

The Czechs, stripped of their morale and their formidable border defenses six months before by the Anglo-French betrayal at Munich, glumly obeyed orders. Not a shot was fired; not a bridge was blown.

At 9:15 that morning, March 15, 1939, the vanguard of the Nazi motorized columns reached the square in front of Hradschin Castle, the ancient seat of Bohemian kings which looks down onto the spires and rooftops of Central Europe's loveliest capital.

While gunners trained their field pieces on the snow-shrouded city below, closed German army trucks carried squads of Gestapo officers to police headquarters to take over security. By midafternoon, Prague was completely occupied and the secret police, armed with lists of potential subversives and other undesirables, were already at work. Some of those who had good reason to believe they would be on the Gestapo lists—mainly Jews who had fled the Nazis once before, from Germany or Austria—preempted arrest by committing suicide.

Though Sudeten Germans and other pro-Nazis waved paper swastikas and cheered as the Wehrmacht rolled along the main traffic arteries to the heart of the city, the great mass of Czechs mourned.

Men and women wept openly in the streets as their twenty-year-old model democracy, built on the ruins of the Hapsburg Empire, was crushed under the boots and tank treads of Hitler's legions. Here and there, onlookers shouted defiance, sang the national anthem, threw snowballs at a German armored vehicle. The conquerors did not respond; they had orders to show restraint should a few locals let off steam—as long as they did so harmlessly.

That evening Hitler himself arrived and, while his personal standard was hoisted over the castle, installed himself in triumph in the apartment that for seventeen years had been occupied by the founder-President of the republic, the late and deeply lamented Tomas Masaryk.

The next day the Fuhrer proclaimed a Nazi "protectorate" over Bohemia and Moravia, the Czech heartland. Slovakia, the other main component of the defunct state, had already declared itself, at Hitler's urging, to be an independent republic under German tutelage. The eastern province of Ruthenia was occupied by the forces of Hitler's ally-to-be, the Hungarian dictator Admiral Horthy. The destruction of Czechoslovakia was complete.

On March 17, when the Nazis permitted the resumption of civilian traffic between their new protectorate and neighboring areas, Zoltan Schalk took the first train to Prague from Bratislava, the Slovak capital. It was a risky undertaking, for security on both sides of the new frontier was intense and Schalk was—by any criteria the SS or its Slovak equivalent, the Hlinka Guard, might apply—an undesirable element.

But Schalk was also a man of experience and resource, of cunning and guile, a man with an impressive talent for getting himself into inaccessible places and unlikely situations and out again unscathed. So when it became clear that someone would have to go to Prague immediately to retrieve a batch of irreplaceable documents before they fell into Nazi hands, he had been the obvious choice to undertake the mission.

It wasn't that Schalk himself—or anyone who knew him—would ever have cast him in the role of selfless hero; but even his detractors had to admit that in addition to being an extremely effective operative, he appeared to be genuinely committed to the work he had been engaged in for the past two years as a member of a semiclandestine organization smuggling Jews out of Nazi-dominated Europe and into British-ruled Palestine.

It was a vocation that so far had fed his taste for picaresque adventure and given him a sense of mission without exposing him to too much danger. He had felt comfortably at home in the ambience of intrigue that prevailed amid the potted palms and faded kitsch of Bucharest's Grand Hotel Lafayette, where the network had its headquarters. His hunger for travel had been appeased by his constant crisscrossing of the Continent, from Prague to Constanza, on the network's subterranean business. And for intrigue of a different kind, there had been women enough on his travels who were drawn to Schalk's dark, faintly sinister good looks, silky, well-tailored style and carefully underplayed air of mystery.

At different times, Schalk's vocation might find him smuggling hard currency—perhaps the most serious of the offenses he was called upon to commit in the service of the cause—dodging the political police of half a dozen nations, blackmailing, coercing or bribing bureaucrats, haggling with venal middlemen or sweating out sale and charter deals with voracious shipowners. He did it all with verve and style.

Secret codes, elaborate deceptions, ludicrous disguises and outrageous bluffs were all part of the repertoire as Schalk and his colleagues pitted sharp wits but slender finances against rapacious middlemen and hostile or at best indifferent bureaucracies, and against the British, who were using all diplomatic and other means to stop the traffic in illegal—or, as the network preferred to say, "free"—immigration.

But for Schalk, so far, membership in the network had not involved anything quite as dangerous as crossing swords with the Gestapo.

Now, as he prepared to enter the lion's den that was Nazi-occupied Prague, he felt the rough edge of a new reality. This time it wasn't the gentlemanly British intelligence or some ramshackle Balkan secret-police organization he would be taking on. This time he was likely to run head on into Himmler's people.

He got his first sight of them when half a dozen SS men—

death's-heads on their hats and double lightning flashes on their lapels—clattered onto the train at Malacky to inspect the passengers before allowing them to cross the frontier between the new Slovak Republic and the Nazi Protectorate of Bohemia and Moravia.

Up to that point the trip had been easy enough. True, there had been Hlinka Guards at the station in Bratislava— rawboned peasant youths in crude, ill-fitting uniforms, the slovenly bullyboys of the ultranationalist Slovak People's Party. But they had been easily awed by his confident manner and his *laissez-passer*—a letter stamped with the seal and signature of a senior police officer, confirming him as a person authorized to leave the territory of the newborn republic and to return at will. Schalk had good friends in Bratislava police headquarters.

It had not been necessary to produce his other safe-conduct document, a letter signed by a friendly official of the Skoda automobile-manufacturing firm, saying he was on his way to Prague on business in connection with his appointment as the Skoda agent in the Slovakian capital. Schalk had good contacts in Bratislava business circles too.

Seated in a first-class carriage, Schalk had sat immersed in the Sudeten German daily *Die Volkstimme* until the train pulled out, appearing to be complacently absorbed in the good news of the Nazi take-over. Now, with the train halted for inspection at Malacky, he made sure that the paper lay at his side, blaring headlines in full view, as two SS men entered the otherwise empty carriage. True to the spirit of his role as a patriotic *Volksdeutscher,* happy to be reunited with his ethnic brothers and free at last from the rule of the despised Slavs, Schalk got to his feet and gave them an enthusiastic raised-arm salute.

"*Heil Hitler!* My, it's good to see you fellows."

"*Heil Hitler.* Your papers, please."

The response was coldly dismissive. The SS did not feel obliged to exchange pleasantries with every provincial zealot who fawned on them.

Schalk produced his passport and the two letters. The SS sergeant took them in with a swift yet intense scrutiny, the eyes cold and gray as his native Baltic, eyes which he then turned on Schalk himself.

Legend had it that the SS were trained to sniff out Jews, like police dogs smelling for drugs or explosives, their senses finely attuned to the nuance of feature, the subtlety of inflection that would betray "racial impurity," however well concealed. Of course, Schalk knew it was pernicious nonsense, an idea encouraged by the Nazis to enhance their omnipotent image and obligingly disseminated by their intended victims. Yet the legend had a terrible, undermining potency, and although there was nothing in his travel documents or his appearance to betray his origins, Schalk felt the sweat of dread and the suffocation of fear as the SS sergeant questioned him skillfully, those Baltic eyes flicking from Schalk's to the documents and back again.

Did he sense the chill damp in the palms of Schalk's hands and the backs of his knees, the constriction in the throat, the trip-hammering inside the rib cage? It began to seem to Schalk that he must, that layer by layer his cover was being stripped away so that soon he would be revealed in all his Semitic vulnerability before this relentless examining angel.

But suddenly, the ordeal was over. Apparently satisfied, the SS sergeant grunted curtly, gave a perfunctory *"Heil Hitler"* and motioned to his subordinate to move on to the next carriage. The legend was just that, after all, a legend—a malevolent fairy tale to frighten guilty children—and the SS sergeant just some unsophisticated farm boy from East Prussia. Schalk lit a cigarette to steady himself and resumed his seat.

Twice more between the frontier and Prague, at Kuty and Breclav, the SS came aboard to make similar checks. Twice more Schalk played the loyal pro-Nazi, rejoicing in the presence of his liberators. Twice more he produced his papers, underwent the scorching scrutiny of the demigods in black and mercifully passed it.

On arrival at Prague's Masaryk Station, Schalk caught a streetcar to a stop on the border between the commercial district and the old Jewish quarter on the east bank of the Vltava River. His destination was a hastily abandoned office in an apartment block on Benediksa Street where he guessed the documents he had come for had been left—probably inside the safe—when its occupants fled from the Nazis.

Schalk was not a religious man, but he muttered a little prayer that he might get there ahead of the Gestapo, who would certainly have put a search of those premises high on their list of priorities. Worse, they might be keeping the place under surveillance or even be inside when he arrived, and how would an honest Slovak *Folksdeutscher*, supposedly on business for the Skoda car company, explain his presence there?

Snow flurries swirled about the streetcar as it clanked through half-deserted streets draped with huge red-and-black swastika flags. The passengers sat in silence, carefully avoiding each other's eyes and the fear and humiliation they knew they would see there.

As Schalk walked the six blocks to his destination from the nearest streetcar stop, through streets turning slushy as the unseasonal snow began to melt, he felt uneasily, if irrationally, conspicuous. At the same time, he was conscious of the cold and damp in his feet and cursed himself for having forgotten to bring overshoes. German soldiers stood on street corners in pairs, hunched up against the driving sleet, but none showed any interest in Schalk as he walked past, head down and collar up.

He reached Benediksa without incident and walked twice past Number 2, looking for parked cars or a light in the second-floor window that might indicate the presence of the Gestapo, while scanning the street furtively for sight of a watcher concealed, maybe, in a vehicle or a basement doorway. On the third pass, he took a deep breath, as though for a plunge into icy water, ran up the six steps to the heavy front door, found it unlocked and entered the dingy hallway.

Smells of cooking and tomcats haunted the stairwell as Schalk, avoiding the noisy elevator, walked up to the second floor. The nameplate, *Aliyabüro,* had been removed from the front door of the office, but there was no sign of a forced entry as Schalk unlocked the door and let himself in.

So far, so good. It seemed the Gestapo had not been there yet. The open filing cabinets and papers strewn about the floor were just as likely to be evidence of a hurried exit as of a Nazi search. A mound of ash in the open grate showed where documents had been burned. The Gestapo would have taken documents away, not destroyed them.

Without switching on the office lights, for these might betray his presence to a passerby outside, Schalk hurried over to the wall safe and began to dial the combination code he had been given in case of just such an emergency. Schalk wondered how much warning his colleagues in Prague had got of the Nazis' coming and whether they had been able to get clear in time. If so, they would be on their way to Bucharest; if not, well . . . best not to think of that right now.

Inside the safe, Schalk found what he had come for. Stacked neatly at the back were the passports of 280 young Slovakian Jews, sent to Prague to be stamped with Paraguayan visas by a bribable consul. The visas, of course, were a blind; they would never have been issued had there been the slightest chance they would actually be used. It was simply that the passport holders had to have an "end destination" before the Slovak authorities would allow them to leave the country. Their real end destination—once a ship had been acquired to take them there in secrecy—was Palestine, for which no visas were obtainable.

Schalk opened the valise he had brought with him, removed the clean shirt and change of underwear and the Skoda brochures and price lists he carried as part of his cover, and put the passports inside.

Then, having replaced the clothes, brochures and lists to cover the passports, he let himself out into the slushy streets of the occupied city.

1

From the time Schalk brought their passports back from Prague, Alexander Citron and his people in Bratislava had to wait another fourteen months for their ship.

In that time, the Nazis crushed Poland, devoured Norway and Denmark, and overran the Netherlands and Belgium. Now, in the second week of May 1940, they were poised to deliver the sword thrust that would send the British fleeing across the Channel from Dunkirk and end the life of the French Third Republic.

By any rational calculation, then, it would seem far too late for escape from Hitler's Europe. But Citron was not a man to be deterred by rational calculation. Notified of the vessel's approach, he hustled from his office, crossed Republikplatz and clipped eagerly along Donaugasse before turning down toward the waterfront to watch it arrive.

His first glimpse of the vessel as it sidled up to its berth at quayside, its paddles churning the dirty gray Danube into a frenzy of foaming scum, was scarcely reassuring. He had, of course, been warned not to expect a Cunarder, but this was something not so much beneath as beyond expectation—a truly ludicrous object, even to Citron's landlubberly eye.

"A caricature of a submarine,' he muttered to himself, somewhere between awe and dismay.

The raddled old sidewheeler couldn't have been much to look at even in its prime and had never been intended to carry human cargo. Now, with its original proportions all but overbalanced by a crude wooden superstructure, hurriedly hammered on to provide passenger accommodation, the ship looked as unsafe as it was ungainly, and far too small for the 400-odd people—100 more than the modifications had speci-fied—who would have to be crammed aboard.

Still, it would have to do; there was no other ship avail-able. And the passengers would embark willingly enough, Citron knew, anxious to get away and expecting to spend no more than ten days or so aboard this unlikely vessel—just long enough to reach the mouth of the Danube, where, they had been told, a regular seagoing ship would be waiting to take them the rest of the way.

Only Citron and a handful of others close to the heart of the operation were aware that in reality there would be no seagoing ship standing by and that the decrepit sidewheeler—which scarcely looked fit to navigate the more difficult stretches of the river, let alone venture out to sea—would have to take them all the way, through the Black Sea, the Aegean and the eastern Mediterranean to their destination: a secret night rendezvous off the coast of Palestine.

The chances of its sinking in the attempt, Citron was forced to concede as he observed the vessel, might be as high as 50–50. Still, though chastened, he was not deterred. *Chutz-pah*—sheer effrontery—is a quality much cherished by the Jews, and there was so much of it implied in the very notion of going to sea in this derelict old tub that somehow, Citron told himself, the good fortune that attended on daring would see them through.

As the vessel drew closer, Citron noticed for the first time the name *Pentcho* newly painted on the arch over the flailing starboard paddle wheel and allowed himself a grunt of annoyance. Only the sight of Zoltan Schalk up on deck alongside the wheelhouse persuaded him that he hadn't met the wrong ship by mistake.

He had been expecting a vessel named the *Stefano,* and dammit, the name had been changed without his having been told. Indeed, he had sent out a circular, only a few days before, to all the prospective passengers notifying them that the *Stefano* was expected soon. How like Schalk, he thought peevishly, to keep even that minor but necessary item of information to himself, as if nobody else could be trusted with it.

As Citron watched the *Pentcho* complete its berthing maneuver, a sudden gust of wind caught the crude superstructure, driving the vessel into the quay with a sudden hollow thump of rubber on concrete as its port-side fenders absorbed the blow. From inside the cabin, just aft of the single tall smokestack, Citron heard a strangled curse in an unknown language. Evidently, the *Pentcho* was every bit as clumsy as it appeared.

Seconds later, as four disreputable-looking crewmen began making fast to bollards fore and aft, Schalk picked up a valise, crossed the deck and jumped easily down onto the quay alongside Citron. They shook hands, Schalk—though of only average height—looming above Citron's slighter figure, his dark head with its widow's peak inclined over the young man's shock of vivid red hair. Anyone observing them might have thought of the Jack of Spades greeting the Jack of Diamonds.

"Hello, Citi."

"Welcome back, Zolli."

Despite the affectionate-sounding diminutives which custom and comradeship demanded, there was a mutual wariness in the greeting. Though dedicated to the same venture and sharing a political ideology, the two had little else in common, and both were uneasily aware, now that it seemed the long-delayed voyage was really about to begin, of the possibility of conflict between them.

There were ample grounds for contention. The thirty-four-year-old Schalk considered Citron, twelve years his junior, to be a brash kid, effective enough in his role as a paramilitary youth leader, playing at soldiers in a fantasy world of uniforms, parades and banners, but hopelessly out of his depth in the real world where subtlety and guile were the tools of survival for a Jew. For his part, Citron, blunt and direct, disdained Schalk's methods and resented his patronizing attitude. Even more, he resented Schalk's secretiveness, his inclination to keep all details of his operations to himself, even those vitally affecting Citron and his followers.

But the real clash, Citron knew, would come once they set sail. Schalk apparently intended to remain in charge of the operation after they had embarked on this strange-looking vessel, even though, as Citron understood the instructions he had received from his superiors abroad, Schalk's overall responsibility should end at that point and he, Citron, was to take over.

Schalk broke the awkward silence that followed the handshake. "Well, what do you think of it?"

There was no question of his bestowing the feminine pronoun on this vessel; the British and other seafaring peoples might refer indiscriminately to all ships as "she"—even such a misshapen hulk as the *Pentcho*—but to so quintessential a Central European as Schalk, it would have seemed a ridiculous affectation.

"What do I think of it?" Citron shrugged ruefully. "Not a lot. But it'll do."

Schalk laughed—a short, sharp bark with little mirth in

it. "If you're not enchanted so far," he said, grinning, "just wait until you meet the captain."

Citron looked up sharply. What the hell did Schalk mean by that? Schalk was pantomiming an explanation, drawing small horizontal circles with one forefinger and rolling his eyes expressively. "Drugs," he said. "The bottle, too. Our skipper's a real hard case. And as for the crew"—Schalk emphasized the point with a dismissive gesture—"the sweepings of the waterfront." He shrugged. "Still, what can you expect? Beggars can't be choosers, after all. Especially if they're Jewish beggars."

Schalk then turned to head off up the quayside toward the exit of the port, waving a mock-cheery farewell over his shoulder. "Go aboard, take a look around, meet the captain. I'll see you in the office later."

Citron felt the last of his elation over the *Pentcho*'s arrival drain away as he went aboard. A crazy scrap heap of a boat, a drug addict for a skipper, a rabble for a crew, an unwanted but perhaps inevitable power struggle with Schalk in the offing, and his the responsibility for the safe arrival of the 400-odd people he would lead aboard this vessel in the next few days.

It was a heavy burden for a man just twenty-two years old.

If the pending voyage of the *Pentcho* represented for Citron a daunting challenge, for Schalk it already amounted to a considerable achievement. Just getting the ship this far—properly documented, modified to carry passengers and ready to spirit them away from the Nazi puppet state of Slovakia—had been a triumph of guile and persistence, the crowning achievement of Schalk's three-year involvement in Aliyah Bet,* as the clandestine traffic in emigrants to British-ruled Palestine was called.

It was more than a mere rescue endeavor, for if the object

* *Aliyah* means literally a "going up"; *bet* is the Hebrew letter B.

had been simply to spirit Jews out of Hitler's Europe, almost any destination would have sufficed. But the ideology involved here demanded that they be taken to Palestine to be future citizens of a Jewish state.

Schalk had come to this work by way of a sudden conversion, in his thirtieth year, to the radical program of illegal emigration and armed struggle advocated by Vladimir Jabotinsky, leader of the Revisionist faction of the Zionist movement, known as the New Zionist Organization. At a meeting in Bratislava he had heard the spellbinding Jabotinsky warn of the holocaust to come and call for massive Jewish settlement in *Eretz Yisrael,* as he called Palestine—"the Land of Israel."

The experience charged Schalk's perceptions, if not his style, of life. He had never felt the slightest interest in the Zionist idea before that moment and had given no more thought than the realities of life in Central Europe had forced on him to the fact of being a Jew. His interests— women, cars, clothes, drink, good food—had been happily hedonistic, determinedly trivial. Unlike most of the young Jews of Bratislava, he considered himself thoroughly assimilated, cosmopolitan, and most of his friends were Gentiles.

The inspiration brought about by Jabotinsky's oratory redirected rather than reformed the raffish Zolli Schalk. In many ways he remained the pleasure-loving bachelor of old— suave and convivial on the surface, secretive and conspiratorial underneath. The difference was that he now turned his talents to a purpose larger than mere personal gratification.

Between 1937, when Aliyah Bet began in a very small way, and the time the *Pentcho* arrived in Bratislava, the organization Schalk belonged to had smuggled some 20,000 European Jews into Palestine. The great majority of these had been fit young men and women with a certain amount of paramilitary and agricultural training—members of the Betar youth movement, of which Citron was the regional commandant for Slovakia. These highly motivated youngsters were settlers and potential guerrilla fighters rather than refugees, though the distinction necessarily became less and less valid as Hitler extended his grip across Europe, either directly or through surrogates like the puppets who now ruled in Slovakia.

Citron and his group had been waiting for their ship to Palestine since the Munich agreement of September 1938, when the ultimate fate of Czechoslovakia became clear to anyone willing to read the signals, and the decision was taken at NZO world headquarters in London to evacuate the Czech and Slovakian youth as soon as transport could be found for them.

A freighter named the *Noemi Julia* had been the first ship earmarked for the Slovakian Betar. They would have sailed on it in August 1939, with the Paraguayan visas obtained in Prague, if their places had not been reallocated at short notice to a group of Polish Jews whose need had appeared more urgent. A second ship, the French coaster *St.-Brienc,* had been acquired and paid for in record time, but just as it was about to sail from Marseille to rendezvous with the group at the Black Sea port of Sulina, the war broke out and the French Government commandeered it.

This had left Citron's group virtually penniless, with the chances of finding another ship slender indeed, now that Europe was at war. Then, in the winter of 1939, an NZO agent in Bulgaria named Reuven Franco heard through the grapevine that the owners of a riverboat lying in the Rumanian Danube port of Braila would be willing to sell if they could get their price. Schalk was summoned from Bratislava to see if the vessel would do for the Slovak contingent.

At Braila he inspected the *Stefano,* a flat-bottomed side-wheel paddle steamer of dubious condition, uncertain age and even more uncertain provenance that had been plying the lower reaches of the Danube since the turn of the century, either hauling coal and livestock or pulling barges. Registered in Naples, it was 165 feet long and 40 wide with a mere 5-foot draft, and no one in his right mind, thought Schalk, would even consider going to sea in it.

True, Aliyah Bet had never been luxury travel and all its ships had been desperately overcrowded, worn-out old hulks, only marginally seaworthy. More than one of them had sunk with all hands, and the Jews of Palestine had named these vessels "the little death ships." The *Stefano*, Schalk felt, surely deserved the description. But he dared not reject it. The situation in Slovakia was becoming more threatening by the day and the *Stefano* might well represent their last chance to get away.

Putting aside his misgivings, he got the next train to Bucharest and proceeded to the Grand Hotel Lafayette, where he recommended that negotiations to acquire the *Stefano* be started as soon as possible.

In the past the NZO transport bureau's policy had been to charter rather than to buy, but with the outbreak of war, and a new British policy to impound any vessel intercepted while carrying illegal immigrants, this was no longer possible. The *Stefano*'s owners, a Greek firm named Anatra, were insisting on a cash sale—a down payment of $10,000, another $5,000 when the vessel had been modified to carry passengers and a final payment of $15,000 when it arrived in Bratislava to pick them up.

It was an outrageous price. The *Stefano* was about at the end of its working life, and its scrap value would have been less than a tenth of what Anatra was demanding. But the owners, well aware that there was nothing else available, refused to haggle and the deal was struck on their terms. Schalk's headquarters had barely sufficient resources to make the down payment; somehow the rest would just have to be found when due.

Work began immediately to modify the *Stefano* to carry

the number of passengers expected: 300 at most. Three sleeping/living levels were created—one in the cargo hold, whose occupants would serve as human ballast, one just below deck level and the third inside the superstructure that was to be built onto the deck.

Down in the hold, rough wooden bunks would be constructed in two tiers on each side of the ship, with the space in between as a living area with toilets and washrooms. This would give each passenger a sleeping space 2 feet 6 inches wide by 5 feet 3 inches long, with 2 feet of headroom. A slave trader from the days of the Middle Passage might have approved of this arrangement, although he would of course have considered the toilets and washrooms a needless luxury.

Schalk remained in Rumania while this work went on, making frequent trips to Braila to check on progress. At the same time he began acquiring the documents the *Stefano* would need to fulfill its unlikely new role.

First of all, the vessel would require a new name and a new nationality. With Mussolini likely to enter the war at any moment on Hitler's side, it did not seem wise for the ship to remain under the Italian flag.

The question of a name was quickly resolved; in recognition of Reuven Franco, who had first located the *Stefano,* it was given his *nom de guerre,* "Pentcho"—a slang term signifying a Bulgarian, much as an Englishman might be called "Limey" or a Frenchman "Froggy." To make the name change official, Schalk's contacts among the Bulgarian maritime authorities were brought into play, and with a good deal of cajoling and palm-greasing—for it could not have passed any inspection—the newly named *Pentcho* was registered under the Bulgarian flag.

Rather more effort and ingenuity were required to obtain a certificate allowing the *Pentcho* to sail upstream to Bratislava. As the *Stefano* it had never been allowed above a point known as the Iron Gate, near the Rumanian–Yugoslavian border, because its hull was not considered sturdy enough to withstand the swift currents which flowed there. With the crude superstructure that had been added, making the vessel visibly top-heavy, the *Pentcho* would be considered even less likely to pass unscathed through the Iron Gate. Yet somehow the permit had to be obtained, for Bratislava is some 400 miles farther upriver.

With the inducement of a moderate bribe, a solution was found when an official in the river-traffic licensing bureau got the bright idea of making the *Pentcho* "safe" to pass through the Iron Gate by filling its hold with heavy rocks. The rationale was that the pressure of the rocks against the inside of the hull would counter the pressure of the powerful currents on the outside.

The next document required was a certificate from the Rumanian maritime authorities permitting the *Pentcho* to sail, outward bound, from Sulina. Paradoxically, this was easier to obtain than the other documents, for while the river authorities were reluctant to license a ship that might sink in the Danube and block the navigation channel, they had few qualms about a similar disaster at sea, beyond their sphere of responsibility. After all, if a boatload of Yids drowned while trying to get illegally to Palestine, who would care?

Finally, there was the matter of a collective Paraguayan visa—which could not be obtained in Bratislava, where only the Axis countries and their most fervent admirers had diplomatic representation. Eventually, this was arranged through a middleman in Sulina, but when Schalk went there to collect the visa he was picked up by the river police and taken off for a none-too-pleasant interrogation. A few uncomfortable hours passed for Schalk before the middleman, Jean Foscolo, turned up at river-police headquarters and sprung him.

As Schalk well understood, anywhere in the Balkans, but

especially in Rumania, one could get anything one wanted with a little *baksheesh*.

By contrast with the shadowy world of Zoltan Schalk, Alexander Citron moved through a brightly lit landscape without dark corners. His environment matched his temperament—assertive and direct, untroubled by doubts, unfettered by ambiguities. He was a born commander, a natural authoritarian, an unswerving ideologue, but not quite a fanatic. Boyish enthusiasm, quirky humor and an easy manner with both superiors and subordinates were the saving graces which made him a leader to be loved as much as feared, admired as much as respected.

Unlike Schalk, he was no latecomer to the cause. A Betar pamphlet brought home by an older brother when he was only ten had set Citron on the rocky road to Jerusalem. Its author was that same Jabotinsky whose spellbinding oratory had redirected Schalk's life.

At about the same time that he discovered Zionism, the precocious Citron abandoned the God of his ancestors, telling his pious father that he was no longer a believer and that he had no intention of studying for his *Bar Mitzvah*. He would submit to the ceremonial confirmation when the time came, if only to spare his family the shame of noncompliance with this essential rite of passage, but he would not waste his time poring over the Torah when there were so many more important things to do.

Abraham Citron threatened, pleaded and cajoled in vain, and at the age of thirteen his youngest son went before the rabbi and the congregation of Berehovo, his hometown, virtually unschooled in the Law. Turning a diplomatically deaf ear to young Citron's willful lack of preparation, the rabbi confirmed him in the Faith, thereby reinforcing the boy's conviction that the whole business was a hollow sham.

Nevertheless, the young atheist realized that the religion

he rejected had served an invaluable function as a cement binding the Jewish people together over the centuries of exile, and he understood intuitively that its outward manifestations—Sabbath observance, the covering of the head, the dietary rules—served well as symbols of a resurgent Jewish nationalism.

Citron's enthusiasm for Jabotinsky's radical brand of Zionism may have been a product as much of environment as of temperament. In the remote, Hungarian-speaking region of Ruthenia, or Carpatho-Russia, where he was born at the end of World War I, the Gentile peasantry imbibed anti-Semitism with their mothers' milk and the substantial Jewish minority were reciprocally hostile, inward-looking and not a little fearful.

In such an environment, the good intentions of the decent liberal statesmen who ran the affairs of Czechoslovakia from faraway Prague seemed to most Jews of the region to be of little relevance. As he grew to manhood, Citron found no reason to doubt that the *goyim* were irredeemably hostile and that, as Jabotinsky preached. the Jews' only salvation lay in getting out of Europe and re-creating their nation-state on ancestral soil.

Scorning the pacific idealism of the mainstream Zionists as wishy-washy parlor socialism, Jabotinsky held that the Jews must regain their ancient homeland—all of it, including the east bank of the Jordan and the desert beyond—by "blood and fire," not by negotiation and compromise. But first the Jews of the Diaspora must acquire a new image—and most importantly a new self-image—to replace that of the meek, downtrodden creature of the ghetto. A new generation must arise, imbued with an aristocratic fighting spirit, who would prepare themselves to seize, colonize and defend the Promised Land, and who would show the Gentiles that Jews were no longer a people to be pushed around.

The vehicle for this transformation was to be Betar—a

name honoring a legendary soldier named Josef Trumpledor who had died in 1923 while defending a Galilee settlement against Arab marauders, and whose feats of valor all Jabotinsky's young followers were exhorted to emulate.*

It was a strident creed that Jabotinsky taught; yet there was a Boy Scout primness about it, too, as when he enjoined the members of Betar to aspire to a quality which he defined by the untranslatable Hebrew word *hadar*—an outward glow of manly *politesse,* reflecting an inner glow of self-confidence. "Be tactful, be noble," he enjoined a group going abroad for naval training. "Learn to speak quietly in school, in the street, at your meetings. . . . You must shave every morning [and] check whether your nails are clean. . . . Your face, hands, ears and your whole body must be clean."

But behind the Rover Boys language lay a lurid purpose: on reaching Palestine, Betar members were expected to join Irgun Zvai Leumi, the terrorist movement that was preparing to fight the British, the Arabs and anyone else who stood in the way of a Jewish state in Palestine.

Betar took root and flourished vigorously in Poland, where there was a large Jewish population, traditionally despised by the Catholic majority, and where a young zealot named Menachem Begin rose quickly to head the movement.

In Czechoslovakia, where the demographics of anti-Semitism were less acute, the movement's growth was slower. The young republic's 350,000 Jews felt generally secure under the benign national leadership of Masaryk and his successor, Eduard Benes. But as Hitler's rise to power and Continent-wide prominence began to stoke the fires of ethnic hatred, the atmosphere in Czechoslovakia began to change for the worse, particularly among the Sudeten Germans, who formed their own Nazi movement, and the Slovaks, whose clerical-Fascist People's Party was as much anti-Semitic as anti-Czech.

* "Betar" is an acronym for the Hebrew B'rit Josef Trumpledor—the Josef Trumpledor League.

> *Pack the Czechs off to Prague,*
> *And the Jews to Palestine,*

bawled the Slovak nationalists, while their Sudeten Nazi counterparts screamed their hatred with

> *When Jewish blood spurts from the knife,*
> *Then all goes well again.*

Even among the stolid and tolerant Czechs, the Jews were occasionally accused, of all things, of being pro-German, since the majority of them spoke German as a first language and did indeed have a cultural bias toward what might be termed a pre-Hitlerian Germanism.

In reaction to all this, the Jewish youth of Slovakia were increasingly drawn toward a movement which, with its uniforms, banners and parades, its mystic nationalism, pugnacious slogans and rousing songs, mirrored and challenged the youth movements of their enemies. It was not a comparison that worried young activists like Citron; the Betar code taught the necessity to fight fire with fire, and if this did not make the *goyim* love them, it might at least teach them a little respect.

Although Citron had become a perfect example of the new, nationalistic Jew—"proud, generous and fierce"—that Jabotinsky was trying to create, his family were less hungry for Zion. In 1929, Citron's oldest brother had emigrated to the United States, and once he had established himself in New York City, the rest of the family prepared to follow. But not the young Alexander. Although his parents and four siblings begged him to go with them when they left for America in 1936, he refused.

By this time he had already enrolled in the medical school of Bratislava University, and he argued that without a knowledge of English he would be at a severe disadvantage in the United States. "Let me graduate first; then I'll join you," he told his father. It was a maneuver to avert a bruising row with his parents: neither then nor later did he have any intention of going to America.

It was an austere existence that Citron led in Bratislava, studying by day and devoting all his evenings to Betar. He lived with a married sister and her husband in their one-room apartment, receiving a monthly allowance of $10 from his oldest brother in New York. Eight dollars of this went to his sister for board and lodging; the remainder was his spending money.

In 1938, Citron was appointed Betar leader for the autonomous Slovak region; the following year, after the Nazi-engineered breakup of the Czech Republic turned Slovakia into an "independent" state, he was appointed Betar's *Natsif,* or national commissioner. Soon afterward the new Slovak Government introduced the legislation which expelled Citron, and all other Jews, from institutes of higher education. From then on he devoted himself full time to Betar, getting ready for the exodus that had become the organization's principal objective.

The refitting of the *Pentcho* had been completed by early January 1940. Only river ice upstream had prevented it from sailing to Bratislava to collect its waiting passengers straightaway. To make maximum use of it before the spring thaw, it was sent downriver to Sulina, where the NZO pressed it into service as a floating dormitory for people waiting to board the largest transport ever organized by the Revisionists—the 1,645-ton *Sakaraya,* which eventually sailed from the Danube estuary in February 1940 with 2,200 Austrian, Czech and Polish Jews.

While waiting to leave aboard the *Sakaraya,* Jabotinsky's son Eri inspected the *Pentcho* and marveled that anyone would consider taking it to sea. "The whole contraption looked like a cross between a submarine and a flea," he was to write in a postwar memoir. "No more extraordinary vessel ever sailed the waters."

His comrade Willi Perl thought it "looked like a toy put together by an eleven-year-old with an Erector Set," while Eli Gleser—also a passenger on the *Sakarya* and formerly Citron's superior as Betar *Natsif* for all Czechoslovakia—would recall only half-jokingly that 'if you changed your keys and loose change from one pocket to the other, the boat tilted over."

While the *Pentcho* was wintering in Sulina, its Greek owners were scouring the dives and taverns of half a dozen Balkan ports for a captain and crew. Since no reputable skipper was likely to risk his license and reputation, not to mention his life, in such a crazy venture, this was not easy. Finally, in a waterfront bar in Piraeus, they found their man.

He was a stateless White Russian whose papers identified him as Igor Markeyevitch; it may have been to protect a once-honored family name that this broken-down hulk of a man chose to be known only by his patronymic. He had lost his master mariner's license because of his addiction to drink and drugs. Now he was willing to take on any command that was offered.

Many aspects of Markeyevitch's past life were as murky as the provenance of the vessel he was to skipper, but it seemed he had been an officer in the Tsarist navy and had lost his right leg during the Russo-Japanese War of 1905, when the Russian fleet met catastrophe at Port Arthur after sailing halfway around the world to do battle with the upstart Japanese.

It had been a rough-and-ready amputation, carried out under battle conditions in the sick bay of his ship. While recovering from it in a hospital in Vladivostok, he had become hopelessly involved with the woman doctor who was to become his wife—and with the morphine that was already their joint addiction.

After the Revolution they had gone into exile, two ravaged orphans chained together by their dependence on each other and the syringe, and she was with him still—a frail, brittle old woman with a dowager's hump and haunted eyes—when he arrived in Braila to take over his command after it returned from Sulina.

Schalk was waiting to meet him, anxious to see what kind of skipper its owners had hired. What he saw was hardly reassuring. Yet derelict though he obviously was, Markeyevitch still bore himself with some shreds of dignity. The eight-man crew—a motley collection of Greeks, Turks and Bulgars—might be riffraff, but Markeyevitch, Schalk decided, remained at least the remnant of a gentleman. He could only hope that Markeyevitch might still prove to be the remnant of a master mariner.

When, toward the end of April, circumstances were right for the *Pentcho* to start upstream for Bratislava, its departure was duly noted by the British Embassy in Bucharest, which was well aware of the purpose for which the vessel had been purchased and refitted. Like other British ambassadors in neutral countries strung out along both banks of the Danube, Sir Reginald Hoare was under pressure from Whitehall to do everything possible to impede the clandestine traffic of emigrants to Palestine, and he passed the word of the *Pentcho*'s departure to his colleagues upstream.

As the British saw it, illegal emigration to Palestine was not primarily a refugee movement, although as a secret government memorandum published two months earlier had conceded, "there are, of course, refugees among the immigrants." Rather, the movement was viewed as a defiant response to the British decision to impose a limit of 75,000 on the number of Jews to be admitted to Palestine over the next five years. Its intention, said the memorandum, was "to defeat the limitation . . . and ultimately to increase the Jewish population of Palestine to a majority, which will give them a dominating position in the country."

The British were aware that various organizations and individuals were involved in the traffic but in their view the principal body concerned was the New Zionist Organization, "the most extreme of Jewish parties, whose programme is a mass immigration into Palestine and Transjordan, and who possess an illegal military organisation in Palestine." The passengers on the NZO's ships were "carefully picked and trained young men of military age, and women, not the old men and women and children who would be in the van of a true refugee movement," said the memorandum.

It was an accurate enough description of the aims and methods of the *Aliyah Bet* Revisionists, even if its tone suggests a frigid indifference to the dimension of sheer necessity created by Hitler's relentless hounding of the Jews.

The British memorandum calculated that during the six months of April through September 1939, more than 11,000 illegals had entered Palestine. There had been a lull during the early months of the war, but now there were signs of a revival in the traffic, and it was assuming the proportions of a major political problem because of its effects on Arab opinion in Palestine and throughout the Middle East. "It might well precipitate a revival of the Arab rebellion and postpone indefinitely a rapprochement between the Arabs and Jews in Palestine," said the memorandum. "Should this occur, British relations with the Arab countries . . . would be seriously jeopardised and troops which are urgently required elsewhere would be immobilised."

But as the British document ruefully noted, the traffic was extremely difficult to stop, and as a result "the impression has been created in some quarters that the Palestine Government and His Majesty's Government are secretly conniving at illegal immigration"—an impression that the document said was being "carefully fostered by the Jews."

This was perfectly true; spreading such an impression was an important part of the psychological warfare being conducted by the inventive spirits of the NZO's bureau in Bucharest. In an effort to counter British pressure on the Balkan governments, they had been putting out the word that, while officially protesting about it, the British were secretly in favor of the traffic, if only because they wanted an influx of young Jews to fight against a possible German invasion of Palestine.

To many neutrals this sounded likely enough, and the very fact that the lumbering, leaky vessels of *Aliyah Bet* were getting through to Palestine, despite the vigilance of the Royal Navy, seemed to give the invention credibility. After all, did not Britannia rule the waves—so how could the Jews get through without her connivance? Consequently, Balkan officials tended to regard a complaint from the British as a *pro forma* diplomatic maneuver, intended only to fool the Arabs.

Meanwhile, Nazi policy at this time was to rob the Jews and kick them out, if they had anywhere to go, rather than to exterminate them. Indeed, one faction inside the Nazi hierarchy believed it to be in Germany's interest to compound Britain's problems with the Arabs by making sure that illegal immigration was not impeded.

For this reason, Austrian riverboat companies under SS control were allowed to ship Jews down the Danube, while strict fiscal regulations were frequently waived to allow Jews to buy the hard currency they needed to acquire vessels. This had been the case with the sale of the *Pentcho,* in which Slovak crowns had been changed in Switzerland into the sterling demanded by the vendors.

The status of the Danube as an international waterway presented yet another problem to the British. Departing Jews needed no transit visas for the riparian countries they would sail through, and the British deplored that this gave the governments concerned "a useful excuse for not interfering with a traffic which helps to rid them of their surplus Jewish population." Even when these governments wanted to be cooperative, the British document complained, "their intentions were liable to be defeated by the inefficiency or venality of subordinate executive officials."

At the end of the line things were scarcely any easier for the British. They had mounted an intensive sea patrol along the Palestine coast to intercept illegal immigrant ships, but realized that in practice they could not exercise their prerogative to use "such force as is necessary" to stop them "in view of the serious political consequences of firing on, and perhaps sinking, a ship filled with 'refugees.' "

In short, they conceded that they could not prevent the landing of illegal immigrants once they reached the coast of Palestine, but only ensure that most of them were detected and arrested on arrival. Once an illegal immigrant had landed, however, it was "almost impossible" to deport him, and certainly, the British document concluded, a prison sentence was no deterrent.

Thus, *Aliyah Bet* may be seen as a cat-and-mouse game in which the cat by no means enjoyed all the advantages.

Despite all these problems, the British kept trying to stamp out the traffic at its source. The safe arrival of the *Sakaraya* had been a major setback, so considerable effort was focused on stopping the *Pentcho*, and it was in response to a complaint initiated by the British that the vessel was detained when it reached Budapest en route to Bratislava.

Schalk, who had traveled ahead of the boat by rail, received an urgent phone call from a contact in Budapest telling him what had happened. Hurrying to the Hungarian capital with a lawyer in tow, he discovered that the British had pressured the Bulgarians into asking the Hungarians to turn the ship back on the ground of irregularities in its registration.

Schalk demanded a hearing, and two full days of legal argument followed. It seemed touch-and-go for a while, but finally the Hungarians ruled—without even the offer of a bribe—that they had no grounds to detain the *Pentcho* or send it back.

Within the hour the *Pentcho* had been released, and Schalk ordered Captain Markeyevitch to resume his journey upstream without delay. This time he remained aboard himself. After what had just occurred he wasn't going to let the *Pentcho* out of his sight.

2

$\mathcal{S}$eated at her elderly Adler typewriter in the dingy office that served as Betar headquarters on Kaplowitz-platz, just across from the Slovak Senate building, Shoshanna Spiegel did her best to stifle her resentment at having been left behind while Citron went to watch the *Pentcho*'s arrival.

True, there was a mountain of paperwork to be done now that the ship was here at last—passenger lists to finalize, inventories of supplies to be typed, telephone queries to be answered, telegrams to be sent out to passengers in the provinces alerting them to stand by for departure.

But surely he could have taken her with him. An hour or so away from her desk wouldn't have made any real difference. After all, she had waited as impatiently, as longingly, as he had for this moment; and she was not just the Betar secretary—the person who, without payment, kept the whole office running virtually single-handed. She was also Citron's fiancée.

Of course, if she had asked he would probably have taken

her along. But she hadn't asked; it was not her way to push herself forward. A woman's place, her mother had taught her—and her father's attitudes and those of her community had always made clear—was in the background, helping her menfolk, never asserting herself.

Coming from a traditional Jewish family in which she was the only daughter, she had always filled the role of assistant to her mother in the running of the household and nurse-maid to her five younger brothers, even though she also held down a job as secretary to the boss of an import-export firm, ran the Betar office and commanded its women's auxiliary wing, and studied part time for a degree in chemistry.

It had never occurred to her father, a Talmudic scholar, trained as a rabbi, who had drifted none too successfully into commerce as a wine merchant, that there was a fundamental inequity in this, any more than it had to her brothers. That was the way things were. Tradition. Shosha had accepted it herself, though not without an occasional flash of resentment.

Even with Citi, it seemed, she was all too often taken for granted. But she could not remain angry with him for long.

They had met at a Betar evening shortly after he came to Bratislava from Berehovo in 1936. There had been a perky self-confidence about him and a boldness in the bright button-brown eyes that made her lower her own when he introduced himself. Although only eighteen and just arrived from the provinces, a Hungarian-speaker with only partial command of the German that was the city's *lingua franca,* he had seemed completely self-possessed and socially at ease—much more so, Shosha recognized, than she could ever be herself, even among familiar company.

For his part, Citron felt drawn immediately to this intense, quicksilver girl and, with his customary lack of self-doubt, "knew straightaway that she would be mine." Whatever reservations Shosha might have had were quickly swept aside. Within a day or two it was tacitly understood that they were informally engaged.

Physically they might have been brother and sister, both trimly built, hyperactive individuals into whose small frames, it seemed, enough dynamism had been compressed to make half a dozen less forceful people. Some who knew them both wondered if they weren't just a little too alike to make a comfortable pair—each with so much drive and fire, so many sharp corners of temperament and personality.

There were differences, of course. Shosha took her religion seriously, and occasionally she was offended by Citron's unconcealed disdain for her beliefs. Politically, their positions were to a limited extent reversed; here it was Citron who was the true believer, a blind follower—as he readily admitted—of the doctrines and instructions handed down from above, while Shosha reserved, and exercised, the right to doubt and question.

But to both of them it seemed inevitable, almost from the start, that they should marry—though not, they agreed, until they reached *Eretz Yisrael*. There, Shosha had heard, women were able to walk side by side with their men, not one step behind.

And now the ship was here at last, and soon they would be going "home" to claim their patrimony. Like Citron, she thought of herself not as a refugee, but as a pioneer. Like Citron, she did not have the slightest doubt that the Holy Land was theirs by right or that they would reach their destination and recover it.

The prospect of their imminent departure sent Shosha back to her work with renewed vigor, and she quickly typed out the telegram which, on Citron's confirmation that everything was in order, she would send out that day to their members in the provinces: "STEAMSHIP ARRIVED STOP FOR-

MALITIES WILL TAKE FEW MORE DAYS STOP WILL NOTIFY YOU
SHORTLY BEFORE DEPARTURE STOP TRANSPORT BUREAU."

She could still only just believe it was true.

The bar fell silent as Imre Lichtenfeld shouldered his way
in. He was not unused to being noticed when he entered a
public place; Bratislava was not, after all, such a big city, and
he was something of a local celebrity. But this was not that
kind of silence.

Otto, the waiter, formed his mouth into a mute "O" of
appeal and shook his head, eyes darting anxiously from side
to side. "Please, Mister Imi," he whispered. "You know we
can't serve you."

As Lichtenfeld pushed past him and perched on a high
stool at the bar, feeling the eyes boring into his back, Fat
Irma, proprietress of the Kit-Kat Bar, bustled over from the
cash register, all bosom and bombazine.

"Please, Imi," she entreated. "I don't want no trouble."

"One drink," he told her. "One drink and I'll go."

She could tell by the set of his jaw that she would get nowhere arguing with him. If she called in Alois, the bouncer,
Imi would make mincemeat of him—and probably smash the
place up in the process. Although he wasn't one to throw
his weight around unless provoked, he was a holy terror
when roused, as just about everyone in Bratislava knew.

So perhaps the best thing was to give him his drink and
encourage him to leave as fast as possible, before one or more
of the customers started making trouble or, God forbid, the
cops arrived.

"All right," she snapped, squinting through the blue veil
of smoke that rose from the cigarette clamped between her
lips. "One drink and then out."

Lichtenfeld flashed her the little-boy-lost smile he knew
to be so effective with older women and was rewarded with
an almost immediate response. The hard carapace seemed to

crack, and Fat Irma said: "Christ, Imi, I'm sorry it's like this. I really am."

Her regret was genuine enough. It was one thing to kick the Yids out of the universities and the professions, where perhaps they did hog too many places. But banning them from restaurants and bars was a bit too much if you asked Irma, especially a lovely young fellow like Imi Lichtenfeld.

She had watched him in the ring, quick and lethal as a striking snake, winning the All-Slovakia lightweight wrestling championship; she had seen him on the dance floor, lean and lithe as a randy tomcat, winning the tango prize in the city ballroom-dancing contest, and she had heard, through the gossip of the town, of his reputation as an accomplished chaser of skirt and regretted only that she was no longer of an age to qualify as quarry.

All in all, Fat Irma thought, he was a damn sight better man than most of the blowhards around town. And yet that gang of priests and perverts who were running the country nowadays had the gall to tell her she couldn't serve him a drink. The injustice of it, and the slivovitz she had been tippling quietly all evening, were having their effect. Yes, she'd serve him a drink, all right. On the house, what was more. "But for Christ's sake, Imi, drink up fast and get out before you drop me in the shit."

"Thanks, Irma. Make it a cognac." As a rule he never touched the stuff, but tonight he really needed it.

Lichtenfeld sat up straight on the high stool, sipping his drink with deliberate slowness, watching in the mirror behind the bar for the first sign of trouble heading his way, but feeling so cool it amazed him.

In the mirror he could see a group of youths in uniform seated in a booth—homegrown Nazis, members of the Volunteer SS, a local version of the real thing and none the less nasty for being an imitation. At the head of the table sat Heini Muller, a husky *Volksdeutscher* whom Lichtenfeld remembered from the days, not so long ago, when they used to compete in gymnastics. He was a decent enough chap, Lichtenfeld thought, before he got into that uniform and let himself be carried away by the hate and hysteria.

Muller made no move, and neither did any of his brown-shirted comrades. They didn't even look in Lichtenfeld's direction, and slowly the rumble of conversation started up again.

For some reason, they seemed to be in no mood for a dustup that night—either that, or they were quite simply intimidated by Lichtenfeld's reputation as a brawler. Just as well, he thought. He wouldn't have a chance if it came to tackling them all at once. But whatever the reason for their lack of response to his presence, it certainly wouldn't do to hang around too long. His drink finished, his point made, Lichtenfeld left the bar and walked out into the night.

By May of 1940, he was one of the very few Jews in Bratislava foolhardy enough to venture out alone after dark—certainly the only one crazy enough to show his face in a bar and certainly the last one who should have done so. For as he knew very well, he was a marked man.

Yes, it was a pretty stupid thing to do, and Lichtenfeld was never quite sure just why he went into the Kit-Kat Bar that night. It might have had something to do with the flinty notions of self-respect dinned into him from earliest childhood by his formidable father. "Never let anybody put you down for being a Jew. Never," the old man used to say.

Certainly it had been a long time since anybody had tried to put the superbly muscled, fiercely mustachioed Samu Lichtenfeld down, for any reason. He had been a circus strong man before joining the police and rising to become Chief of Detectives for the city of Bratislava, famous throughout Czechoslovakia for having brought some of the republic's most notorious criminals to justice.

As soon as Imi was old enough, Samu had taught him to

box and wrestle and coached him in track, gymnastics and swimming. Imi excelled in all and in time had become almost as celebrated as his father, though not so much for his athletic prowess as for his role in the violent street disturbances that began to rack the Slovak capital from the mid-'30s on.

Bratislava at that time had a population of 140,000, of whom some 20,000 were Jews and the rest about equally Slovaks, Czechs and Germans. The pretext for the first major anti-Semitic outbreak in 1936 had been the showing of a film about the Golem of Prague—a fabled monster created by a seventeenth-century rabbi to protect his people from the city's hostile Christians.

The Slovak nationalists and the local Nazis, finding the film altogether too sympathetic to the Jews, staged violent protest demonstrations outside the cinema where it was being shown, and soon running street battles broke out. When followers of the Slovak nationalist leader Father Andreas Hlinka tried to invade the Jewish quarter, Imi Lichtenfeld organized an *ad hoc* defense of the district, and in pitched street battles he and a squad of scrappy young boxers and wrestlers drove the invaders out. The next day, the nationalist party newspaper carried headlines saying: "JEWS MAKING POGROM. CHRISTIAN BLOOD FLOWS IN JEWISH STREETS."

The street fighting continued intermittently. Long periods of calm were followed by short, sharp bursts of violence as one pretext or another inspired a fresh eruption of ethnic hatred. To the Jewish youth of the city, Imi Lichtenfeld became an emblem and a hero, idealized and emulated by youngsters who flocked to join Jewish sports and athletic clubs and the paramilitary Betar, determined to prove their manhood and train to defend themselves and their turf.

Although the ethnic violence that plagued Bratislava was common enough wherever Nazi influence had inflamed indigenous nationalist feelings, the street clashes in the Slovak capital lacked something of the viciousness seen elsewhere.

Bratislava remained essentially a small town where everyone knew everyone else and where consequently the antagonists felt constrained to use fists and boots rather than guns and knives.

But by the spring of 1940, as the war spread and the Slovak puppet regime moved even closer to the Nazis, it had become clear that the old restraints would not hold much longer, and Lichtenfeld knew his reputation as a fighter ensured that he would be among the first to fall victim once the gloves were off.

Although not a member of Betar, whose flags, uniforms and parades did not appeal to him, he had been offered a place on the *Pentcho*. For months he had been undecided, and until the ship actually arrived, there had been no need to make a final decision. But now he would have to make up his mind, and having made his grand gesture of defiance in the Kit-Kat Bar, he realized that the time had come to heed the urgent advice of his father—now retired on pension—and get out of Slovakia while he had the chance.

On his family's 400-acre farm near Plavec, close to the Polish frontier, Marcel Friedmann, stripped to the waist in the heat of the forge, hammered the last small dent out of the white-hot harrow disk and plunged it into the vat to temper. He had been working for a year now under the tutelage of his father's blacksmith, Mikhal Zvanziger, and the muscles rippled like a nest of snakes under the skin of his arms and torso.

Adolf Friedmann had intended his boy for something better than manual labor, and could well have afforded to see him through law school or medical college, but by the time Marcel graduated from the Gymnasium at Presov in 1939, Jews were banned from the universities.

Resurgent anti-Semitism had already moved young Friedmann to desert the Boy Scouts for Betar where he was urged to prepare himself to be a useful settler by learning a trade. Since he could no longer be admitted to a university, he decided to learn the blacksmith's craft, working in Zvanziger's forge while he waited for the ship to Palestine.

As his muscles hardened in the smithy and his hands grew callused, the pace of events quickened. After the Slovak puppet state was set up, the ripples reached Plavec, where there were ugly demonstrations against the Friedmanns and the three or four other Jewish families who had lived there for centuries. But the tension soon died down, and Adolf Friedmann persuaded himself that the trouble was as much social as ethnic, a case of the poor peasants' giving vent to their envy of the better off, rather than a warning of systematic persecution to come.

In September 1939, German troops came through Plavec on their way to join the invasion of Poland, and for three days a unit of infantry and horse-drawn artillery billeted themselves on the Friedmann farm before crossing the frontier in a flurry of dust and field gray. The enlisted men were well-enough behaved and the officers correct, especially so when they learned that Adolf Friedmann had been a warrant officer in the Austro-Hungarian Army during World War I.

Before they moved on, a young lieutenant from Munich gave the Friedmanns some friendly advice: "Today it's Poland and before long it'll be Russia. If you're Jews, you'd better move out of here while you can."

Though troubled by the warning, and by what he knew was happening elsewhere in Slovakia, Adolf Friedmann was not troubled enough to consider abandoning the farm that was his life's work. Like most of the Jews of Slovakia, he was prepared to sit things out until the storm blew over—and he was in a better position to do so than most, isolated on his remote farm. But for the young people it was different; it would be good for Marcel to go and start a new life, he thought, free from the role of eternal scapegoat which the Gentiles seemed determined to impose upon the Jews.

Now, as Marcel trudged into the house that warm May evening, still sweating from the forge, it seemed that the moment had come. Wordlessly, the old man handed him the telegram from Shosha Spiegel that had arrived an hour before.

In the three years since she had last seen her husband, Gisella Farkas had often imagined their reunion.

She would spot him from far off as the tugboats ushered her great liner into the harbor at Haifa—an unmistakably elegant and slender figure in a smart, freshly pressed linen suit that proclaimed his newfound prosperity. And as the ship drew alongside the quay, she would see again his loved and longed-for features, handsome and as eager for her as he had been on their wedding night.

He would be scanning the figures on the deck, intent for a first sight of her and their little boy, Karci. And, yes, their eyes would at last find each other's, they would wave and cry, and soon she would be in her Shani's arms again and the years of loneliness would be over. They would laugh and they would cry some more, and then Shani would pick up little Karci and hold him up to the slanting rays of the morning sun rising over Mount Carmel so that they would light up his blond head like a beacon. And he would say, "What a fine little *mensch* he has become, my Karci."

And they would be together, a family again.

Only Gisella now knew it would not be like that at all. Those reunion fantasies had belonged to the early years of their separation when she had believed that Shani would soon fix things so that she and Karci could go openly and legally to join him in Palestine. Now she knew that if she was to get there at all, it would be secretly, and in great danger and discomfort; that if they ever did get that far, she and

Karci would have to wade ashore one dark night off some stretch of deserted beach, with always the chance that they might be caught by patrolling British soldiers or, worse still, by marauding Arabs.

She knew, too, in her innermost heart, that far from looking prosperous and elegant, Shani was all too likely to appear threadbare and anxious—though enraptured, of course, to see her and Karci again. For reading between the lines of his letters, she could tell that he had not found the streets of Tel Aviv to be paved with gold.

Alexander Farkas had gone to Palestine in the spring of 1937, not driven by any fervent belief in the Jewish people's right and overwhelming need to return to Zion, but because he was disappointed and restless; after a series of business failures he had convinced himself that he should make a fresh start abroad, and Palestine seemed a likely place to do it.

Since immigration was severely restricted, he had bought a round-trip ticket, and had obtained a tourist visa by representing himself as a business visitor with a special interest in an international trade fair that was being held in Haifa. Once in Palestine, he had melted into the general Jewish population, intending to set himself up in business with what he had been able to salvage from the collapse of his unsuccessful enterprises in Czechoslovakia, and then to send for his wife and only child.

But he had underestimated the difficulties of establishing himself in a Palestine still suffering severely from the effects of the world Depression, and of getting his wife and child into a country where his own status was, to say the least, not quite "official."

On his departure, Gisella had taken seven-year-old Karci to her hometown of Kezmarok, a little resort center in the High Tatra mountains, where they lived with her married sister while waiting to hear from Palestine that their passages and entry certificates had been arranged. Always, she was sure they would be going in just a couple of weeks. Always she was disappointed.

So the weeks turned to months and the months to years and all that came from her husband was promises, assurances that he was trying his best to arrange things, and small sums of money. Meanwhile the international scene darkened, and even in remote and picturesque Kezmarok, where her late father had been a prosperous timber merchant and her family enjoyed some status among the *goyim,* Gisella could sense the chill of coming events.

The ardent wish to be reunited with her husband was now reinforced by fear for the future; and tired of waiting passively, Gisella decided to take matters into her own hands.

Hearing rumors of an illegal transport due to sail soon from Bratislava, she collected her savings, said goodbye to her family and took a train to the capital, with little Karci in tow. There she found that a transport was indeed being organized by a free-lance operator and that the price for two places aboard it would be a hefty 30,000 crowns—about $1,000. Gisella paid, exhausting most of her savings, then went to the three-room apartment of her brother and sister-in-law and their five children to wait for word that it was time to embark.

Again she waited in vain. With the outbreak of war in September 1939, the organizers cancelled the transport.

At that point a less determined woman might have given up. Her family were urging her to forget about going to Palestine for the time being, to return to Kezmarok, where the war and the anti-Semitic ravings of the new regime in Bratislava would seem but distant echoes. Maybe it's a blessing that that ship never sailed, said her brother. Why go to sea in some leaky old tub and risk your lives? So go home and sit it out until the storm blows over.

It was the kind of counsel that seemed to make sense to most Slovak Jews at that time. Not all their Gentile neighbors were hostile, and support for the pro-Nazi regime was far from unanimous. We've lived through hard times before, the Jews told themselves, and we'll do it again. So there had been no mass panic to get away, and when the free-lance transport was cancelled, there was no shortage of those who were ready to say "I told you so. Now forget that stupid idea."

But Gisella Farkas was not a woman to listen to such sensible advice. Driven partly by fear but mostly by the ever-more-compelling need to rejoin her husband, she began to look around for new options. And when she heard that the Betar people were organizing their own transport, she marched into Citron's office and demanded to be put on his list.

Citron and Schalk had agreed to make a limited number of places available to people from the cancelled transport, but Gisella and her child were not the kind of passenger they were looking for; Betar policy was wherever possible to make room only for the strong and the fit who would be best able to withstand the rigors of the journey and make good settler material on arrival.

But Gisella was not to be denied. She pleaded, she argued, she wheedled, she demanded. Finally she wore them down, and the fact that her husband was already in Palestine tipped the scales for her. Their names on the list, she and Karci went back to her brother's flat to resume waiting.

It was a long wait. Once winter set in and the river iced up, everyone realized there would be months of delay, and even then there was no guarantee—and, it seemed, less and less likelihood—that the ship would ever arrive.

For Karci, a bright and active little boy, there were the distractions of cousins to play with and, for a while, of school. Although Jewish children were now barred from the schools of the Slovakian state, controls were not rigorous, and it was easy enough for any child not obviously Jewish by name or appearance to enroll. To relieve the overcrowding in her brother's flat and keep Karci off the street, Gisella decided to let him attend classes.

A bizarre incident cut short this phase of Karci's education. Early in 1940, the Hitler Youth leader Baldur von Shirach paid a visit to Bratislava. Eager to impress their distinguished guest, the city fathers arranged for a couple of hundred of their brightest, most Aryan-looking children to greet him at the station. Each of the city's schools was asked to provide a contingent, and Karci was one of those chosen.

Hardly aware of what it was all about, and swept up in the excitement of the occasion, Karci had stood in line with the others, giving the raised-arm salute and shouting *"Heil"* as instructed when Hitler's blond godling strode by.

When she heard about it, the outraged and fearful Gisella immediately withdrew Karci from school. This made life more difficult than ever. Karci was either forever underfoot in the overcrowded apartment or else out playing in the street where he might get into heaven knew what kind of trouble. Whenever he was late home for meals, Gisella grew anxious.

She was particularly anxious this beautiful early evening in May, for Karci should have been home for supper half an hour ago and her brother's children had no idea where he might be. "So much hate there is," she fretted, "that even a little boy can't walk the streets in safety." Then, just as her imagination was beginning to create fearful scenarios of injury or death, the apartment door burst open and there was Karci, unkempt and excited, his eyes afire with good news.

"Mamouka, Mamouka," he gasped. "Guess what? The boat is here. The boat to take us to Papa!"

Although it was early May, snow still lingered in the foothills of the High Tatras, and a sawtoothed wind ripped across the muddy, potholed parade ground of the camp where Oskar Salomon, the son of a rabbi, was one of a company of young Jews performing the menial labor of the Slovak Army—

digging trenches and latrines, filling sandbags and throwing up earthworks for their betters.

That morning Salomon was on latrine duty, long-handled mop in one hand, galvanized bucket in the other. "I want that shithouse floor so clean you could eat your dinner off it!" Sergeant Voytech had commanded in the strangled scream that seemed to be his sole mode of addressing his subordinates. "And as for those toilet bowls, I want them sweet and fresh enough to drink out of. Understand, Salomon, you dirty little Yid?"

"Yessir, Sergeant," Salomon rapped back, wearing the inane, good-natured grin he always affected for Voytech's benefit.

"Don't smile at me, you horrible little Jew-boy," screeched Voytech as he stomped off, leaving Salomon alone with the acrid effluvia of his morning task.

Such was life in the Slovak Army's Labor Corps, a device for the "useful" employment of young Jews who would otherwise be denied the privilege of serving in their country's armed forces. It would hardly do to conscript young Catholic Slovaks and leave the Jews to their soft civilian life; on the other hand, it would hardly do to give the Jews guns and instruction in how to use them. So the answer was the shovel and the mop, the latrine and the sandbag.

As he swabbed the floor, Salomon reflected ruefully that if, like his Betar commander Citron, he had come from the Carpathians, he would have been exempt from this demeaning service. Since the Hungarians had annexed the region, those born there were officially regarded as foreigners and therefore not liable for the draft.

Still, the crude rigors of camp life didn't worry him unduly. It might be unpleasant, but it wasn't Dachau or Mauthausen, and Salomon was able to relieve the tedium and deflect the crude bullying of Voytech and the other NCOs by acting out a disingenuous "Good Soldier Schweik" role, accepting all tasks with a willing grin and then executing them with a total incompetence which drove his masters to a frenzy of frustration.

It was a risky game, but one he had learned to play to perfection, so that his fellow draftees would shake their heads and wonder how that *shaigetz*—that scamp—Oskar got away with it.

What worried him most was not the filthy work, the vile food, the harsh and capricious discipline but the fear that because of this enforced service he would miss the Betar transport he had signed up for more than a year before. He knew by letters from home that the ship had not yet arrived, so there was still a chance. But it didn't seem like much of a chance, and cooped up in camp in the mountains, how would he and the other Betar members serving in his company ever know if the ship had sailed or not? Even the irrepressible Salomon was beginning to lose hope.

Afterward he would reflect on the irony that the detested Voytech should be the bearer of such totally unexpected good news that morning as he swabbed the lavatory floor. Voytech entered the latrine, his meaty peasant face furrowed in a frown of concentration, a pink signal form in his hand. "Salomon," he shrieked, "put down that mop, get to your hut and start packing your kit."

"Packing, Sergeant?"

"You heard me. Packing. It says here that you're leaving, Salomon. You and"—he stopped to look at the signal form in his hand—"Arnstein, Fahn, Kohn, Klein, Mittelmann and Rosenberg. Be outside the company office at twelve hundred hours sharp, ready to go."

"Where are we going, Sergeant?"

Voytech snorted with disgust. "May the Devil fuck your mother, Jew-boy, but it seems someone's been pulling strings and you're going home."

"Home?"

"Yes, home, you lucky little Yid—all the way to Palestine. There's a ship waiting for you and we're getting rid of you at last!"

Unlike the young stalwarts of Betar, Daniel Hamburger hadn't the slightest interest in going to Palestine. All he wanted was to go—anywhere, at any cost. He had seen the Nazis up close in his native Germany and he knew from painful experience what they were capable of.

Within days of Hitler's coming to power in January 1933, a bunch of brown-shirted thugs had punched and kicked Hamburger half to death in the street near his home in Frankfurt-am-Main. As he lay in a hospital recovering, he had decided to leave the country before something worse happened.

It had not been difficult for Hamburger, a solitary thirty-one-year-old bachelor with no immovable possessions, to tear up his roots and leave for what he thought would be a safe haven, Czechoslovakia. He chose German-speaking Bratislava as a suitable spot to stay, rented a furnished room and set himself up in business in a small way—a shy, timid man, tall and ungainly, shunning the company of others, growing more fearful as the stain of Nazism spread outward from Germany to infiltrate the borders of his sanctuary.

Hamburger would never forget the day the Nazis had marched into Vienna, on the opposite bank of the Danube. Austrian Jews had thrown themselves into the river to get away and tried to swim across to the Slovakian shore. He had seen three of them dragged ashore half-dead, and he knew then that his Slovak sanctuary wouldn't be safe a lot longer, that he must get away.

But how? Hamburger was a badly frightened but not, it seemed, an especially resourceful man.

His salvation was a sudden financial crisis which affected the Betar evacuation plan even as the *Pentcho* was panting and wheezing upriver toward Bratislava. The *Pentcho*'s owners were due a final payment of $15,000 before they would authorize the captain to leave with his passengers, and the NZO transport bureau in Bucharest found itself completely out of funds. If the money was not raised within a couple of weeks, the deal would be off and the boat would be lost. A phone call to Schalk from Bucharest broke the news.

He was horrified. The financial arrangements had been handled entirely by *Aliyah* headquarters in Bucharest and he had assumed the money was on hand for the final payment. But the bureau had always led a hand-to-mouth existence, performing a juggling act with insufficient funds, and at last things had caught up with it.

There was nothing for it but to raise the money by taking on paying passengers at whatever price the market would bear, even at the risk of overloading the ship. In a transit camp at Patronka, on the outskirts of Bratislava, and in private lodgings in the city, there were many refugees who had left Austria and, earlier, Germany, with sufficient funds to buy themselves a place on the *Pentcho*.

As news spread that there were 100 or so places available, the Betar office was besieged. Selecting who should be allowed to go and who not was a nightmare. Citron and Schalk had well-established guidelines and tried to stick to them— no one over forty-five, no one in poor health, no small children; in short, no one who might not be able to stand the hardships of the voyage. But in practice it wasn't possible to be too rigid. They found it expedient to sell places at inflated prices to the rich and elderly as a way to subsidize more suitable young people who had little or no money. One merchant paid enough for his passage to allow four other people to travel free. And one young couple was allowed aboard even though the wife was seven months pregnant.

One applicant who elbowed his way into the line and was willing to pay enough to cover someone else's passage as well as his own was Daniel Hamburger. He knew he wasn't the kind of settler Betar was looking for; "But they needed my money and that's why they took me.

"I didn't know anything about Betar and I cared even less," he would recall. "Palestine, Peru, legal, illegal—it was all the same to me. I just wanted to get away. I'd have gone to Shanghai or anywhere else if that was the way out. As for Jabotinsky, the little that I knew of him I thought he was a crazy man—a *meshuggeneh.*"

Nonetheless, when he had secured his place aboard the *Pentcho,* Hamburger—a devout man, never without his skull-cap and prayer shawl—offered thanks to the Almighty for creating the madman Jabotinsky, whose wild notions had made his escape possible.

Imre Lichtenfeld, Marcel Friedmann, Gisella and Karci Farkas, Oskar Salomon, Daniel Hamburger just six of the 400 whose names appeared on the embarkation list of "the little death ship," the S.S. *Pentcho.* Mostly they were perfectly ordinary people propelled by historical circumstances into a most extraordinary situation—some moved by simple self-preservation, others driven by a blinding ideal; some equipped to respond positively to the trials of the journey, others in every sense of the word mere passengers.

What all of them had in common—those who were chasing a dream and those who were fleeing a nightmare—was simply that to the power that dominated the continent they were about to leave, they were equally worthless as members of the same condemned species, the European Jew.

3

On Saturday, May 18, 1940, as the *Pentcho* churned away from quayside at Bratislava and out into the Danube's main navigation channel, the Nazis' grip on Europe was tightening convulsively. That day, the Belgian Government fled from Brussels to Ostend to escape from the path of Hitler's *Blitzkrieg,* while the Allied commander-in-chief, General Maurice Gamelin of France, declared in an order of the day that "the destiny of the world depends on the battles now being fought."

Amid such titanic events, the departure of the *Pentcho* from Bratislava necessarily attracted very little local attention.

To make doubly sure that it left unnoticed, the Slovak authorities had barred all mention of the transport in their tightly censored news media, while the vessel itself had been diverted to the winter port, where few, if any, dockworkers would be on hand to see it load up and leave. And to prevent any large-scale emotional send-off by friends and relatives, all but those who were actually sailing were barred entrance to the port.

There was a good deal of ambivalence about the *Pentcho* in official circles, but on the whole the authorities were glad to be rid of another 400 Jews as long as the affair could be kept quiet. Even the Nazi advisers by now attached to all government ministries and the Gestapo officers attached to the police had not objected. The policy of Endlosung—Final Solution—was still eighteen months in the future. Also, there remained a handful of individual officials who were genuinely sympathetic to the plight of the Jews, despite the anti-Semitic obsessions of the ruling People's Party and their Nazi patrons.

Zoltan Schalk's friend Police Commissioner Yosef Yakouboczy of the Aliens Department, was one of these. He had been instrumental in clearing the way for the *Pentcho*'s departure after two earlier transports, organized by the Zionist Maccabi sports club, had been stopped by bureaucratic obstacles. It was Yakouboczy, too, who pulled the strings that got Oskar Salomon and some four dozen other Betar youngsters released from Labor Corps service in time to join the transport.

But Yakouboczy had reason to wonder whether he had done the humane thing when he went down to the winter port with Schalk to get his first, and last, sight of the *Pentcho* on the day the passengers embarked.

He seemed horrified at the vessel's makeshift appearance and dilapidated condition, and when Schalk confided that contrary to the general belief, they would have to make their entire journey in the *Pentcho,* Yakouboczy clapped his hand to his forehead in a gesture of incredulity: "In *this* ship you plan to go to Palestine? Unbelievable!"

Matters between Schalk and Citron had come to a head two days before embarkation. Citron had been making a final inspection of the *Pentcho*'s living and sleeping quarters when Schalk announced that he intended to sell another 50 places on board.

"Impossible," said Citron. "We have as many as we can carry already."

"We must make room," countered Schalk. "We need the money for supplies and provisions."

Citron stood firm. He was not going to take responsibility for the extra people and risk the success of the entire project for the sake of a little more cash, however badly needed. They would have to manage without it. But Schalk was insistent; they couldn't rely on the transport bureau in Bucharest for any more financial assistance. To be sure that they would be able to buy food, fuel and other essential supplies on the trip downstream, they must sell the extra places. In any case, said Schalk, the decision was his to make. He was the Transport Director.

Citron eyed him levelly. "Not once we leave, you're not," he snapped. "This is a Betar transport, I'm the Betar commander and I say 'No more passengers.'"

A carpenter at work sawing supports for extra bunks stopped to listen, and Citron decided to cut the argument short. "We'd better continue this discussion in the office," he said.

Further argument in the privacy of Betar headquarters failed to break the deadlock. Finally it was agreed to submit the dispute to the arbitration of Artur Yanowitz, senior among the Revisionist officials who were to remain in Bratislava.

At a meeting in his office the next day Yanowitz delivered his verdict: Citron was to be in charge of the running of the ship and its finances, while Schalk was to have charge of all external affairs, including liaison with local Jewish communities en route, the police, port and river authorities and suppliers of food, fuel and other necessities. As for the number of passengers, it would remain finalized at 400—300 of them members and sympathizers of Betar and the rest nonaffiliated refugees.

It was a solution that still left room for ambiguity. Each man was responsible for his own part of the operation, but there was still no one in overall command. Far from creating permanent peace between Citron and Schalk, it merely set the agenda for further conflict later on.

Schalk spent the night before embarkation in the Café Blaha, a popular riverside restaurant, as host of a farewell party to which he had invited, among others, a trio of convivial secret policemen—Simo, Klobuscicky and Sucsky. He wasn't taking any chances on a last-minute hitch, and anyway, he had favors to repay to his friends of the *Tainapolizia*.

There were a Gypsy orchestra, bowls of steaming goulash, an abundance of the rich, fruity wines of the region and willing girls to dance and sport with. The party went on until 5 A.M. and the secret policemen got reeling drunk. Schalk only pretended to. However good one's relations with the *goyim*—especially the likes of Simo, Klobuscicky and Sucsky—it never did to let one's guard down.

By contrast, Citron spent his last night ashore at the office, giving final instructions to those who would attempt to carry on Betar after the transport left, before walking over to the transport bureau in nearby Fochovastrasse to discuss final details for the voyage. Shosha was already at home, packing for herself and the two younger brothers—Alexander, aged seventeen, and ten-year-old Leopold—who would accompany her on the *Pentcho*.

By the time Citron had finished his business at the transport office the last streetcars had stopped running, and he walked home to his brother-in-law's apartment. All was peaceful in the moonlit streets of the baroque Old Town, which presented a scene of picture-postcard beauty marred only by the ubiquitous posters denouncing Jewish "crimes" against the Slovak people or exhorting the citizens of the puppet republic to an all-out war effort. "SLOVAKIA IS MOBILIZING," read one. "LET THE WORLD TREMBLE."

That night Citron slept soundly, confident that they would leave this time and certain that they would eventually reach their destination, "though not without a good deal of difficulty."

Like Schalk, Marcel Friedmann, the farmer's son from Plavec, spent his last night ashore partying. He had come to Bratislava a day early, traveling on the overnight train from Presov with his father, so that they could spend the day in town together before he embarked.

As they strolled across the Republikplatz, where the streetcars lurched and clattered to and fro, they were accosted. "Hey, Marci. Marci Friedmann! What are you doing here?"

It was an ex-classmate from the Gymnasium at Presov, a friend who was now studying law at the Slovak University in Bratislava. Friedmann felt no resentment toward the other youth, who seemed eager, for his part, to distance himself, if only implicitly, from the official policy of discrimination which had allowed him to attend the university while excluding Marcel. When Friedmann mentioned that he was embarking for Palestine the following day, he insisted on rounding up some other ex-classmates for a farewell party.

"That's all right," said Adolf Friedmann. "Go, enjoy yourself with your friends. We have the whole day to spend together and I have people to see tonight."

That evening, like any group of youngsters seeing a comrade off, Friedmann's friends bore him off to the Golden Cockerel, a wine cellar in the Old Town, and caroused the night away with songs, toasts and student high jinks. Next morning, like any youngster who has celebrated rather too energetically, Friedmann awoke with happy memories and a sore head.

When he and his father walked together to the river to say their farewells at the entrance to the winter port, there was no sense of catastrophe to come. Like any parent wishing Godspeed to an emigrating son, Adolf Friedmann told his boy, "Remember, if things don't work out for you over there, you always have a home here with your mother and me."

There might have been no war, no Hitler, no "Jewish Question." And had the elder man been able to see the condition of the *Pentcho*, he might well have been a good deal more worried about his son's safety than about his own.

The Jews of Central Europe had, after all, survived hard times before, and few could imagine the fire storm that was to descend upon them.

Karci Farkas went to bed early the night before, too excited to sleep, while his mother packed and baked cakes and biscuits for the journey. Lying awake in the dark, whispering and giggling with his cousins who were staying behind, he savored the rich kitchen odors of yeast and cinnammon, raisins and caraway.

The next morning, skipping onto the quayside alongside *Mamouka*, clutching his valise and a box of cookies, he was almost delirious with the excitement of it all. The *Pentcho* looked magnificent to him—a marvelous, magical vessel to transport them all to a fabulous land of sunshine, sandy beaches and orange groves.

Mamouka looked happy, happier than he could remember, despite the sadness of saying goodbye to the family. Her eyes were bright because at last they were on their way to Papa, the Papa they both missed so much. And everywhere he looked there were happy, laughing, confident people—brawny young men and pretty young women, most of them in leather coats, all with rucksacks on their backs, partners with him in the great adventure that was about to begin. How splendid they all looked!

See, there was Imi Lichtenfeld, the famous wrestler and street fighter, scourge of the Jew-haters; and there was Cibi Braun, the footballer, who used to play center half for Spartacus of Prague; and there were Ernst Schillinger, the Maccabi boxing champion, and Yoni Kaufmann, captain of the Bar Kochba water polo team.

And standing by the gangplank, directing them to their places on board, crossing their names off his list one by one, was the man even these heroes all looked up to—Commandant Citron, with his flaming hair and soldierly bearing. And next to him, with more lists and her little brother Poldi in tow, was Shosha Spiegel, who everybody knew would one day marry him.

And look again, there was Karci's friend Walti Ehrlich, going aboard with his parents, while up on deck a couple of Betarim had put down their packs and were strumming guitars. Someone else played an accordion, and once they were all aboard they began singing the songs they had learned at Betar. Then, led by the strong, true tenor voice of Citron, they were singing "Hatikva"—"The Hope"—the anthem of what would one day be the Jewish state. And if there were tears—and Karci saw quite a few moist eyes—they were tears of happiness and pride, not of sorrow at leaving.

Those were the memories of one who was a child at the time. The reality, as described by those who were older, seems to have been somewhat different.

Passengers began to arrive at the winter port at about 9 A.M., and by the time Citron turned up at midmorning, more than 300 of them were milling around outside the barred gates, kept from entering by the port authorities, who had not yet received final word from the government that the *Pentcho* would be allowed to leave.

It was a gray, damp day, and it was four in the afternoon before the gates were opened and the passengers, frustrated and footsore, were able to proceed to the big customs shed where processing could begin. Schalk, who knew more about the ways of Slovak officialdom than did Citron and the others, chose that moment to make his first appearance.

The customs officers checked everyone and everything thoroughly, looking in particular for hard currency and cameras. They confiscated Citron's camera and took articles of gold and other valuables from other passengers. They even confiscated items of food: Schalk's younger brother Tibor had a salami and a jar of jam taken from him.

Schalk himself carried the "hottest" item of contraband—a shoulder bag containing seven handguns and 250 rounds of ammunition in case of trouble on board. He did not attempt to smuggle it past the overzealous customs officers but merely handed it to his friend Commissioner Yakouboczy, who carried the bag aboard for him.

Passport checks were as rigorous as customs, but here too Schalk managed to circumvent the regulations. With Citron's tacit approval—but without his formal knowledge, so that he could not be held responsible—11 people without passports or any other kind of documentation, including two girls who had fled into Slovakia from Nazi-occupied Poland, were smuggled aboard. And the customs officers were persuaded to give back Citron's camera.

It was late that night before everyone was aboard, and a good deal later still before everyone was settled for the night, amid a certain amount of confusion and complaining about the accommodations.

Although Daniel Hamburger, the refugee from Frankfurt, felt a surge of claustrophobic panic at his first descent into the hold where his bunk was located, the boisterous young-sters of Betar who would sleep and live there with him—and with whom he had so little in common—seemed unaffected by the suffocating dark. They nicknamed the hold Akko, after the fortress (better known as Acre) in Palestine where the British jailed their more dangerous political prisoners.

The comparison was not entirely fair to the British: living conditions in the hold were measurably worse than in the prison. Because of the extra passengers taken on to enable the final payment to be made on the *Pentcho,* there were now three men to a bunk instead of two, allowing each man a space 20 inches wide instead of 30.

At such close quarters, each trio slept like stacked chairs; when one turned, all turned. Each man had one thin blanket, and rucksacks or valises served as pillows. There were no mattresses, just the rough, bare boards beneath them, though some had had the foresight to bring inflatable mattresses.

The hold was dimly lit by oil lamps, and when it was crammed to capacity with 200 men and boys, the atmosphere rapidly became fetid and suffocatingly airless. Common "liv-ing" space was the area between the rows of bunks, minus what was taken up by washrooms and toilets and the com-panionway leading up to the next level. This was nicknamed Ilava, after a notorious Slovakian prison camp, and there more than 100 women were sleeping—the Betar girls, plus wives and fiancées of men down below in Akko and the younger refugee women. The older refugee women and men were located in the top level, abovedecks, where there was the most air.

Like Daniel Hamburger, Karci Farkas did not like what he found down below in Akko. His embarkation euphoria evaporated instantly when he was consigned to the hold. *"Mamouka, Mamouka,"* he wailed from his bunk. "I want to be with you." Efforts to soothe him only made him wail even louder.

On the upper level Karci's cries were heard by his mother, who had allowed him to be taken below only with great misgivings. She did not wait long before marching off to find Citron. "Rules, rules?" she said. "You should choke on your rules. Either you send that child up to sleep with his mother or I'm going down to sleep with him."

Backed to the wall, his iron resolve already beginning to crack under the relentless onslaught of Jewish motherhood personified, Citron pointed out that there were other small boys in Akko—Poldi Spiegel and Walti Ehrlich, for example.

"The others?" Gisella Farkas snorted. "The others? Others who have their fathers to keep them company? Others who have their big brothers to keep them company? Let me ask you, where is my Karci's big brother? He hasn't one. Where is his father? He's in the Land of Israel, the good Lord should bless him, a pioneer in the Land of Israel. Isn't it enough that for three years my Karci should not see his father? Now you want to separate him from his mother too? A shame on you, young man."

At this point Citron capitulated. Within minutes, the still-sobbing Karci had been liberated from the hold and restored to the arms of his formidable mother.

Oskar Salomon's stay in Akko was equally brief. He wasn't going to spend the voyage cooped up down there in the dark with 200 others if he could help it. The way to get out, and make himself useful at the same time, was to attach himself to the crew. That might mean a lot of hard work, but it would give him the run of the ship and a place in the crew's quarters in the forecastle, where there would be a good deal more air than in the hold. It would also give him a chance to keep tabs on the crew, a villainous-looking lot, he thought, who might well have mutiny or desertion in mind.

He wasn't sure yet how he was going to work it, but he decided to make the attempt without delay. Self-interest was turned into a good deed when he encountered one of the 11 "stowaways" among the men crowded into Akko like cattle in a stockyard pen and learned that he had nowhere to sleep. Meyer Steinmetz, he said his name was, and Salomon immediately offered him his bunk.

"But where will you sleep?"

"Don't worry about that," said Salomon. "I've got other plans."

He made his way up on deck and stood watching the captain for a few minutes at his place inside the wheelhouse while he considered his next move. What he had heard about Markeyevitch, while hanging around the Betar office a few days before sailing, had given Salomon the germ of an idea. Now it rapidly ripened.

Markeyevitch looked just as he had heard Schalk describe him: an aristocratic ruin, a man who had fallen a long way. What would such a man miss most of his past life as an officer in the Imperial Russian Navy? A fine ship, smart uniforms, a disciplined crew, a personal servant. That was it, thought Salomon, a personal servant: that was the one want he could fill. He would offer himself as the captain's orderly. It would tickle the poor old bastard's vanity, make him feel important again, to have someone fetch and carry and run personal errands for him.

Confident that he had found the key, Salomon strode boldly to the wheelhouse, where Markeyevitch stood gloomily watching a crate of supplies being winched aboard. Stepping forward with a smart salute, the young Betari introduced himself, and speaking in Czech—a language close enough to the captain's native Russian for him to understand—he launched into an impromptu monologue.

He expatiated on his consuming interest in ships and the sea and his unquenchable ambition to follow a maritime career. Markeyevitch gave him one bleak glance before transferring his attention once more to the loading of supplies. Undeterred by this total lack of response, Salomon plowed ahead, promising to prove an apt pupil and a valuable addition to the crew if given the chance. Wearily, Markeyevitch cut him short. "No good," he interjected. "Too busy. You go below. Goodbye."

Even the finality of that curt "goodbye" failed to halt Salomon's flow. Ever the realist, he had been expecting an initial rebuff and knew that the way to success was to wear the Russian down.

Of course, he said, he realized very well that the captain and crew would be far too busy to show the ropes to a landlubber like him and he wouldn't for a moment expect them to waste any time on his instruction. All he wanted was the opportunity to observe at close quarters how a ship was run and how a master mariner handled his command. He would absolutely keep out of everybody's way, and in return for the privilege he would be happy to act as cabin boy/valet/batman for the captain.

A glimpse of the hunched figure of Ludmilla Markeyevitch, surveying him doubtfully from the half-open door of the captain's cabin, inspired Salomon to amend his offer of personal service hurriedly to include the captain's lady. It was an inspired piece of improvisation. The old woman emerged from the doorway, shuffled over to her husband and muttered a few words in Russian. The captain bent his gaunt 6-foot-3 frame close to that of his tiny wife, grunted two or three times, then shrugged and nodded.

"All right," he said to Salomon, more resigned than enthusiastic, as his wife shuffled back to the cabin. "You can try your luck. But watch your step and don't come crying to me if you get all the shitty jobs. Right?"

Salomon snapped to attention and threw the captain a crisp salute. "Aye, aye, sir," he said in English—a phrase he had picked up from a Hollywood costume drama he had seen a year or two back about a mutiny on a British man-of-war. "I'll bring up my gear."

Although he was exhausted, Citron found himself too tense for sleep and sat on deck all that first night, sheltered under an awning from the continuing drizzle. Shosha was able to snatch half an hour from her duties with the women and children to be with him, and they sat looking at the lights of the city they would soon leave forever, side by side and holding hands—the only physical contact they would permit themselves, for they considered it essential to set an example of proper behavior to all on board.

They spent much of the next day making sure everyone was properly settled for the start of the journey, allotting duties, and giving instructions to the dozen men—mainly ex-soldiers, older than the Betar cadets—who would act as stewards, men like Imi Lichtenfeld, Schalk's brother-in-law Stefan Braun and Emerich Dukas, a fifty-year-old World War veteran who had been a sergeant major in the Austro-Hungarian Army.

That evening, before sundown and the start of the Sabbath, Shosha typed out the first of the military-style daily orders Citron would issue throughout the trip: ablutions would be carried out in strict rotation, section by section; comrades were requested to comport themselves respectfully during prayers; Hans Goldberger would be in overall charge of the ship's cleanliness while Karol Hoffmann would supervise the passengers' personal hygiene, both of them being empowered to take "any measures necessary" to carry out their duties.

Passengers would be divided into seven groups who would take turns to go on deck. It was strictly forbidden to send letters from the ship while on the Danube. All fraternizing with the crew was strictly forbidden, and in general it should be understood that all official instructions must be obeyed at all times "in order to permit us to avoid taking strong and strict measures."

Citron was determined to run a tight ship, and the orders were addressed to all its passengers, not just the Betar. The older refugees might resent taking orders from a twenty-two-year-old but they would just have to learn to live with it. Without discipline, he knew, the *Pentcho* didn't stand a chance.

That night, with the commencement of the Sabbath, candles were lit and prayers and blessings said. Many of the passengers felt pangs of nostalgia for the homes and families they were leaving behind in the land where their ancestors had lived for a thousand years and more.

Some of the Betar girls wept, but not eighteen-year-old Grete Ehrenfeld; she was going with no regrets at all, for she was leaving absolutely nothing behind. Her only brother had already gone to Palestine on an earlier transport; her parents were with her on this one, and so was the young man she was engaged to marry.

Grete had come to Bratislava with her family from Vienna more than two years before, after the Nazi occupation of Austria. The Slovak capital had proved to be a close and convenient refuge, but the Ehrenfelds never had any intention of staying there longer than they had to. They were convinced that Czechoslovakia would before long share the fate of Austria; they had strong connections with the Revisionist movement, and their aim was to get to Palestine on the first available Betar ship.

Grete's older brother, Fritz, was soon on his way. He had been a leading member of the Austrian Betar, which qualified him for a free place in a Revisionist transport that set out from Brno in November 1938. While they awaited their turn, the rest of the family made what they could of life in Bratislava, a city which any Viennese—even penniless refugees, like the Ehrenfelds—felt bound to consider irredeemably provincial.

Josef Ehrenfeld, a stonemason and jack-of-all-trades, was able to find work as a roofer, and Grete labored alongside him as his assistant, clad in overalls which disguised her ripening figure and with her long brown hair piled up under a workman's cap so that she could pass as a boy. But though they could earn enough to live, it was impossible to save. There was no way that they could pay their passage to Palestine when the time came.

Like her brother, Fritz, Grete had been an active member of Betar in Vienna, and now she joined the Bratislava brigade, turning up for parades and lectures four and five nights a week after a hard day's work aloft. Her zeal, her past connections with the movement in Austria and her family's reduced circumstances guaranteed that like Fritz, she would get a free place on the next transport.

But what about her parents? The number of free places was strictly limited, said Citron, and only the young and the fit were eligible. Grete protested. "I won't go without them," she said. Citron shrugged. "I'm sorry. There's nothing I can do. Be thankful there's a place for you."

Grete was not to be put off that easily. Without her parents' knowledge she wrote to Jabotinsky's headquarters in London, citing her family's services to the movement and making the case for her mother and father. Some weeks later, Citron received a message from London: all three Ehrenfelds were to travel free.

While the dynamic Grete was working alongside her father on the rooftops, keeping up with Betar and ensuring her parents' survival, she did not neglect her personal affairs. First she outraged her parents by falling for the debonair street brawler and thoroughly unsuitable ladies' man Imi Lichtenfeld, a cousin by marriage. Then she delighted them by becoming engaged to the respectable, good-looking and extremely eligible Karol Hoffmann, the son of well-to-do parents, who was also to sail on the *Pentcho*.

Karol's parents were scarcely less pleased. Despite her family's straitened circumstances, they thought Grete "a fine girl," and although they disapproved of "this crazy plan to go to Palestine," they were glad their Karli would have his fiancée with him on the voyage. So here were the Ehrenfelds together on the *Pentcho*—Grete, her parents and her husband-to-be—with a bright future in prospect and no one and nothing left behind. Despite the conditions on board, which she already found "pretty horrifying," Grete Ehrenfeld's only feeling, as her bunkmates cried themselves to sleep that night, was impatience to get away.

As for her fiancé, although he was leaving his parents and two older brothers behind, Karol Hoffmann was no less eager to get away than Grete.

While some, like his father and brothers, were determined to sit things out, hopeful that the good days would return, Karol could entertain no such illusions. The once-loved city of his birth and boyhood—the city in which his father had been able to rise from humble beginnings to a position of wealth and prominence—had turned into a hostile place since the events of 1938 brought the People's Party to power.

The narrow streets of the Old Town where he had loved to wander alone, weaving tapestries of a splendid past in his imagination, finding there the evidences of a heritage he considered as much his own as anyone else's, had become filled with menace. The tavern signs which had once suggested warmth and conviviality now signaled only rejection and contempt. The Gentile friends he had known since childhood had turned first cold then hostile. Bratislava no longer felt like home to him, and Karol had rejected the city as the city had rejected him.

In the gloom of Akko, using the bare boards of his bunk as a writing desk, he jotted down his bitter parting thoughts. *"So glad to get away from my home, where I was born and raised and schooled and where I had all my friends and memories,"* he wrote. *"Friends have turned into enemies and every landscape so familiar to me has turned into their parade ground. No, this cannot be my home, though I have never known any other."*

Of his father—*"still unbelieving and telling me to abandon this foolish idea"*—Karol noted: *"He remains an optimist to the end. He refuses to believe that things have changed."* But his mother seemed glad that he was going, even though she wept profusely at their parting. *"I am her youngest son and very much attached to her,"* he wrote, *"but she seems to have a premonition that I am saving myself by going away."*

At about ten the next morning, the *Pentcho's* tired old engines coughed and spluttered into life and the whole ship began to vibrate. Fifteen minutes later the paddle wheels turned noisily as the vessel cast off from quayside and moved slowly out into the stream.

Apart from the crew, no more than 20 people were on deck, including Schalk, Citron and Shosha. The others had strict instructions to remain below. Being denied a last view of their homeland did not seem to worry the youngsters in Akko. Karol Hoffmann noted that among the young men at least, *"nobody seems to be sad, everybody laughs and is radiant; all we feel is hope and optimism for the future."*

As they drew clear of the port area, Citron could see that a small crowd of relatives and friends, not more than 30 or so, had gathered on the embankment to see them go. Among them was Shosha's mother, who walked briskly after the *Pentcho* until she reached the end of the embankment, then stood there watching the vessel clatter out into the main channel.

Shosha brushed away a tear, and Citron squeezed her hand wordlessly as the embankment slipped away behind them and the small, still figure of Charlotte Spiegel slowly merged into the background of the receding city, capped by the ruins of its ancient castle.

From below, Citron could hear the boys in Akko singing a Betar pioneering song, accompanied by Karol Hoffmann on the mandolin: "There, in our promised land, all our hopes will be fulfilled."

As far as they and Citron were concerned, they were not leaving home. They were going home.

4

The *Pentcho*'s first two days' run downriver from Bratislava—through the glittering twin cities of Buda and Pest, across the great, featureless Hungarian Plain and on to the undistinguished little coaling port of Mohacs—were uneventful enough. Uneventful, that is, if one discounts the time the vessel ran into a sandbank and later, after freeing itself, all but capsized as its passengers shifted en masse from one side of the boat to the other for a better view of the approaching Hungarian capital.

"*Nadrugu strano, nadrugu strano*—Move to the other side!" the captain yelled, lapsing into his native Russian as the *Pentcho* dipped almost to its port gunwales, lifting the starboard paddle clear of the water. There was a panic rush for the other side of the boat, which then dipped crazily in that direction. "*Nadrugu strano, nadrugu strano,*" yelled Markeyevitch again.

Citron immediately ordered everyone below, and from then on stewards were posted around the clock to make sure that nobody went on deck except at the time allotted for his group, and that when passengers were on deck there was no crowding to one side or the other.

These measures were enough to keep the ship from actually turning over, but of course could not cure the overladen *Pentcho*'s chronic instability. Its crazy, lurching progress and the frantic cries of *"Nadrugu strano"* from Markeyevitch, echoed by the stewards, were to become a feature of the voyage downriver and the subject of much high-spirited joking by Citron's young Betarim.

Inevitably, the ship's drunken gait attracted the attention of the authorities. When the *Pentcho* reached Mohacs it was stopped and ordered into port, where the Hungarians detained it for five days while they decided whether it should be allowed to proceed. The rank-and-file passengers were not informed of the reason for the delay, Karol Hoffmann noting that *"there is not much use to try and find out what is holding us up; nobody knows and the few who do won't tell you."*

While Schalk argued and pleaded with the authorities on shore, Citron concentrated on shipboard discipline. His daily orders recorded that five Betarim would receive black marks for disobedience, and warned that "the next time very strict punishment will be exacted." Ideology sessions were started, with discussions limited to Jewish national themes, since "all other subjects are superfluous." Order on ship was "slowly coming up to Betar standards," but nevertheless two men were barred from going on deck for two days as punishment for breaches of regulations.

On the *Pentcho*'s last day in Mohacs, one male Betari earned himself four days below decks and two Betar girls were barred for three days after they were found visiting the men's quarters.

Two registered and paid-up passengers who had failed to catch the boat at Bratislava caught up with it at Mohacs: a youngster named Pal Lorenz and Dr. Paul von Heller, an elderly and eccentric Viennese professor, who convulsed the younger Betar boys by arriving at quayside with his belongings in three cardboard boxes and asking, "Where is my cabin?" Marcel Friedmann picked up two of his boxes and took him below to Akko.

The first inclination of the authorities at Mohacs had been to send the *Pentcho* back to Bratislava, but they discarded this option, fearing that the overladen vessel might well sink on the return journey while still in Hungarian waters. They might not have been particularly concerned about the safety of the passengers, but they did have to worry about the very real possibility of the *Pentcho*'s overturning and blocking the shipping channel before it passed out of their jurisdiction.

Another option might be to terminate the *Pentcho*'s voyage altogether, but the Hungarians quickly discarded that idea too, lest they be saddled with 400 Jews whom no country wanted. The best way out of the quandary was obviously to pass the problem on to someone else, and this was the option the Hungarians finally took.

The Yugoslav border was only a few miles distant, and just beyond that lay the first Yugoslav river port, Bezdan. It should be possible to see that the *Pentcho* got that far safely. To make absolutely sure, the Royal Hungarian Navy's Danube flotilla would be asked to send an officer aboard to pilot the ship as far as Bezdan. Once there, the *Pentcho* would become the Yugoslavs' headache. The decision relieved Citron and Schalk. At least they would be on the move again, and if the *Pentcho* ran into similar trouble with the Yugoslavs, they would be in less hostile territory there than in pro-Nazi Hungary.

When Hungarian Navy Lieutenant Zalan Petnehazy went aboard the *Pentcho* the next day to take it to Bezdan, he came quickly to the conclusion that everyone on it must be insane. Who but a bunch of lunatics would travel voluntarily on such a vessel? Sure, he realized that things were not so good for the Jews nowadays, either where this lot came from or in his own country. But to sail in such a death trap? Surely things were not *that* bad.

Making a closer inspection, he was surprised to find that despite the acute overcrowding, sanitary and health conditions were good enough. It was when he went below to inspect the engine room that he got a shock. He found it, as he reported later, "in terrible condition—the engines clogged with grease and filth and steam escaping from the pipes."

Nonetheless, he was "deeply impressed by the passengers' almost fanatical certainty that they would reach their final destination."

Some hours later, having delivered the *Pentcho* into Yugoslav jurisdiction at Bezdan, Petnehazy returned home by road, thankful that he did not have to proceed any farther on such an unstable craft. The experience obviously left a deep impression, for almost forty years later Petnehazy recalled his brief encounter with Citron's "caricature of a submarine" in an article in the Hungarian magazine *Uj Elet*. "I wonder if any of them survived the voyage?" he wrote.

But if the professional sailor was appalled by the *Pentcho,* the younger passengers at least were still able to regard it all as something of a lark. To the great approval of his shipmates, Karol Hoffmann wrote a lighthearted lyric which he set to the tune of a popular ditty of the day:

> Pentcho, *you are the world's most lovely boat.*
> Pentcho, *you are the sweetest thing afloat.*
> *One day forward, then six days you're stuck,*
> *When you move you waddle like a duck. . . .*

That verse and the phrase *"nadruga strano"* were to remain in the memory of *Pentcho* survivors long after time had blurred other fine details of their strange odyssey.

* * *

Before they left Mohacs, an alarming rumor had swept the *Pentcho* that between 75 and 100 more people were being sent from Bratislava to join them. *"This is bad news,"* Tibor Schalk wrote in his diary. *"There is absolutely no room for them."*

Shortly after they reached Bezdan the rumor was confirmed. When Zoltan Schalk went ashore to telephone a progress report to the NZO office in Belgrade, he was given firm instructions, endorsed by the Revisionists' world headquarters in London, that room simply had to be made for another 101 passengers—a group of German, Austrian and Polish Jews just released from Dachau after long and difficult negotiations, through Swiss intermediaries, between the New Zionists and the SS.

"But it's impossible," Schalk protested. "We're almost literally hanging over the sides as it is, and the Hungarians held us up for five days because of overloading."

"Listen," said the voice on the other end of the line. "These people are free on condition that we get them out of Europe immediately. The SS told us, 'Either they go on the Danube or they go in the Danube.' I don't have to tell you they weren't bluffing. You'll just have to squeeze up and make room for them."

That ended the argument as far as Schalk was concerned, and when Schalk returned to the *Pentcho,* Citron took out his tape measure and went below to see how and where another 101 bodies could be fitted in. He didn't dare to consider the even more critical question of how the *Pentcho* could be expected to remain afloat in such a grossly overladen condition. It was "insanity," he knew; but what else could they do but obey instructions, take the extra people on and hope for a miracle?

Not everyone aboard the *Pentcho* took the news with such stoicism. There was open protest among the refugee element, and even Citron's tightly disciplined Betarim muttered resentfully among themselves that it would be impossible to crowd any more bodies onto the ship.

A group of refugees, sensing that they had a majority behind them, went to Citron and Schalk with a demand that no new passengers be taken on until there had been a vote among all those presently aboard. Neither man was in the mood for a plebiscite. "There'll be no vote," Citron ruled. "This is an order, not a request. These people will sail with us."

During a seven-day wait in Bezdan for the new passengers, Citron turned his full attention to growing problems of morale and discipline. But for the delays they might well have been at the Black Sea by now, and there was a good deal of discontent about that, quite apart from continued grumbling about having to make room for the newcomers. In his daily orders for June 3, Citron warned against "creating problems" over the holdup. "As soon as we get instructions we will continue our journey," he said.

The next day, he found it necessary to denounce an "absolutely abominable" act of vandalism: someone had cut up another passenger's inflatable mattress, and "if this kind of thing happens again we will be obliged to use disciplinary measures not so far employed." The warning against men's visiting the women's quarters had to be repeated, and on June 5, Citron threatened "very strict consequences" if anyone tried to circumvent the ban on sending unauthorized mail.

In his orders of June 6, Citron gave a stern warning against black-marketeering and the "unprincipled and un-Revisionistic practice of exploiting the poverty of fellow travelers to do business at their expense."

Though adequate, the official ration was small, and there was hunger aboard. Racketeers were buying valuables at knock-down prices from people needing cash for extra food, which could be purchased ashore. To put a stop to this, Citron forbade individuals to go ashore to shop and warned them "not to sell your property to greedy people."

There was also a certain amount of petty theft. People were "careless" about handing in lost property, said the June 6 orders, which contained the warning that some missing blankets must be handed in by nine the following morning or there would be a search operation "which will be quite disagreeable for some of you."

Again Citron felt obliged to stifle dissent over the arrival of the new passengers, who were now expected the following day. "You are kindly requested not to create any difficulties, nor to discuss the locations of the new arrivals, since this is absolutely pointless," said the orders. "Try to put yourselves in their place. We are prepared to accept any discomfort, and a display of un-Jewish selfishness will only reflect badly on all of us."

On June 7 the freed Dachau prisoners arrived in Bezdan from the Patronka transit camp near Bratislava aboard a small steamer named the *Oriole—"mostly old people, but one family with many children,"* Tibor Schalk noted in his diary.

They did not begin boarding until late that night when the *Oriole* drew alongside the *Pentcho,* which was anchored in midstream, and a gangplank was thrown between the two vessels. A searchlight bathed the scene as the new arrivals made their way aboard, one by one, to be met by the *Pentcho*'s medical team before being assigned to their places. Many were old and weak. Cold, wet and miserable in the driving night rain, they moved haltingly from one vessel to the other, and it took two hours to get them and their luggage transferred.

Despite his admonition to "put yourselves in their place," Citron felt resentful at having so many obviously unfit people imposed on his transport. He recognized many of them as the type of refugee who, once freed from immediate danger, made a point of complaining about the current conditions and harking back to the "good old days." Further, the ship's doctors found on examination that some of them were suffering from heart disease, and even tuberculosis—ailments that would ordinarily have made them ineligible for a place on board.

The boys down in Akko didn't think too highly of the newcomers either. Hoffmann thought the situation *"almost intolerable—we are packed like sardines and you can hardly move a step without bumping into somebody."* To make matters worse, *"these people are not a disciplined group like us and are noisy and quarrelsome."* He did, however, allow that *"apparently they have endured more hardships than we who are fresh from home and to whom this whole thing still looks very much like a romantic adventure."*

Attempting to hide his misgivings, Citron made a brief welcoming address to the newly freed prisoners. He reminded them that the *Pentcho* was a Revisionist ship but told them they should feel themselves to be among family and called on them to try to fit in with the arrangements on board, since they would all share a common fate.

In a status report to the emigration office in Bucharest five days later, Citron noted that the *Pentcho* now carried 514 passengers, of whom 12 were children under five, 15 were children between five and twelve, 130 were women and 98 were old men. He complained that while his original 300 were "good human material," the refugees they had brought with them for financial reasons from Bratislava, and especially the latest arrivals, were "substandard."

"It was heartless to send these people on such a journey," he wrote. *"They were accommodated only with extraordinary difficulty and 46 people, for whom there are no places below, will have to sleep on deck."* Discipline, which had been satisfactory up to that time, had been impaired by the arrival of the additional passengers, he added.

After giving an account of the state of the *Pentcho*'s dwindling food supplies and health conditions, which he called adequate, Citron reported that the boat was *"uncomfortable in the strongest sense of the word and shockingly unstable."* But despite all this, morale was *"generally unimpaired."*

Paradoxically, one whose morale certainly did not suffer was the claustrophobic Daniel Hamburger. For him the new arrivals brought a measure of relief. Volunteers were needed to sleep on deck, and Hamburger was quick to step forward.

"I was the first to go up on deck," he would recall. "It really saved me, because I couldn't breathe in that hellhole down there. Even when it was cold or rainy I didn't worry. I had an inflatable mattress and a leather coat to keep me warm and dry. After Akko it was like paradise for me on deck."

As the *Pentcho* lurched and clattered slowly on down the Danube, through a landscape of silver birch forests and picturesque villages where storks nested on the rooftops, it became clear to the handful of passengers who were aware of the power struggle between Citron and Schalk that Citron held all the cards.

Not only did Schalk lack the constituency to enable him to exert the control he thought was rightly his; he was also personally unpopular. Despite his gift for cultivating policemen and bureaucrats, he had less talent for gaining the good opinion of his fellow travelers, to whom he perhaps appeared slightly shadier than he really was. As the one known to have organized the voyage, he was held personally responsible for the overcrowding, the discomfort, the poor food, the noisome toilets. The dissatisfaction had to find a focus and Schalk was the obvious candidate.

Even the veterans, including his brother-in-law, whom Schalk had brought aboard to act as his "police force," were not supporting him. As Imi Lichtenfeld saw it, "Although it was Schalk who had invited me to sail with the *Pentcho* and although it was Schalk who had organized the transport and made it possible for it to leave, I felt bound to accept the control and leadership of Betar, and so did the others."

So while Schalk continued to handle the *Pentcho*'s negotiations with the authorities ashore and the emigration bureau in Bucharest, in the tight, enclosed world of the *Pentcho* itself Citron was king.

With 514 passengers now jammed on board and unexpected delays all along their route, it was an even slower and more uncomfortable journey than Citron had anticipated. In the intense summer heat, conditions below were stifling, yet because of the shortage of deck space, the Betarim in Akko could come up only in relays and for strictly limited periods for fresh air and exercise.

Constant cleaning and cookhouse details and regular parades helped to counter the morale-eroding effects of enforced inactivity. The Betarim would muster in full uniform—brown pants and shirts with Sam Browne belts and peaked caps—every evening just before sunset, to line up in platoons and parade the Betar colors: a blue flag emblazoned with a menorah and the slogan "IN BLOOD AND FIRE JUDEA FELL; IN BLOOD AND FIRE JUDEA WILL ARISE AGAIN."

As the Betarim marched and wheeled on deck, taking great care to keep the ship's balance even, some of the other passengers would mutter scornful remarks about "playing at soldiers." Citron was well aware that there was a feeling among the refugees that drilling and marching were not suitable pastimes for "nice Jewish boys." Some of them thought it almost blasphemous that military commands should be barked out in Hebrew, the language of the Torah.

Citron had issued strict instructions to his ranks not to allow themselves to be provoked by such attitudes. "They don't understand," he said; "remember, it's *our* discipline and *our* morale that will pull us all through."

5

The *Pentcho* had set out from Bratislava hoping to reach the coast of Palestine by the end of June. In the event, it took almost five weeks to get as far as the Yugoslav-Rumanian frontier, little more than halfway between Bratislava and the Black Sea.

The frontier coincides roughly with the entrance to the most spectacular and difficult stretch of the Danube's 1,776-mile length—the Kazan Defile, known also as the Kataract, where the river narrows abruptly to run at breakneck speed for more than 100 miles through a rocky, winding gorge.

Although the *Pentcho* had been able to battle its way through the defile unladen on its way upstream a couple of months before, the international commission regulating river traffic now needed to make only a cursory inspection of the vessel in the no-man's-land between the two frontiers to rule that it could not be allowed to proceed into the defile. One of the commissioners was heard to comment that the vessel was a danger to shipping and should not be afloat at all.

As with the Hungarian authorities at Mohacs, the commission members may have been less concerned for the safety of the *Pentcho*'s 514 passengers than afraid that if the vessel came to grief it would block the narrow shipping channel. Oil from Rumania's Black Sea oil fields was flowing upstream by barge and shallow-draft tanker to fuel the Nazi war machine; any interruption of this flow—especially as a result of the passage of a boatload of Jews—would be calculated to enrage the Germans, who held all Europe in terror after their lightning defeat of France.

Whatever the commissioners' true concerns, their order to the *Pentcho* to turn back was the start of a holdup that would last six weeks, bringing the entire project to the brink of failure.

Three days of fruitless haggling with the authorities preceded the *Pentcho*'s enforced return to the Yugoslav port of Moldava. From Moldava it was sent another 20 miles upstream to Vishnia-Graditska. At Vishnia-Graditska there was a further official change of mind, and the vessel was directed downstream toward the frontier. Finally, the *Pentcho* came to rest at the little port of Dobra, just short of no-man's-land, where it was ordered to anchor in midstream while its fate was decided.

Schalk went ashore to contact the emigration bureau in Bucharest, the Jewish community in Belgrade and anyone else who might be expected to help get them moving again. To some of those aboard, it seemed that this time the *Pentcho* must finally have run out of luck. *"People are very anxious,"* Tibor Schalk noted in his diary, and a few days later he observed gloomily that *"our leaders are helpless in this situation."*

The men quartered in the depths of the ship were the hardest hit. As the *Pentcho* lay motionless in the heat of an unusually sunny June, their quarters turned into a fetid oven in which lice and bedbugs proliferated alarmingly. For Karol

Hoffmann, as for most of the young men in Akko, the infestation was an unpleasantly novel experience.

"After the first shock there was nothing to do but accept the unavoidable," he recalled later. "Lying on my bunk and trying to sleep in the stench of the hold I could feel them all the time, but after a while I didn't even bother to try and catch them, since they didn't bite me—apparently my blood was not to their taste." It took Hoffmann some days to get used to having to shake the bugs out of his cup before lining up with it for his morning coffee.

Conditions were becoming unbearable by the time the Yugoslavs offered some relief by allowing the *Pentcho* people to go ashore to take exercise, and by bringing an open barge which tied up alongside the *Pentcho* and became a temporary substitute dormitory for the 300 men and boys of Akko. This arrangement had the dual advantage of allowing the Betarim the luxury of breathing fresh air at night and permitting Akko to be thoroughly cleaned and disinfected, so that by June 29, Tibor Schalk was able to record that the Dobra harbormaster had been aboard and had remarked how clean and orderly the ship was.

Citron's orders of the day for this period indicate no serious disciplinary problems, apart from that of "certain gentlemen who find themselves in the ladies' quarters" and continued attempts to send out letters and postcards through unauthorized persons. "If we intercept such correspondence, it will be destroyed," warned Citron.

He also found it necessary to complain about certain individuals' lack of respect for *Hatikva* and the Betar hymn. They should stand still and keep quiet while these were being sung, said Citron. "This courtesy, which is observed by other nations, should be observed by the Jewish nation."

Concern for such fine details of discipline was, however, far from being Citron's major preoccupation. By this time some of the passengers were in a state of almost open revolt, demanding that the transport be abandoned, and Citron was sufficiently worried to start considering the desperate expedient of making a dash for the Kataract in the hope that once they were in the narrow defile it would be impossible for the Rumanian river authorities to turn them back.

When Schalk returned empty-handed from a trip to Belgrade on the first of July, Citron discussed the possibility with him. Schalk shrugged. "Why not?" he said. "As things stand we have nothing to lose."

The next person Citron consulted was the captain. Perhaps made reckless by morphine euphoria, Markeyevitch agreed to make an attempt to gate-crash the defile before dawn, when the troops manning two blockhouses at the entrance to the gorge would probably be at their least vigilant.

In the small hours of the morning of July 3, the *Pentcho*'s engines started up, and a few minutes later the old paddleboat slipped its moorings and began heading downstream toward no-man's-land, a few hundred yards away, and the entrance to the gorge a couple of miles beyond that.

But the *Pentcho* was hardly capable of stealth. The clank and rumble of its antique and neglected engines and the rattle and splashing of its paddles were sufficient to awaken Captain Arpad Biecescu. the harbormaster of Dobra. Jumping out of bed to find out what was afoot, he was in time to see the shadowy bulk of the *Pentcho* heading downstream in the murky predawn light. Snatching up his service revolver, but without stopping to dress, the pajama-clad harbormaster leaped onto his motorcycle and gave chase, roaring along the towpath behind the *Pentcho*, bellowing at it to heave to.

In the wheelhouse, where he stood alongside the captain and the Greek helmsman, Costas, Citron heard the roar of Biecescu's motorcycle and his outraged cries rising above the rumble of the *Pentcho*'s engines. "Keep going," he said.

When the *Pentcho* failed to obey his orders to stop, the harbormaster drew his revolver from his waistband and began firing. Still the *Pentcho* pressed on.

By now the entrance to the gorge and the two blockhouses guarding it were visible in the strengthening light. Inside the blockhouses, dozing sentries were alerted by the rumpus upstream. Citron realized this when they started firing warning shots in the *Pentcho*'s direction.

With Biecescu roaring along behind them and the Rumanian troops ahead now thoroughly alert, the attempt seemed doomed. There was nothing for it, Citron decided reluctantly, but to turn back.

Shortly after they had returned to their moorings, tied up and cut off the engines, Captain Biecescu—now wearing his harbormaster's uniform—came out to the *Pentcho* in his launch, accompanied by two armed policemen. In a blind fury he stormed into the wheelhouse and, failing to find the captain, who was in his cabin taking a shot of morphine to calm himself after the morning's excitement, he turned on Costas, the helmsman, and felled him with a blow.

Biecescu posted the two policemen on board to make sure they did not try to breach the defile again and, as a parting shot, accused Citron and Schalk of traveling under forged documents, warning them of retribution ahead.

The *Pentcho* was to be detained at Dobra for the next six weeks, a period in which morale would sag and relations between the transport leadership and the refugee groups would plummet in an atmosphere of backbiting and recrimination.

But while their elders complained and their leaders argued, the youngsters of Akko and Ilava, at least, had something of a holiday. No longer cooped up in their respective quarters below, they were able to mix together freely for the first time since the *Pentcho* had sailed. Especially for the courting couples—for whom shipboard restrictions and the utter lack of privacy had made it difficult to have much more contact than a smile, a wave, a quick hand-squeeze or an occasional peck on the cheek—it was an idyllic time.

Grete Ehrenfeld would recall how, with another engaged couple, Sidney Fahn and Regina Sonnenfeld, she and Karol spent long, lazy afternoons swimming in the Danube and wandering in the woods that ran down to the riverbank, imagining their future in the far-off Promised Land which, despite present difficulties, they were sure they would reach. "It was like a wonderful holiday," she said—"the sunshine, the swimming, the woods. For a while we didn't care if we never moved on. What was more, we were on neutral territory, safe from the Nazis."

But there was danger in the Danube, and after one near-fatality, Citron felt obliged to ban diving and swimming.

It happened one afternoon as a group of Betar girls and youths were diving from the upper deck of the *Pentcho* and sporting in the cool green waters of the river. On the after-deck the *Pentcho*'s best swimmer, Imi Lichtenfeld, dozing in the sun after a vigorous gymnastics workout, was awakened by shouts of alarm—"Imi, come quick! Benny's drowning!"

Benny Willinger, a novice swimmer, had failed to surface after diving in. His companions were searching frantically, but inexpertly, unable to reach the bottom, where Willinger lay tangled in a forest of weed. Lichtenfeld jackknifed over the side into 20 feet of water to join the rescue attempt, swallowing to equalize the pressure on his ears as he searched the bottom for the missing youth.

In the dark green murk, visibility was limited, and his first two dives proved fruitless. On the third, he spotted Willinger, no longer struggling, and began to free him from the clinging weeds. The boy, though barely conscious, reached out and—where a drowning person might be expected to clutch convulsively—touched his rescuer lightly on the arm.

In seconds, Lichtenfeld had him loose and was bearing him to the surface. Not long after that, the water forced from his lungs by artificial respiration, Willinger was sitting up thanking his rescuer.

Lichtenfeld was the hero of the *Pentcho,* though he considered the rescue to have been an easy enough matter for a swimmer of his ability. What struck him most about the episode was the extraordinary trust implicit in Willinger's gentle, panic-free touch as he had reached out for him on the riverbed.

As the *Pentcho*'s enforced stay at Dobra dragged on, health conditions aboard remained surprisingly good, despite the stifling summer heat, the overcrowding, the primitive sanitary and cooking facilities and the poor diet.

The three ship's doctors were relieved to find that though they were kept busy with minor ailments and injuries there were no serious medical problems, apart from growing infestations of lice and bedbugs which, as Dr. Erwin Gross would recall, "we somehow managed to keep at supportable levels." Both sexes washed their hair in fuel oil to get rid of the lice and scrubbed their bunks and blankets with disinfectant to keep down the bedbugs.

It was during this period that Aviva Blumenfeld, the *Pentcho*'s first baby, was born—an event that some of the older and more traditional among the passengers saw as a good omen.

The child, born to the couple Citron had allowed on board against the rules, knowing the wife to be seven months pregnant, was delivered safely by Dr. Lili Frischer, one of the three physicians aboard the *Pentcho,* in the tiny cabin on deck that served as her clinic. Betar member Ladislav Kurti, the ship's dentist, who witnessed the birth, was intrigued to see that the child was delivered still covered by the amniotic sac, which Dr. Frischer "peeled off like a plastic wrapping."

Medical supplies were adequate, if basic. Kurti, who had been detailed by Citron to provide a pharmacy for the boat before they left, had managed to scrounge a trunkful of various medicines—sulfa drugs, iodine, aspirin and other pain-killers, bandages and dressings.

These were supposed originally to be enough for a journey of six weeks at most, and inevitably certain items began to run short while the *Pentcho* was stranded at Dobra. When Kurti, working with a primitive, foot-operated drill, ran out of material for filling cavities, he improvised by using arsenic paste, covered with absorbent cotton wool and sealed with pitch which he picked from between the planks of the "infirmary."

Dr. Gross and his two colleagues had also brought aboard whatever medical supplies and drugs they could muster, including morphine. Captain Markeyevitch and his wife had been quick to ascertain this, and as their own jealously guarded supply of drugs began to dwindle, they badgered Kurti and the ship's doctors constantly for anything, from aspirin to morphine, to feed their addiction.

As one week followed another and there was no sign of an end to the impasse, the older passengers renewed their argument that they should abandon the *Pentcho* and petition the Yugoslav authorities to house them in a camp for the duration of the war—which they thought would not last long—or until they could arrange more suitable transport.

Some even wanted to turn the *Pentcho* around and head back to Bratislava, encouraged by news in letters from home that "things weren't so bad" in Slovakia and wasn't it time to consider giving up this "crazy idea" of going to Palestine and coming home? Word had not yet reached them of a meeting on July 28 between Hitler and the Slovak President, at which the latter agreed to institute a full-blooded "National Socialist" regime, with Adolf Eichmann's principal assistant, SS Major Dieter Wisliceny, as his government's "adviser on Jewish affairs."

Some of those who wanted to go back to Slovakia became so insistent that Citron had some vital engine parts removed and hidden, in case they tried to hijack the ship. Discontent came to a climax at a noisy mass meeting at which the refugees confronted Citron and Schalk with their demands, forcing them to set aside their differences and stand together. Dr. Gross was one of the most vociferous advocates of abandoning the voyage. At one point, when Citron rose to speak, Gross shouted, "Don't let him talk! He hypnotizes the youngsters." Gross argued that even if they reached Sulina, the *Pentcho* would never survive a sea journey. Schalk and Citron insisted that there was a seagoing vessel waiting at Sulina for them, but Gross no longer believed this.

Some of his strongest supporters were among the group of former concentration-camp prisoners who had come aboard at Bezdan—"the Turkish group," as Citron satirically called them. In his words, "they were troublemakers, always complaining." Finding himself in rare agreement with Citron, Schalk observed that "one of them literally kissed my boots when he came aboard, but soon he became one of the worst troublemakers."

The refugees thought the Yugoslavs might be willing to let them stay at a transit camp at Kladovo, on a tributary of the Danube, where 1,200 Jews from an abandoned earlier transport were living. Citron's and Schalk's insistence that the only way was forward, that to start splitting up now would be fatal, and their tongue-in-cheek assurances that a seagoing ship was waiting to take them on from Sulina finally won over the majority, and the meeting voted in favor of staying together and hanging on until the deadlock was resolved.

Having won the battle to keep the *Pentcho* people together—even the troublesome "Turkish group," whom he was determined not to abandon if he could help it—Citron decided it was time for a conciliatory move. So to placate the dissident groups, he agreed to the setting up of a five-man advisory committee that would have a say in, if no authority over, the future running of the ship. Its members, older men with experience in business and the professions, represented all the definable factions that had grown up over the past few weeks. This did not please Schalk, however, who vowed that he would allow no interference in his conduct of the ship's external affairs.

Without question, Citron and Schalk saved the lives of those who wanted to abandon the voyage and join their co-religionists at Kladovo, for the inmates of that camp were slaughtered on the spot after the Nazis overran Yugoslavia in the spring of 1941.

According to evidence presented to a war-crimes inquiry in 1945, they were marched to a field adjoining the river, put up against stakes in batches of 50 and shot. Serbian peasants, brought to the scene by the Nazis, were ordered to rifle the bodies of any valuables, including rings which were torn from the fingers of the dead and gold teeth which were ripped out of their mouths.

The killing and looting went on for two days, until all 1,200 had been dispatched. "During the whole period of the shooting," one of the Serbian eyewitnesses would testify, "the Germans took pictures of various moments, like victims before the shooting, how they were marched to the stakes, the bodies lying next to the stakes, us carrying the bodies to the ditch, the lineup of the marksmen and other moments."

The *Pentcho* had been at Dobra for five weeks when Schalk, on a trip ashore to report to his office in Bucharest, learned that the fifty-nine-year-old Revisionist leader Jabotinsky had died of a heart attack while on a lecture tour of the United States.

Shocked by the death of the man who had so influenced his life, and concerned at the effect it would have on morale, Schalk told no one for two days. When it could be suppressed no longer, he broke the news first to Citron. For the young Betar commander the death of his idol was a shattering blow. He went to a quiet corner of the ship, and for the first time since early childhood, he wept.

Others wept too. Coming on top of all their tribulations, it seemed like an omen that their voyage was doomed to end in failure.

Pulling himself together, Citron ordered a period of official mourning on board and had a mock catafalque constructed on which he and his comrades stood round-the-clock guard for seven days. Though absurd to some of the refugee element, who held Jabotinsky in little regard, the ceremonial served a double purpose in Citron's mind: to honor the fallen leader and to stiffen the resolve of his rank-and-file.

And one day after the end of his vigil over Jabotinsky's "coffin," Citron's steadfastness was rewarded when the deadlock was unexpectedly broken and the *Pentcho* was suddenly free to continue its journey downriver.

It was the Yugoslav Government which took the initiative that got the *Pentcho* moving again. After consultations with the international Danube commission, it sent the government-owned tug *Cibija* and two barges to escort the *Pentcho* through the gorge. The barges were to be lashed to either side of the *Pentcho* to give it lateral stability and protect its fragile hull while the tug towed it through the defile.

The strange convoy set out from Dobra for the Kataract on the morning of August 14. In the almost three months since the *Pentcho* had left Bratislava, France had capitulated, Italy had joined the war on Germany's side and the British, the last obstacle to Hitler's victory, were fighting on alone, waiting for a Nazi invasion.

▲ *The twelfth-century castle dominating the ancient city of Bratislava, capital of the Nazi puppet state of Slovakia. The last view of their homeland the passengers on the* Pentcho *saw as they began their perilous odyssey to Palestine.*

▶ *Alexander Citron, the fiery young Zionist who led 514 Jewish refugees on their flight to freedom.*

▲ *Citron with his fiancée, Shoshanna Spiegel, who proved an un-flagging source of strength on the voyage.*

▲ *Zoltan Schalk, Citron's colleague and rival, acquired the* Pentcho *and outmaneuvered the authorities who tried to prevent its passage.*

▲ *Karol Hoffmann, the poet of the* Pentcho, *and his fiancée Grete Ehrenfeld. Both survived the voyage, although their engagement did not.*

▶ *Imre Lichtenfeld, wrestler, gymnast, dancer and ladies' man, whose courage and daring inspired his fellow passengers.*

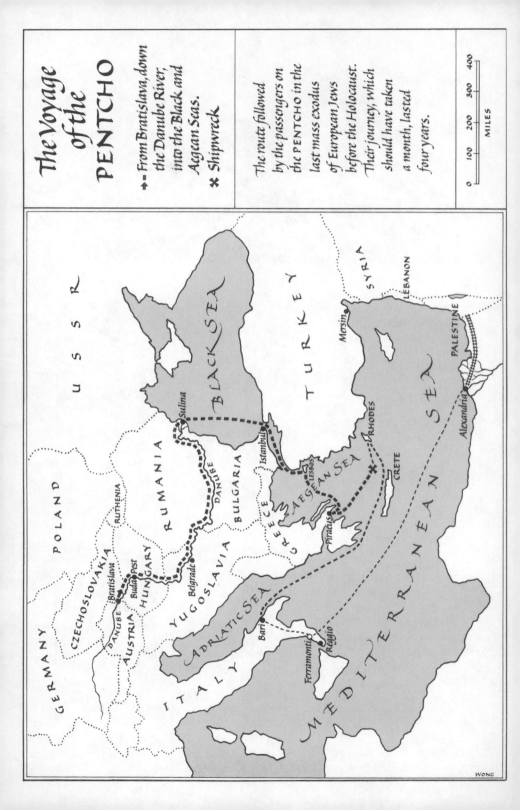

The Voyage
of the
PENTCHO

→— From Bratislava, down
the Danube River,
into the Black and
Aegean Seas.
✕ Shipwreck

The route followed
by the passengers on
the PENTCHO in the
last mass exodus
of European Jews
before the Holocaust.
Their journey, which
should have taken
a month, lasted
four years.

0   100   200   300   400
MILES

GERMANY
POLAND
CZECHOSLOVAKIA
RUTHENIA
U S S R
AUSTRIA
DANUBE
Bratislava
Buda Pest
HUNGARY
DANUBE
RUMANIA
Belgrade
YUGOSLAVIA
BULGARIA
Sulina
BLACK SEA
Istanbul
TURKEY
SYRIA
LEBANON
Mersin
GREECE
Piraeus
LESBOS
AEGEAN SEA
RHODES
CRETE
PALESTINE
Alexandria
ITALY
Ferramonti
Reggio
Bari
ADRIATIC SEA
MEDITERRANEAN SEA

WONG

▲ *Listing and dangerously overcrowded, the* Pentcho *on the Danube at Dobra, delayed for six weeks while authorities debated the problems that would result if the boat sank in the channel.*

▶ *Delousing on deck with a paraffin "shampoo." Lice and bedbugs were a constant torment to the Pentcho's passengers.*

▲ *Despite overcrowding and squalor, morale remained high on board, and there were moments of calm and beauty as the* Pentcho *steamed down the Danube.*

◀*Captain Igor Markeye-vitch, the one-legged White Russian morphine addict who skillfully skippered the unwieldy riverboat through Danube rapids and out into the open sea.*

▲ *Thrown off course by violent storms and crippled by an explosion, the* Pentcho *ran aground on the rocks of the tiny uninhabited island of Kamilanisi in the Aegean Sea.*

▲ *Survival on the island depended upon salvaging the contents of the stricken vessel before it broke up and sank.*

▲ *A field kitchen, complete with stovepipes, was improvised on the beach of the deserted island, where both food and water were in dangerously short supply.*

◄An SOS flag fluttered under stormy skies in an appeal for rescue that went unanswered for ten days.

▲Citron's strong command and discipline prevented chaos and panic among the survivors.

◀ *As food supplies dwindled, the women of the Pentcho wove a net in the hope of catching fish.*

◀ *Still no sign of rescue, and the survivors of the shipwreck looked out over a bleak vista of naked rock and empty sea.*

▶ *In the single lifeboat salvaged from the Pentcho, Schalk, Lichtenfeld and three others rowed away from the island in a desperate search for help.*

▲ *When rescue finally came, it was by the "enemy"—the Italians, who herded the survivors of the* Pentcho *into a hastily constructed camp at the soccer stadium on Rhodes.*

▶ *A guard posed happily with his prisoners—a sign of the unusually humane treatment the survivors received at the hands of their Italian captors.*

▲ *Transported to Italy, the survivors were next detained in a camp at Ferramonti in Calabria, where winter rains kept the site waterlogged for months.*

▲ *Apart from his amorous pursuit of female prisoners, soccer was the camp commandant's passion—and the principal recreation of the young men of the Pentcho during their long imprisonment.*

◀The Papal Nuncio, Cardinal Borgongini-Duca, visited the camp and told the prisoners prophetically, "You will return to Zion, God willing."

▲ Ironically, an air raid in which the Allies mistook Ferramonti for a military installation set the huts on fire and claimed four lives.

◀ *A British Army vehicle bearing the shield of David brought Jewish soldiers from Palestine to visit the prisoners soon after the camp was liberated in the Allied invasion of Italy.*

▼ *Free at last, the passengers of the Pentcho packed up their belongings to leave Ferramonti for the final leg of their journey to Palestine.*

▲ Sidney Fahn and his bride, Regina. The Fahns alone among the survivors of the Pentcho were permitted to remain on Rhodes. With Sidney's brother, Rudolf, the couple and their infant son were transported to Auschwitz just as their comrades arrived in Palestine. Only Sidney survived.

▲ A jubilant Citron and other passengers of the Pentcho were welcomed at Athlit in Palestine, their new homeland.

6

The Kazan Defile offers some of the most wildly beautiful scenery in Europe. It is located where the end of the Transylvanian Alps plunges almost vertically into the Danube, and the river narrows from a breadth of 2 miles to 200 yards as it enters a gorge that twists and turns for almost 100 miles.

It is a place of river mists and sheer granite palisades, of swooping falcons and hovering eagles, where the current runs unchecked over saw-toothed rocks. Halfway through the defile, the name of Trajan, carved in huge letters on the sheer cliff wall, commemorates the passing of the Roman Emperor with his legions two thousand years ago on an expedition that was to bring the entire Danube Basin under the Roman imperium.

Exhilarated to be on the move again, after it had seemed that their journey might end in futility, the *Pentcho* people responded to the wild scenery, savoring their pell-mell trip, towed by the *Cibija* and flanked by the two barges, through the defile and into the Iron Gate. This is a less spectacular but even more difficult stretch where, although the river widens out considerably, it now runs over dangerous shallows.

Once through the Iron Gate's narrow navigation channel, bounded by a concrete wall, the *Pentcho*'s triple escort was no longer needed. The two barges disengaged from the sides, the tug cast off with a farewell toot and the old sidewheeler was free to continue alone, heading for the sea.

Up on deck as they lay at anchor that evening, the ship's musicians gave an impromptu concert to celebrate the end of their six weeks' detention. *Pentcho* veterans retain a wistful memory of Imi Lichtenfeld, no less a dancer than a wrestler, swimmer and athlete, shuffling rhythmically across the deck while the plangent notes of "In a Persian Market," played on the accordion, drifted out across the water.

And in the tiny "office" that had been created for her at one end of Ilava, Shosha Spiegel sat at her faithful Adler transcribing Citron's stolid account of their vicissitudes to date for the ship's newspaper, *Iton Pentcho*—a compendium of poems, essays, articles and songs which she typed in triplicate on toilet paper. For the same edition Karol Hoffmann had contributed another offering, somewhat more poetic than his *Pentcho* theme song.

> *O little ship,*
> *My little ship,*
> *Whither doest thou sail?*
> *To Ofir, golden Ofir,**
> *Thither do I sail.*

As those lines suggested, the young bloods of Betar, if not the older passengers, were beginning to develop a sneaking affection for the raddled old riverboat which had now been

* Legendary seaport to which King Solomon sent his fleet to obtain "gold for Beth-Horon."

their home for more than three months. At the same time, Citron and the other Betar officers were beginning to realize that the *Pentcho*'s scarcely less derelict captain had unsuspected qualities too.

Despite his addiction, Markeyevitch had proved to be skillful, conscientious and unexpectedly willing to carry out whatever lunatic orders he might receive, provided he got his daily shot of morphine and was left alone in his cabin to sleep it off. Schalk even thought it possible that through the fog of pain and morphine which clouded his perceptions, Markeyevitch might be relishing the madcap mission for which he had signed on. He knew he would be expected to take the *Pentcho* all the way to Palestine, and so far he had given no evidence that he was of a mind to desert them at the mouth of the river—if they ever got that far.

Not that anyone imagined that Markeyevitch was particularly fond of Jews: very few if any White Russians were, if only because an inbred anti-Semitism had been reinforced by the fact that many of the leaders of the Communist revolution were Jews. But Salomon—who, as Markeyevitch's self-appointed orderly, was closer to the dour, laconic Russian than any of the rest—thought it possible that the ex-officer in him at least appreciated Citron's leadership qualities and the *esprit de corps* of the Betarim. He might also have been intrigued by the strange coincidence which linked his past to that of the Russian-Jewish soldier Josef Trumpledor, for whom Betar was named.

One day, fighting the *ennui* of their long wait at Dobra, Markeyevitch had questioned Salomon in a desultory way about Betar. He showed little interest in Salomon's account of the origins and objectives of Revisionist Zionism, but pricked up his ears when he heard that Trumpledor had been, like him, a Tsarist officer.

"Not possible," Markeyevitch grunted dismissively. "Never was a Jew an officer under the Tsars."

"Well, this one was," Salomon insisted, "and he lost his left arm in battle against the Japanese at Port Arthur."

"No, no. Never was a Jewish officer in the Imperial Navy."

"Not the navy—he was an officer in the army."

"No, no. Not possible."

Salomon shrugged. That seemed to be the end of the discussion. But obviously Markeyevitch gave this curious matter some thought over the next few days, for about a week later he asked Salomon: "You are sure he was an officer, this Jew Trumpledor?"

"Sure. No doubt about it. It's a well-established fact."

"And he lost an arm fighting the Japs?"

"That's right."

The captain shook his head, wonderingly. "And I lost a leg, same war, same Japs."

Markeyevitch thought about this for a few moments, then allowed himself a deep, tombstone chuckle. "Must have been some goddamn Jew, this Trumpledor!"

Despite increasingly good opinions of the captain, no one had any illusions about the ragtag crew. As a precautionary measure, Citron ordered a dozen of his men to follow Salomon's example and find out as much as they could about the details of a deckhand's job and the peculiarities of the ship. Two others with some experience as mechanics, Salomon's friends Meyer Steinmetz and Tibi Laufer, were sent below with Grete Ehrenfeld's father to familiarize themselves with the engine room. Citron intended to be prepared in case of desertion or mutiny.

If the *Pentcho* was none too popular with the Rumanian authorities for its attempt to crash the Kazan Defile some weeks earlier, it was even less in the good books of the Bulgarians, on the south bank of the river, because of the irregularities concerning its registration.

Thus, when the *Pentcho* put into the Bulgarian port of

Vidin, about 100 miles downstream from the Iron Gate, hoping to take on oil and supplies, it got a hostile reception. The harbormaster came aboard, accompanied by armed police, informed the captain that the vessel's registration had been revoked and forthwith performed a bizarre little ceremony on deck. The police stood to attention and saluted while the harbormaster lowered the flag of registry, folded it up and took it ashore. For good measure, he also removed part of the steering gear to prevent the *Pentcho* from leaving until he had found out from the appropriate government department whether it wanted to prosecute.

Citron and Schalk waited, close to despair, for the outcome of this latest disaster. The project could hardly survive another extended delay, and if the Bulgarians exacted a heavy fine, how could they possibly pay?

This time, however, the delay was mercifully brief and the outcome favorable. The harbormaster returned within a day, bringing the steering parts with him, and issuing peremptory instructions for the *Pentcho* to be on its way. His government had decided not to trouble to prosecute, no doubt fearing that an embarrassing tale of official corruption might emerge. It just wanted the *Pentcho* to leave immediately—without the Bulgarian flag, of course, and without even the fuel oil it badly needed.

From now on the *Pentcho* was stateless, like its passengers, though as Karol Hoffmann observed, it didn't make much difference whether they flew a flag or not. *"We don't belong anywhere and we know it,"* he noted bitterly.

When the last of the fuel oil ran out, the crew fired the boiler with wood, and the *Pentcho* proceeded downriver at a snail's pace until, five days and 200 miles farther on, they ran out of wood too and were forced to drop anchor by a deserted shore, swampy and alive with mosquitoes. To many, it seemed they had reached journey's end.

Karol Hoffmann noted that morale was at a very low ebb

and people were becoming *"more and more desperate."* There they were, in the middle of Europe, yet *"isolated as in the midst of a desert—no prospects and no hope. People get increasingly quarrelsome,"* he added, *"and the first serious attacks against the organizers of the trip are voiced. 'Cheats, crooks and murderers,' and so on."*

After three days, a Rumanian police launch arrived to investigate, transferred enough fuel oil to get the *Pentcho's* engines going again and ordered the old sidewheeler to follow it. An hour's steaming downstream brought them to a spot where they were ordered to anchor offshore, between the Rumanian town of Giurgiu on their left and its Bulgarian twin, Ruschuk, on their right.

The Rumanian police boat pulled away, with instructions to the *Pentcho* not to leave. These were hardly necessary; the paddleboat was out of fuel again. The next morning the *Pentcho* people noticed that a small military detachment had been posted on the Rumanian bank, overlooking their mooring—obviously to prevent anyone from swimming ashore. It was the start of another long and agonizing delay.

It was late August and oppressively hot. Food and drinking water were severely rationed. Some began drinking polluted river water, which they tried to disinfect with chlorine and potassium permanganate. Soon they were coming down with intestinal infection.

Citron issued instructions "in your own and the common interest to attend to the cleanliness of your person, bedding, clothes and food even more than previously." But despite tight discipline and scrupulous attention to hygiene, conditions were becoming intolerable. The ship's doctors and nurses were working to the point of exhaustion, medical supplies were running dangerously short and the decks and dormitories were crammed with the sick and the hungry.

To add to their growing misery and apprehension, they saw steamers going past them downriver loaded with German soldiers and carrying signs bearing the Nazi slogan "STRENGTH THROUGH JOY." Rumania was coming increasingly under the Germans' thumb, and although the troops were ostensibly on their way to rest-and-rehabilitation leave at Black Sea resorts, they were essentially part of an infiltration force sent to secure Nazi control of the Rumanian oil fields. Even here, it seemed, so far from their point of departure, the hand of the Nazis was reaching out to seize them.

By August 26, the *Pentcho* was completely without bread and most other foodstuffs, and Citron noted in his diary that if the situation got any worse *"we will have to take drastic measures to obtain the attention of the world."* The next morning a Red Cross flag was flown from the *Pentcho*'s stern to signal hunger aboard, and a huge banner made from sheets was displayed along each side of the vessel, bearing a desperate message in red paint: "500 PEOPLE WITHOUT FOOD ON THIS SHIP—PLEASE HELP."

Almost worse than the hunger were the bedbugs. All over the ship, but especially in the heat and gloom of Akko, they had proliferated to plague proportions, swarming over the sleeping or waking bodies of the passengers as they lay on their bunks, raising welts on their bodies and spotting their blankets with blood. "They were everywhere, perpetually voracious," Sidney Fahn would recall with a shudder. "If your mouth fell open while you slept they would drop into it from the bunk above; if you turned on your side they'd drop into your ear."

Soon conditions had become so appalling that even some of the tightly disciplined Betarim began jumping ship. Using inflatable mattresses as floats, one small group slipped over the side during the night with some of their belongings and made for the Bulgarian shore.

When their disappearance was discovered next morning, another group decided to follow suit, jumped overboard in broad daylight and began swimming. The soldiers guarding the Rumanian bank began shooting at them, even though they were heading for the distant Bulgarian shore. Luckily, no one was hit.

The commotion alerted the Bulgarians on the other side of the river, and by the time the swimmers arrived there, the police were waiting to receive them. Later that day a Bulgarian police launch brought back all the deserters except one, named Jan Guttmann,* who managed to evade arrest.

But the attempt had not been entirely in vain. The overnight escapees had used their few hours of freedom well, getting to the palace of the Bishop of Ruschuk, where they had told of the *Pentcho*'s plight. The Bishop appeared sympathetic and promised to help arrange relief supplies.

That evening he delivered on his promise. Two motorboats arrived from the Bulgarian side, crammed with supplies. *"A sincere act of humanity and no strings attached,"* noted Hoffmann. *"In spite of all, there are still some decent people left."*

The Bulgarian bishop's display of Christian charity appeared to shame the Rumanians into action of their own. After having ignored the *Pentcho*'s existence for eight days—except to post the guards to prevent its passengers from coming ashore—they sent an official party to see what needed to be done to speed it on its way.

Schalk asked them to contact the Revisionist transport bureau in Bucharest, and a few days later the *Pentcho* was towed into port, where fuel was pumped into its tanks—so much of it, Hoffmann noted, that *"the whole ship smells like an oil field and you can't take a step without stepping in it."* After the oil came cases of food, *"dry vegetables, margarine, etc., there seems to be no end to it. They must have succeeded in locating our organizers and compelled them to supply all our needs, or else."*

* He made his way to Greece on foot and survived the war, eventually emigrating to Canada.

The sudden improvement in their circumstances produced a corresponding upsurge of morale. *"It's strange how fast the mood of people can change,"* Hoffmann noted, *"from the deepest despair to the peaks of joy and enthusiasm, but it is probably this elasticity which makes people able to endure so much."*

The *Pentcho* was now on the last leg of its journey to the Black Sea, and soon it was sailing through the 1,000-square-mile wilderness of the Danube Delta, down a deepwater channel that cut through a seemingly limitless expanse of swamp and marsh, covered by tall reeds, through which the river's many silt-laden distributaries meandered. On September 14, without further incident, they reached the scruffy little seaport of Sulina.

This was where most of those who had endured four months aboard the *Pentcho* had been hoping to transfer to the often-promised seagoing ship. This was where Citron and Schalk had to confess that there was no such ship and, when pressed, that there never had been.

The Betar contingent took the news stoically. The holiday mood with which they had started out had long since evaporated. It was now a question of endurance, and luck. No one had illusions that the *Pentcho* was seaworthy—but what was the alternative? Many of them realized that there was a risk that they would die at sea; but there was no way back, and the only way forward was in the *Pentcho*.

Schalk and Citron had to spell that out plainly to the refugees, who predictably were less willing to accept the realities of their situation. They protested bitterly that they had been misled, fed false promises. They argued angrily that they should remain in port, living aboard the *Pentcho*, while more suitable transport was arranged to take them the rest of the way.

Schalk assured them impatiently that there was no chance

of this. The transport bureau in Bucharest would soon be forced to close. The *Pentcho* was their last chance of escape from Europe. And if they were thinking of staying in Rumania, they had better forget it. The authorities would not let any of them ashore—and even if they did, what could they hope for?

Only a week previously, the Rumanian King Carol had been deposed by the pro-Axis General Ion Antonescu and forced to flee the country with his red-haired Jewish mistress, Magda Lupescu. The violently anti-Semitic Iron Guard was now running wild, and Rumania had become a virtual Nazi satellite, if not yet a formal ally. Sulina's remoteness and inaccessibility, except by water, meant that they were temporarily safe, but they had better not hang about too long.

Faced with such arguments, there was little the critics could do but comply, even if they did not stop complaining. It was the *Pentcho* or nothing.

If the passengers had no choice in the matter, there was always the possibility that the crew might balk at the last moment and refuse to take the *Pentcho* to sea. The original crew had been paid off at Braila and seven new men had been taken on—four Greeks, two Turks and a Rumanian Jew named Yossi Rosenberg. No one knew what they were thinking, but however much they might be inclined to desert rather than face a sea crossing in the *Pentcho,* they knew they would be paid only when they had delivered their human cargo to the Irgun group who would be watching for their arrival off the Palestine coast. That and the knowledge that a shadow crew of Betarim was ready to take over seemed a good enough insurance against mass desertion.

As for Markeyevitch, he had known all along what was expected of him and showed no signs of having second thoughts. Perhaps the drug-and-alcohol haze in which he lived made the risks seem unimportant. Perhaps the kind of life he had been reduced to stripped death of its terrors. Perhaps, with the suicidal recklessness of the Slav, and what remained of the pride and professionalism of the naval officer, he relished the challenge of attempting a sea passage in the *Pentcho*. Whatever his motives, he was ready to go.

The *Pentcho* itself scarcely was. It had been given one week to leave Sulina—just long enough to carry out essential repairs to the paddle blades, which had been damaged in a collision with the police launch at Giurgiu—but far more than that was needed to make it even remotely fit for the sea passage that lay ahead. It had no radio, no navigational aids, not even any proper charts. Just one of its four lifeboats, capable of holding only six people, was in a fit state to be launched. They also needed welding equipment for repairs at sea, and an auxiliary engine.

The British, meanwhile, were still hoping to prevent the *Pentcho*'s departure, but not for humanitarian reasons. Although they had by now lost their diplomatic clout with the Rumanians, and could thus expect no further help from that quarter, they had not quite given up. While the repair work was going on, His Britannic Majesty's Consul, a Mr. Evans, turned up at the quayside, demanding to know where they were bound.

"Paraguay," Schalk told him with a straight face.

The consul laughed and said, "We know very well that you're going to Palestine."

"Then why did you bother to ask?" responded Schalk.

The consul turned on his heel and walked off.

The next day Evans delivered formal warning in writing to Markeyevitch and his crew that they faced long prison sentences if they were caught carrying illegal immigrants in Palestine waters. The captain shrugged indifferently, crumpled up the consul's warning notice and tossed it over the side, downed half a tumblerful of slivovitz and retired to his cabin.

On Saturday, September 21, as the frustrated Evans looked

on, the *Pentcho* sailed out into the Black Sea, its passengers sick, weary and for the most part dispirited. Their four months afloat on the Danube—a shipload of outcasts—had been a bitter experience of rejection that would remain in the memory long after the physical hardships had been forgotten.

As they left the harbor, three patrol boats of the Rumanian Navy closed in to escort the *Pentcho* out of territorial waters. Karol Hoffmann noted: *"We have been ordered to lie down on our bunks to ensure maximum equilibrium and we don't dare move. We are like a herd of sheep being led to the slaughterhouse."*

7

*B*efore the *Pentcho* left Sulina, the 46 passengers who had been sleeping on deck since the Dachau prisoners had come aboard were ordered below for the rest of the voyage—a grievous blow to the claustrophobic Hamburger, who would lament that "suddenly my paradise was over."

Much as this aggravated the dreadful overcrowding, it was a very necessary precaution. Within a couple of hours of the *Pentcho*'s departure, the clear skies under which it had sailed were dark and full of menace. By dusk a ferocious gale erupted, sending huge waves crashing over the vessel's flimsy superstructure, causing even the optimistic Citron to wonder if his original description of the ship as "a caricature of a submarine" might not prove to be horribly prophetic.

One particularly large wave lifted the *Pentcho* high and spun it around 180 degrees. As the ship turned sickeningly under him, Marcel Friedmann muttered the prayer *"Sh'ma Yisrael*—Hear, O Israel"—fearing the vessel might founder at any moment. All around him in the pitching, lurching hellhole of Akko others were intoning the same prayer.

Up in the wheelhouse, Markeyevitch met the challenge with extraordinary skill, bringing the staggering *Pentcho* carefully about to put it back on course as the huge seas battered it broadside. Drug addict and drunk he might be, but a professional seaman above all, thought Citron as he stood alongside the captain, anxiously monitoring the *Pentcho*'s labored progress through the punishing waves.

Down below in the engine room, Steinmetz and Laufer stood watch with the ship's engineer—a villainous-looking Greek named Yannis who boasted of being a convicted murderer—keeping an anxious eye on the dials and gauges. Any loss of power now would leave the *Pentcho* helpless before the storm's fury.

In one of the two small sick bays located on either side of the dormitory area known as Ilava, Oskar Salomon lay with a 104-degree temperature, the result of a bout of pneumonia brought on by an accidental ducking in the harbor at Sulina. As in an evil dream, he was aware, through the semidelirium of his illness, of the screaming of the storm outside and the terrifying rise and fall, lurch and shudder of the ship.

One level above, amid the retching and vomiting, weeping and praying, and with the waves battering the flimsy walls of the wooden superstructure, little Karci Farkas clung to his mother and whimpered, *"Mamouka, Mamouka,* we're going to die." "Hush, *bubeleh,"* she replied. "God will protect us."

Citron, characteristically, had no thought of divine intervention. One of the few not affected by seasickness, he left the wheelhouse to move among the terrified women, children and elderly with Shosha, giving what encouragement he could.

Remarkably, the *Pentcho*'s abused and neglected engines maintained a steady rhythm, while up in the wheelhouse Markeyevitch too drew on unsuspected reserves of dependability, holding the old riverboat's bow head on into the massive seas for hour after hour in a storm that screamed as if in rage and frustration at being cheated of so likely a victim.

When it had blown itself out, he went to his cabin, took a shot of morphine and slept the clock around. By the time he emerged blearily on deck, the *Pentcho* was sailing into the calm of the Bosporus, and his passengers, storm-battered, drained and exhausted—but above all thankful to be alive— were beginning to appreciate that both he and the *Pentcho* had unexpected resources of survival.

"We almost begin to like and admire the little ship which, despite all handicaps, tries so bravely to defend us against the hostile world around us," noted Karol Hoffmann. *"In spite of all, it is the only place where we are allowed to be, and for the time being our only home and refuge."* How true that was would soon be demonstrated once again.

As the wooded shores of the Bosporus slipped past, studded with the ornate villas and walled gardens of pashas and mer- chants, and the domes and minarets of Istanbul came into view, the *Pentcho* people looked forward eagerly to the chance to go ashore and feel dry land beneath their feet while the vessel replenished its supplies of bread and water. Grete Ehrenfeld wanted to stop so badly that "it was like a physical ache—the city looked so beautiful and I felt so envious of the people there who had a place of their own and were able to live normal lives."

But the Turkish authorities had other ideas. As the *Pent- cho* neared the Galata Bridge, hoping to tie up alongside the quay facing the Golden Horn, two police vessels approached and waved them off with angry shouts of *"Yalla, yalla!—*Go away!"

On Citron's instructions, the captain ignored the warn- ing, hove to and dropped anchor. "At least, let us take on drinking water," Citron appealed. The Turks were adamant, the two police boats circling angrily as an officer bawled a warning through a megaphone: "Lift your anchor right away or we'll cut it loose."

Clearly, the Turks knew all about the *Pentcho* and its illegal destination and wanted no part of it. As neutrals they were determined to avoid annoying either the British or the Germans, and their solution to the problem of what to do about the *Pentcho* was to get rid of it fast. The fact that the vessel was now desperately short of drinking water and in need of an opportunity to repair some of the storm damage seemed to concern them not at all. *"Yalla, yalla!"* cried the harbor police, and there was nothing for it but to up anchor as ordered and sail on, past the Golden Horn and into the Sea of Marmora.

There, the next day, under mercifully clear skies, Karci Farkas and his friends Walti Ehrlich and Poldi Spiegel momentarily forgot their hunger as they heard for the first time the story of Ulysses and the Siege of Troy, which lay on the eastern shore, told to them by the eccentric Viennese professor Paul von Heller.

The following day they passed through the Dardanelles, where it was Citron's turn to instruct the children in the exploits of a more recent—and to him more personal—hero. As they steamed by Gallipoli, he told them how the legendary Trumpledor had served there alongside the British in World War I as deputy commander of the Zion Mule Corps during the ill-fated Gallipoli campaign.

Then they were out in the Aegean and heading south for Lesbos, the first of the Greek islands that hug the coast of Asia Minor. If they failed to find temporary refuge there and the water, fuel and provisions they needed, they would be in a truly desperate situation.

As they drew near to Lesbos, a Greek gunboat came out to intercept, circling around like a suspicious watchdog guarding his master's yard. With neighboring Italy now in the war alongside the Nazis, the neutral Greeks were understandably jumpy, and since the *Pentcho* was flying no flag to signify its country of registration, they fired a warning shot across its bow.

The *Pentcho* hove to and the Greek ship came cautiously closer to inspect it. It wasn't until he was close enough to see the diapers and women's underwear, strung up on the *Pentcho*'s deck to dry in the sun, that the Greek skipper's suspicion began to evaporate. He came alongside, and after a brief interrogation by megaphone the gunboat took up position to escort the *Pentcho* into Mitilini, the main port of Lesbos.

On the way there, Citron gave belated instructions for a new flag to be made in the Bulgarian colors of red, green and white. One of the Betar girls, handy with a needle, made the flag out of an apron and a set of her boyfriend's underwear.

By the time they reached Mitilini, word of their approach had been spread, and the dock was crowded with curious islanders eager for a glimpse of a vessel the like of which they had never seen before. The sidewheeler caused such a sensation as it churned and wheezed into the harbor that the event was turned into an impromptu festival.

As the *Pentcho* people watched in reciprocal astonishment, the town band turned out in full uniform and began playing jaunty tunes on the quayside, while black-clad peasant women descended on the waterfront with baskets of fresh fruit and vegetables, which they sold—and in some cases gave away—to the grateful passengers.

Some of the *Pentcho* people broke down and wept, overwhelmed by the truly novel experience of being treated as welcome guests instead of pariahs. *"It seems almost too good to be true,"* Karol Hoffmann noted in his journal.

The *Pentcho* remained at Lesbos for two days—a briefly idyllic period for its passengers, a time of laughter, music, sunshine and song to weigh against the weeks of misery, torment and rejection of their journey down the Danube. But for Schalk it was a moment of truth—a time when, faced with the united opposition of both Citron and his advisory committee, he would angrily relinquish his joint leadership of the expedition.

Unable to challenge Citron's authority on board, Schalk had become all the more insistent on handling his contacts ashore without interference or consultation. Not only did he refuse to consult beforehand, Citron and the committee complained, but he wouldn't even discuss what he had done on their behalf after the event.

Encouraged by Citron, the committee decided it was time to clip Schalk's wings and gain some control for themselves over the way the transport was run. The showdown came when Schalk asked the refugees—many of whom still had cash and valuables with them—to provide the money to buy fuel oil, but refused to take their representative ashore with him to negotiate the deal.

Out of sight and earshot of the rank-and-file passengers, a furious argument raged in Schalk's cabin as Citron and the committee confronted him. Schalk was outraged when the refugee faction more than hinted that they believed some of their money would stick to his fingers if they didn't keep an eye on the negotiations. Citron supported their demand that two committee members, Adolf Waldner and Ignatz Dromlewitz, should go with Schalk to buy the fuel.

Schalk refused point-blank, bitterly angry that his honesty should be impugned by people who, as he saw it, owed their escape from Nazi Europe to his efforts. But eventually—outvoted and with no constituency of his own aboard—he had to accept defeat. In his own words, he was "tired, overwrought,

I'd had enough, I couldn't operate under those conditions."

The next day, as the *Pentcho* sailed between Lesbos and Piraeus, he wrote a formal declaration relinquishing all authority over the transport. *"I agree that in future, negotiations with port authorities should take place without me,"* he wrote, *"but I cannot be responsible for the outcome of such negotiations. I therefore give up any future role, either active or passive."*

Among his personal papers, Schalk would keep that resignation document—salt-stained and bearing the verifying signatures of Citron, Waldner and Dromlewitz—as a bitter memento. He was "completely disillusioned by the experience."

At Piraeus, the Athens seaport, two days' sail to the southwest from Mitilini, the *Pentcho* was met by two leaders of the Greek Jewish community. Citron thought they did not seem too helpful at first, but that their attitude changed when they learned that money was coming from the American Joint Distribution Committee to pay for the food and fuel the *Pentcho* needed before starting the next phase of its journey.

As for the Greek authorities, they were clearly uneasy about the *Pentcho*'s presence, refusing to allow the passengers ashore, except to exercise on the quayside close to their ship, and insisting politely but firmly that they leave as soon as possible. Since October 2, two days after their arrival, was Rosh Hashanah, the Jewish New Year, Citron asked to be allowed to remain long enough to celebrate the occasion. Permission was granted on condition they leave at once when the holiday was over.

Meanwhile, the Jews of Athens sent a gift of freshly slaughtered meat to the port for the *Pentcho*'s New Year festivities—a well-intentioned gesture which was nevertheless to be the cause of trouble. As the meat came aboard, some of the more devout among the refugees protested that it could not be properly kosher. After all, they asked, what would the Sephardic Greek Jews know of the finer points of dietary law?

The devout considered that no self-respecting Jew, however secular-minded, should even consider eating such suspect viands on a High Holy Day. The most fanatical among them went further, insisting that the meat should not even be allowed aboard lest it defile the *Pentcho* and everyone on it. This started a violent scuffle as the less religious, lusting for meat after more than four months on beans, macaroni and a very occasional piece of fish, tried to stop the zealots from throwing the sides of beef and lamb into the harbor.

Things were getting out of hand when Citron stepped in with a solution worthy of a Solomon: the meat should not remain on the ship, but should be cooked on the quayside. Those who wanted meat could eat it there, not on the *Pentcho*. For himself, said Citron, he would stay on board and eat only kosher food. He didn't need to spell it out that he expected his Betarim to do likewise. They knew that to the agnostic Citron the observance of Jewish custom aboard ship was a matter of political ideology, not religion.

To eat with one's head covered and observe the ancient dietary laws—as to learn, and wherever possible speak, Hebrew—was to assert one's national identity, even if one rejected the theology behind it. To Citron and his fellow ideologues, it was a matter of patriotic duty rather than spiritual necessity to observe those practices which set the Jews apart from other peoples.

Not all of the passengers found these arguments strong enough to overcome their hunger for meat. Grete Ehrenfeld, for one, ate her fill of it without feeling a moment's remorse, though later that High Holy Day she was surprised to find herself assailed by guilt feelings after going for an unlawful swim in the harbor.

On the evening tide at the end of the second day of Rosh Hashanah, the start of the year 5701 by the Jewish calendar, the *Pentcho* paddled out of Piraeus with a Greek naval escort to see it through the minefield that had been laid at the approaches to the harbor.

On the advice of the Revisionist leadership, relayed through the leaders of the Jewish community at Piraeus, they were heading toward Turkey, the idea being to hug the Turkish coast, hoping to be allowed to refuel and resupply at the port of Mersin, before heading farther east then south along the Syrian coastline to Palestine, keeping always in sight of land because of their lack of navigational equipment. Although this route would take them through the Aegean islands which at that time belonged to Hitler's Italian allies, Citron had been informed that under British naval pressure, they had been evacuated. This information could scarcely have been more incorrect.

When, after three days' uneventful steaming through calm waters, they were nearing the island of Stampalia— Astipalia to the Greeks, to whom it reverted after the war— two Italian torpedo boats knifed out to intercept them. Aboard the *Pentcho,* there was considerable apprehension as the Italian warships came alongside. Aboard the torpedo boats, there was a good deal of suspicion, mixed with unconcealed astonishment at the sight of a riverboat so far out to sea.

The *Pentcho* was boarded by a party of armed sailors led by a heavily bearded young officer. "Who are you? Where are you bound?" he demanded. Citron decided there was nothing to be gained by deception: only the truth was bizarre enough to carry credibility. He instructed the multilingual Professor Heller, acting as interpreter, to give the Italian a truthful answer.

Told the *Pentcho*'s destination, the officer shook his head wonderingly, echoing the words of Police Commissioner Yakouboczy on the quay at Bratislava: "In this ship you are going to Palestine? Impossible!" Then, still suspicious, he asked Citron, "Do you realize you have just sailed through a minefield? How did you find your way through it?"

Citron went cold at the realization of how close they had come to disaster, but managed a perky riposte. "Perhaps," he replied through Heller, "we got through because we didn't know about the mines and the mines didn't know about us."

What had saved the *Pentcho* was the fact that it drew only 5 feet of water; it had been able to sail right over the tops of the tethered mines without touching them—something no seagoing vessel with adequate draft would have been able to accomplish.

By now, the bearded Italian officer was beginning to find the *Pentcho*'s story a little more credible. At first he had been wary of a British ruse to take Stampalia's defenses by surprise; now he suspected that this ship full of disheveled maniacs might be just what it purported to be, if only because no one could possibly have invented such a farfetched tale.

"You don't know how lucky you are," he said as he ordered the *Pentcho* to follow him into port. "If you'd shown up half an hour later, after sunset, we'd have fired first and asked questions afterward." And he gestured meaningfully toward the two torpedo tubes in the bow of his boat as it bobbed alongside.

The two Italian warships then escorted the *Pentcho* into the heavily fortified harbor, where later that evening a stream of sympathetic and friendly officers and enlisted men came aboard to look at this crazy craft and the people who were insane enough to have put to sea in it. *"Sorprendente!"* exclaimed one officer. "Amazing! We thought we were having a hard war fighting the British, but you—you are the heroes of this war!"

To the *Pentcho* people's astonishment, the Italians brought with them gifts of wine, fresh fruit and vegetables. One officer came aboard with a present for the children—a box of chocolate bars and candy The Italian had tears in his eyes as he handed them out.

Next morning, one of the same two torpedo boats escorted the *Pentcho* out of the harbor, led it through the minefield and gave it bearings for the safest route to Palestine—south toward Crete, then due east, so that it would avoid the heavily mined Italian islands which, far from having been evacuated, were more strongly defended than ever.

The *Pentcho* people waved farewell and sailed on, wondering at the warmth and cordiality they had encountered as guests of the Nazis' unlikely comrades-in-arms.

8

After their narrow escape from the minefields guarding Stampalia, Citron began to appreciate just what it meant to sail through a war zone. He mounted a round-the-clock watch, posting his Betar men along both sides of the ship with long poles, cushioned at the end with rags, to ward off drifting mines. It was a quite different hazard, however, that was to bring the *Pentcho* to grief two days later.

When they left the Danube, Markeyevitch had warned Citron that supplying the *Pentcho*'s boiler with water for any lengthy period would seriously deplete their drinking supplies. On the Danube this had not been a problem, but now that they were at sea the boiler would have to be fed from their freshwater tanks, which would empty rapidly. Seawater, of course, could not be used; it would leave salt deposits which would rapidly block the steam pipes.

Citron went below to discuss the problem with Yannis, the ship's engineer, and his shadows. Steinmetz and Laufer were sanguine. Even if seawater were to be pumped into the boiler, it would take some time, they argued, for the deposits to build up significantly—time enough for them to reach their destination. Yannis, who was no doubt thinking about the return journey from the Palestine coast, disagreed. It was too risky, he said.

Citron considered the problem and then delivered another of his Solomon-like judgments: why not feed the boiler a 50–50 mixture of sea and fresh water?

It seemed like a good enough solution, but this time his ruling was less inspired than at Piraeus. It failed to take into account the unusually high salinity of the Aegean.

Steadily, as they sailed from Istanbul to Lesbos, from Lesbos to Piraeus and from Piraeus to Stampalia, the deposits had been building up inside the main artery of the *Pentcho*'s heart, the pipe carrying high-pressure steam from the boiler to the engine room. Two days out of Stampalia, disaster struck.

The first Citron knew of the trouble was when he heard a muffled thud that shook the ship. Simultaneously, the throb of the engines ceased, and moments later Yannis came panting up on deck, drenched in grease and sweat, to report to the captain that there was "bad business below." Citron sent Laufer, Steinmetz and Josef Ehrenfeld down to see for themselves, and soon they reported to him that the damage seemed irreparable, unless they could get to a port where it could receive professional attention.

They were lucky the boiler had not exploded violently enough to do a good deal more damage. As it was, their situation was bad enough—adrift in a war zone, with only one lifeboat, no means of sending a distress signal and the weather beginning to look threatening.

According to Markeyevitch's calculations, which were very approximate because of their lack of navigational equipment, their position was some 100 miles west of Rhodes, the main island of the Italian Aegean, and about 60 miles north of Crete, then in Greek hands. The nearest land appeared to be a tiny island called Kamilanisi, which should lie just over the horizon, about 20 miles south.

Their chances of reaching Kamilanisi seemed slender. If they weighed anchor and allowed themselves to drift, the prevailing winds and currents would take them not toward the island, but southeast into the Mediterranean, where there might well be no landfall for hundreds of miles.

Markeyevitch suggested a solution—not a very credible-sounding one, but it was better than doing nothing. "Collect sheets, blankets, anything you can find and sew them together to make a sail," he said. "Then I'll see if we can steer for the island. Not easy with such a ship, but it's the only possibility."

Teams of women, organized by Citron and Shosha, were sewing blankets together under the captain's supervision when Schalk emerged from the bitter isolation in which he had wrapped himself since the argument on Lesbos and, disregarding the fact that he had resigned from the leadership, announced his intention of taking the lifeboat to Kamilanisi. If he could find help there for the *Pentcho* he would return with it. If not, he could at least light a fire on the island to guide the *Pentcho* in.

Citron saw no reason to object. It was a prudent suggestion, and given the numbers aboard the *Pentcho,* there was no better use to which its solitary lifeboat could be put. Schalk chose four men to go with him—Imi Lichtenfeld, Yosef Hercz, Ferdinand Lanes and a crew member known as Ali the Turk—and they left with the young commander's blessing.

As the lifeboat was lowered into the swell and slowly pulled away from the ship, Karol Hoffmann reflected how strange it was that now that the worst had happened and the ship was totally disabled, *"everyone seems calm and accepts it as inevitable."*

By midafternoon the sail was ready and, under Markeyevitch's supervision, rigged from the *Pentcho*'s foremast. A steady breeze filled it out, and the ship began tacking clumsily toward Kamilanisi, which gradually became a vague blur on the horizon.

Unresponsive enough under power, the *Pentcho* was infinitely harder to handle under sail. Progress was agonizingly slow, and when night fell the crippled vessel was still zigzagging toward the island like some drunk staggering home in the dark.

Some time after 11 P.M., Schalk and Lichtenfeld, now themselves on Kamilanisi with their three companions, saw the *Pentcho*'s navigation lights. They had hoped to find habitation on the island—perhaps some fishing boats, whose owners could be persuaded to go out and tow the *Pentcho* to safety. But Kamilanisi had turned out to be completely deserted. All they could do to help now was try to guide the vessel to a safe anchorage.

The island was about 2 miles long by half a mile wide, and crescent-shaped. The inside of the crescent was a gently shelving, sandy bay, where the *Pentcho* could anchor safely; the outside, a wave-battered wall of solid rock, fringed by patches of reef. As the red and green navigation lights of the crippled *Pentcho* drew closer, Schalk realized to his horror that the ship was heading for the wrong side of the island.

There seemed to be no way to stop it. Schalk and his companions shouted themselves hoarse, leaping and gesticulating wildly in the light of their signal fire. But they soon realized that even if the helmsman saw, heard and understood their warnings, there was little he could do to correct the *Pentcho*'s course.

At Schalk's command they rushed down to the beach, manhandled the lifeboat into the water and rowed out toward the *Pentcho,* hoping to head it off and get it to anchor clear of the reef. It was too late. As they rounded the tip of the island, Schalk heard "a terrible grating, sawing sound" and realized that the *Pentcho* had run aground.

•   •   •

To those on watch aboard the *Pentcho,* the ship seemed to go to its doom in slow motion. Citron was on deck, next to the captain, peering into the dark for a glimpse of the shoreline. They were almost on top of it before he saw the bulk of the rock wall and the white foam around the reef and realized that there was no way a disastrous impact could now be averted.

Markeyevitch saw the danger at the same time and shouted an order for the anchor to be lowered. It went over the side with a clatter and a splash, but failed to find purchase on the bottom. As the deckhands cranked it up for a second attempt, the *Pentcho* drifted closer to disaster.

Marcel Friedmann, who was on deck as a watchkeeper while most of his fellows remained below in Akko, was all but pitched over the side when the ship ran onto the reef.

Oskar Salomon, sleeping in the crew's quarters in the forecastle, was thrown out of his bunk and momentarily stunned as the hull grounded on rock and the prow reared up.

Gisella Farkas, sleeping with the other women and children on the upper level, woke only some minutes later when the husband of her neighbor leaned over her to shake his wife with whispered news of the *Pentcho*'s grounding. Karci slept through it too, and when his mother tried to wake him he mumbled, "Leave me alone, let me sleep."

In Ilava, Grete Ehrenfeld and the other Betar girls, too nervous to sleep at all, were huddling in their bunks. When the *Pentcho* struck, Grete was pitched onto the deck and her two bunkmates landed on top of her.

Down below in Akko, Daniel Hamburger had been suffering from the claustrophobic terror that had him in its almost permanent grip since he had lost his sleeping place on deck. He was calculating his chances of sneaking up on deck without being caught and turned back by one of the ubiquitous Betar watchkeepers, when to his horror he felt the iron hull of the *Pentcho* strike rock just beneath his bunk.

On deck, frantic crewmen were still trying to get the anchor to catch as the *Pentcho*'s hull was dragged across the submerged rocks, ever closer to the island's sheer wall. On the fourth attempt, the anchor at last grabbed bottom and the vessel's drift was checked, its shattered starboard paddle within a yard or two of the cliff.

By now the ship was alive with the symptoms of alarm, as everywhere people began stirring, lighting lamps, asking one another what was going on, groping for their belongings. Betar officers moved among the women, children and old folk on the upper levels to calm them. "It's all right. No cause for alarm. We'll get you ashore as soon as possible."

In the airless gloom of Akko, with its iron floor scraping ominously against bare rock, Citron told everybody, except those detailed for specific tasks aloft, to stay put until the women, children and old men had been put ashore. According to Citron, "there was fear, naturally, but no sign of panic."

If there was no panic, there was a good deal of hubbub, and Citron quickly realized that, little as he knew about ships and the sea, he was going to have to make all the major decisions on his own. Markeyevitch was in tears, distraught at the loss of his ship, and had "completely gone to pieces." The crew, though for different reasons, were little better. They could not be relied on to think of anything other than their own skins.

In this moment of crisis, Citron took complete charge and, to his surprise and relief, found that things could have been a good deal worse. The *Pentcho* seemed relatively stable now that it had been anchored fore and aft. Mercifully, the sea was not rough, and despite the damage it had sustained, the ship seemed to be in no immediate danger of breaking up and lay close enough to the rock wall for the passengers to scramble ashore if they were evacuated in an orderly fashion.

But first, lines would have to be put ashore to steady the

vessel further. Cibi Braun, the soccer star, volunteered to shimmy along one of the anti-mine poles with a rope around his waist to make the *Pentcho* fast.

When that had been done, Citron ordered four of his Betar boys to manhandle the gangplank out to form a bridge between ship and shore. Four other Betarim rushed forward to prevent the mainmast, which had broken under the impact of the collision, from crashing down onto the deck where the women and children, summoned from their bunks by Shosha, were preparing to go ashore.

Daniel Hamburger, driven by panic and ignoring the order to remain below until the women and children had been evacuated, was already up on deck. "The gangplank broke like matchwood as the ship yawed," he would recall. "A second bridge was thrown out. It was our last hope. If it had broken we wouldn't have been able to get ashore. But it held, and I think I was the first to cross it."

Although the Farkases' bunk was next to the exit, Karci and his mother were the last of the women and children to leave. Karci had insisted on taking with him a book of psalms that had been given to him by his grandfather, pulling his valise out from under the bunk to search for it and blocking the exit. As the women waiting to get out shrieked their protests, *Mamouka* dragged her son back onto the bunk to let them pass.

In the ensuing rush, she and Karci were unable to leave until all the others had gone on deck. This gave them time to find their topcoats, which would prove to be welcome in the chill of the October night. "You see, *Mamouka*," Karci said later, "God rewarded us because I wouldn't leave without my holy book."

Up to now the evacuation—directed through a megaphone by Citron—had been going remarkably smoothly, but as the women, children and old men got ashore they created a dangerous bottleneck by crowding around the end of the gangplank. Huddled in the dark, halfway up the cliff and afraid to climb higher, they were obstructing the exit of the girls and young men who were waiting to come up on deck to make their own escape.

If panic were to erupt below, where seawater was now beginning to trickle into Akko through the sprung plates of the battered hull, the consequences would be disastrous—a wild rush for the companionway, with men and boys tearing at one another to get out. Citron decided on drastic action to clear the bottleneck.

Drawing the revolver he carried under his jacket, he pushed his way to the end of the gangplank and ordered those huddled there to the top of the cliff at gunpoint. Shosha helped them to make the short but tricky ascent by directing a flashlight beam to the summit.

At the top of the rock wall, Gisella Farkas found it "very dark and scary." Not knowing where they were, she and some of the other women "edged across the rocks on our backsides, terrified of falling into the sea."

Hamburger was "in terrible shape." He went forward a few hundred feet, lay down on the bare rock and remained there until the next morning, "totally unaware of what was happening around me."

By now the men from Akko were emerging on deck to await their turn to go ashore. The congestion at the gangplank was still so great that some of them, afraid to wait any longer, dived over the side, clear of the reef, and swam around to the cliff, where despite the surge of the sea against it, they were all able to clamber out unharmed.

The evacuation, under Citron's direction, proceeded steadily throughout the night. It was about 4 A.M. when Emerich Dukas, the last of the men from Akko, went ashore, followed by Markeyevitch, who emerged from his cabin— "drunk, drugged and absolutely despairing," as Citron observed—holding his wife by the hand. Together, they walked unsteadily to safety along the gangplank, old Ludmilla clutching the first-aid box which contained their syringes and morphine.

Citron watched the old couple ashore before making his own way along the gangplank and clambering, exhausted by the night's exertions, to the cliff top, where Dukas was waiting for him. "Why didn't you find some place to sleep?" Citron asked Dukas. "I don't sleep till you sleep," replied the old soldier.

Then Shosha arrived with a blanket she had brought ashore with her and wrapped Citron in it. He lay down on the bare rock and slept until dawn broke an hour later.

As the first rays of the sun began to warm them after their ordeal in the cold and the dark, the *Pentcho* people fanned out over the rocky carapace of the island to discover what kind of place fate had brought them to.

It was not an encouraging sight. As far as they could tell, Kamilanisi was nothing more than a large, barren rock, reminding Karol Hoffmann of the surface of the moon, totally without vegetation or animal life except some scrub and thorns and a few snails. Small groups of Betarim set out to search for water, while the others huddled together, contemplating a bleak vista of naked rock and empty sea.

By daylight, Citron and his lieutenants were better able to assess the condition of the *Pentcho*. Although buffeted by the sea and breached by the reef, it still seemed in no immediate danger of breaking up. Citron moved fast to organize the Betarim into groups who would go back aboard and strip the vessel as quickly and efficiently as possible of everything that would help them survive.

Soon Citron's men were swarming all over the dying *Pentcho*, first removing food, water barrels and medical supplies, then dismantling the four cooking stoves which were bolted to the deck. They went below, ripped out the wooden bunks and hauled the lumber ashore for firewood and to make shelters. Then followed drums of fuel oil, coils of rope, sheets of tarpaulin, tools, cooking utensils, blankets, clothes and luggage.

The work had its hazards. By now there was deep water inside Akko, and there was a real danger that the *Pentcho* might break up suddenly, without warning, trapping anyone who happened to be below. The water inside the hull was oily and evil-smelling, alive with the wriggling bodies of the *Pentcho*'s multitudinous army of bedbugs. Salvage teams had to dive in total darkness under loose planks with long, exposed nails to retrieve sacks of macaroni and onions, while the ship lurched from side to side with the incoming seas.

Salomon, Steinmetz and Laufer entered the flooded engine room, where they dived to salvage a hammer, two pairs of pliers, a grinding wheel and a soldering iron. On a later foray they found the sick bay two-thirds full of murky water, into which they dived repeatedly to recover urgently needed medical equipment.

Ashore, Citron was directing the setting up of field kitchens and organizing food stores. He gave Emerich Dukas his handgun and put him in charge of guarding the food. "I'll kill anyone who tries to pilfer so much as a dried pea," growled the old soldier.

The first meal on the island, a huge caldron of boiled macaroni and onions, was cooked in seawater and was so salty that it was virtually uneatable. Yet the castaways did not dare use their meager reserves of salvaged drinking water for cooking. The island was still being searched for fresh water. If they didn't find it, they could not expect to last more than a few days.

Sundown that evening, October 9, was the start of Yom Kippur, the Day of Atonement, the holiest day of the Jewish year, on which even the skeptical feel obliged to make some observance, and on which most Jews fast and avoid all work.

Under the circumstances, keeping the fast posed few problems, but work was a matter of survival, and the salvage operation went on well into the night and through the next day, despite the objections of the devout.

Salomon overheard two men from his hometown talking about him as he walked by with a large wooden beam on one shoulder. "Look," said one indignantly, "a rabbi's son and he's working on Yom Kippur!"

By midmorning their most pressing problem had been solved. As two dozen of the Betarim scoured the island in ones and twos looking for water, Sidney Fahn's younger brother Rudi stumbled across a well, hidden from view inside a cave, its opening concealed by a heavy flat stone. Peering inside, Fahn could see a bucket with a rope attached—presumably left behind by the Greek fishermen who must have sunk the well—and lowered it to retrieve a sample. He found the water brackish but good enough for cooking and rushed off to tell Citron the news of his discovery.

Throughout the day, as the younger men and women got on with the job of stripping the ship, building shelters, making signal fires and searching for water, Yom Kippur services were conducted under a lowering sky by two cantors from Bratislava. Every so often the workers would take a break and join in the prayers, which were a good deal more fervent than they might have been under other circumstances. Even the nonbelievers joined in—though not Citron.

By midafternoon the *Pentcho* had been stripped bare, and Citron went aboard for the last time with a cleaning party to swab down the decks. He knew the ship couldn't last much longer, and he felt, however incongruously, that the *Pentcho* should go to its death clean.

From the rocks above, others watched in amazement as Citron and his cleanup squad laid out the *Pentcho* for its funeral as if it were a member of the family. "If it was up to me, I'd squat in the middle of the deck and crap on it," said Salomon.

Professor Heller protested. "No, no," he said, "you shouldn't talk like that. The *Pentcho* was a good ship. It saved our lives." Said Turo Neumann: "At least when it goes down it'll take a couple of million bedbugs with it."

By the time the sun set, bringing the Day of Atonement to a close, shelter was available for all, either in makeshift tents and huts or in caves, with which the island was dotted. And the kitchens were working. As they lined up to break their fast with a cup of hot soup and half a boiled egg each, Salomon accosted the two zealots he had overheard criticizing him earlier in the day.

"Hypocrites," he said. "If I hadn't been working then, you wouldn't be eating now."

Late that night, while most of the castaways slept, Citron and a handful of others witnessed the death of the *Pentcho* from a vantage point on the rocks above.

It was a still night with a swell running, and in the pale light of a new moon they could see the old sidewheeler, its decks now awash and its back broken, moving to and fro with the slow heaving of the sea. Then, about midnight, it seemed to shudder and rear up momentarily before falling back onto the reef with a jarring crash. The impact broke the *Pentcho* apart, and within minutes the two halves slid off the reef and sank, leaving nothing but a few pieces of debris.

Citron would claim that he felt no emotion at the death of the vessel which, against all odds, had brought them this far and which he had laid out so carefully for its funeral. After all, who could have any feelings for a wretched, reeking old scow like the *Pentcho*?

Grete Ehrenfeld's only thought as she watched it go was to thank God the bedbugs had gone down with the ship.

When she slipped away early next morning from the tent she shared with her parents and her fiancé to take another look, a few scraps of floating debris were still to be seen—and what at first looked like a huge, ragged red carpet, covering the reef. She scrambled down the rocks to see what it could be and recoiled in horror.

The "carpet" was composed of the floating bodies of hundreds of thousands of the bedbugs that had become such a hateful obsession for her and the others who sailed on the *Pentcho*.

9

For almost a year—since he had first looked it over in the shipyard at Braila—Schalk had eaten, slept, breathed and lived the *Pentcho*. Acquiring it, modifying it, licensing it, getting it upriver to Bratislava, then smoothing its way downriver with its passengers to the sea, past all the obstacles that ill fortune, prejudice and an indifferent or hostile officialdom could place in their way, had been the focus of his entire existence.

All that had changed once they left the sick embrace of Europe and found themselves at sea, where in more ways than one Schalk was out of his element. He may even have been acknowledging that subconsciously when he renounced all further responsibility for the transport after the row on Lesbos. In a sense, his resignation merely formalized what must have become painfully apparent to him and others— that Schalk the Operator, Schalk the Wheeler-Dealer no longer had a role to play in the fortunes of the S.S. *Pentcho*.

If his venture by lifeboat to guide the *Pentcho* to safety after its boiler burst was intended to show that he was still indispensable, it had been overshadowed by his inability to prevent the shipwreck and Citron's compelling display of leadership that followed. Now, as he huddled in his shelter on Kamilanisi, Schalk made up his mind to try again. While Citron and the others waited and prayed for rescue, he would go out and get it.

After all, he told himself, he was the one who had arranged the transport, he was the one who had kept insisting that they must push on, so it was his responsibility to take the lifeboat and look for help "even though I thought we'd probably never make it."

Rounding up Lichtenfeld, Hercz, Lanes and Ali the Turk, he proposed that they leave the morning after Yom Kippur and strike out for Crete, some 40 miles to the south. It would be no pleasure trip, to be sure, for gathering clouds suggested bad weather to come. But with two pairs of strong men rowing in relays while a fifth manned the tiller, he calculated that they should reach their goal within 24 to 36 hours.

A stiff wind was whipping up whitecaps as they set out at first light, and the clouds seemed dark and menacing. But there could be no question of postponing or abandoning the mission. The coming storm might last for days, and help must reach Kamilanisi before the castaways' food and drinking water ran out.

Watching them row off toward the horizon, Karol Hoffmann thought it "quite a courageous gesture, considering the odds against them," and with other castaways he stood on the cliff top waving until they were out of sight.

All day Schalk and his crew rowed south against mounting seas and a headwind which made each yard gained an exhausting effort. Though tormented by the pain of an ear infection which had been troubling him since the day he had dived into the Danube to rescue young Benny Willinger, Lichtenfeld insisted on rowing nonstop while his companions spelled each other.

That night the storm gathered full force, and to the five men, tossed and buffeted, soaked and terrified, in their tiny craft it seemed that awesome force was directed entirely, malevolently, against them. The suffering Lichtenfeld was horrified by the size of the waves—"a solid wall of water, several meters high, constantly bearing down on us."

Some time after midnight, as they struggled on through a haze of pain and exhaustion, they found themselves close enough to the Cretan shore to see the lights of a small harbor. Schalk roused the two off-duty oarsmen, and the four of them pulled for land while he called the stroke.

It was painfully hard work, for they were now contending not merely with wind and waves, but with a powerful current running parallel with the coast, dragging them toward the eastern tip of the island. Lungs heaving, palms rubbed raw with the effort, they threw everything into a last attempt to reach the harbor whose lights twinkled so invitingly yet so mockingly.

They might conceivably have made it if Ali's oar had not snapped suddenly under pressure flipping him heels over head off his bench. At the limits of their strength and with only three oars functioning, they now had no chance to beat the current. Remorselessly, the harbor lights fell away to their right. They collapsed over their oars and slept.

By dawn they were past the tip of the island, which receded to the west and vanished as they went into the Straits of Kasos and were swept southeastward into the Mediterranean. All that day they tried to thwart the winds and currents that continued pushing them eastward, still hoping to circle back toward the southern coast of Crete. By nightfall, totally exhausted and now without food or water, they gave up and drifted.

Some time later, Schalk awoke to find that the storm had abated. The lifeboat was bobbing gently on a sea that seemed no longer hostile, and the moon was peeping through a rent in the dark cloud cover. But the relief Schalk felt was short-lived. Struggling back to full consciousness, he became aware that water was swirling around his ankles. With a start of horror he realized that the boat was shipping water from beneath the floorboards.

Screaming to the others to wake up, he began bailing frantically with cupped hands. Lichtenfeld grabbed a bucket from under the forepeak and joined in. Ali used his hat to bail. Hercz groped underwater in the dark to find the cause of the leak. He soon located it: a bilge plug, a couple of inches in diameter, had obviously worked loose during the storm and popped out while they slept. Water was coming in fast, and the plug itself was nowhere to be found.

Frantically, Hercz forced his fingers and thumb into the hole to stanch the flow while the others went on bailing. Lanes grabbed the handle of Ali's broken oar, pulled out a clasp knife and, gripping it in a raw and blistered palm, began whittling the end of the oar handle to fashion a plug that would fit the hole.

It was agonizingly slow work. Schalk lost track of time. It seemed to him that they were bailing all night while Lanes worked away at carving the plug. At last they had something that fitted well enough and Lanes jammed the oar upright into the hole, reducing the flow to a manageable trickle. By that time they were all limp with exhaustion and fear.

Dawn of the third day brought no sight of land or ship. Lichtenfeld was now in a delirium of pain from his ear infection. All of them were suffering acutely from saltwater sores and thirst. And they were cold. A piercing wind penetrated to the bone as they lay, wet and exhausted, in the tiny, bobbing craft.

That day, they discussed the possibility of ending their suffering by committing suicide. Schalk had brought two handguns with him. But when he checked them he found their mechanisms so corroded by saltwater that they were useless.

On the morning of the fourth day, there was more talk of suicide. Hercz and Lanes were contemplating going over the side, swimming away from the boat and drowning. But now, somehow finding a new determination to survive, Schalk had turned against the idea of suicide. "No no," he said, "we must stay with the boat."

Later the same day, while they were lying in the bottom of the boat, huddled together for warmth, Lanes roused them. "Listen," he said, "I hear something—an engine."

The others heard nothing. Schalk thought Lanes might be going out of his mind and beginning to hallucinate. But a few moments later, he imagined he heard something himself.

Heaving himself painfully to his feet by means of the broken oar which now stood upright like a small mast, he looked about him, trying to locate the source of the sound. Soon, Lanes and Hercz were on their feet too. Now they could all hear it—unmistakably, the sound of an aircraft engine coming closer.

The Fairey Swordfish torpedo bomber was at the end of its reconnaissance arc and about to turn back toward its carrier, His Majesty's Ship *Illustrious,* steaming 60 miles away over the northern horizon. After the exhilarating experience of action against the Italians a couple of days before, the aircraft's two-man crew were finding patrol duty more than usually irksome and monotonous.

The Swordfish, affectionately known as "Stringbag" to the men of Britain's Fleet Air Arm, was not luxury travel at the best of times. In weather like this—with high winds buffeting the elderly biplane as it cruised at 65 miles an hour and driving rain lashing the faces of the pilot and navigator in their open cockpits—it was decidedly uncomfortable. The prospect of a prompt return to the carrier, with hot showers and pink gins in the wardroom afterward, was more than usually appealing.

The pilot was beginning to bank to the left to start the homeward run when he spotted the open boat among the whitecaps, about 200 feet below. Looking over his shoulder to the navigator, he gestured downward with a gloved hand and eased the joy stick forward for a closer look.

At 50 feet he could see that there were five men in the boat, two of them lying down, three standing up and waving frantically. One held up a white flag with a red cross on it. The pilot waggled his wings to acknowledge having seen them, and to reinforce the message he circled the boat three times, the navigator leaning over the side and giving them a reassuring thumbs-up before the Swordfish climbed and headed northward toward the *Illustrious*.

In the boat, Schalk and his companions went wild with joy, embracing and slapping each other on the back. Within fifteen minutes smoke began to smudge the horizon in the direction the aircraft had taken, and as they watched, the smudges changed slowly into shapes, and the shapes into the outlines of ships—many ships, and all heading in their direction.

Before long the Royal Navy's entire Eastern Mediterranean battle fleet was bearing down on the *Pentcho*'s lifeboat—more than twenty ships of the line, including the aircraft carriers *Illustrious* and *Eagle,* the cruisers *Ajax, Achilles* and *Newcastle,* six or seven destroyers and assorted frigates, corvettes and minesweepers, returning to Alexandria from a foray in which the *Ajax* had sunk two Italian destroyers while planes from *Illustrious* and *Eagle* had bombed and torpedoed the Italians' Aegean naval base at Leros.

As the fleet neared them, the destroyer *Nubian* broke formation and raced toward the *Pentcho*'s lifeboat. Soon it was alongside, a rope ladder was lowered and painfully, the rungs biting into the blistered flesh of bare feet and hands, the five men climbed up the gray, heaving flank of the British warship. They were barely on deck before a heavy-machine-gun crew sank their boat with a burst of fire and the *Nubian* was racing back to resume its station alongside one of the carriers.

Stewards brought Schalk and his companions mugs of hot, sweet tea before they were taken below for a medical checkup. As sick-berth attendants bandaged their tortured hands and administered pain-killing drugs to alleviate the agony of Lichtenfeld's ear infection, Schalk broke into a prolonged fit of uncontrollable sobbing.

Later, they were interrogated by a young officer who spoke flawless German. Like the Italians at Stampalia, he seemed to have some initial doubts about their story. Five hundred people trying to get to Palestine on a Danube river steamer? Impossible. Yet again the very unlikeliness of the story gave it credibility, and the Englishman was soon satisfied that Schalk and company were what they claimed to be, rather than German seamen posing as refugees. Their plea for help to be sent to their shipmates on Kamilanisi was radioed to the flagship, and some time later Schalk was notified that the British commander, Admiral Sir Lumley St. George Lister, had promised to see what could be done about sending a rescue party.

But Admiral Lister had a shooting war on his hands. The next day Italian planes and submarines, out to avenge the losses inflicted by the British, moved in to attack his battle group. A brisk engagement ensued during which an Italian plane scored a crippling hit on the *Newcastle,* causing many casualties and so badly damaging the cruiser's bow that it had to be towed stern-first into port.

Lichtenfeld was particularly impressed by the composure of the *Nubian*'s crew under fire—"like nothing much was happening, laughing and joking. It gave us a good feeling." Schalk's lasting impression of the *Nubian* was of "the kindness and care we received from people I had always thought of as hostile because of our differences over Palestine."

When the fleet reached Alexandria, Schalk and company were removed from the *Nubian* on a cutter manned by British military police and taken ashore to become the first inmates of Alexandria's new Mustafa POW camp—5 prisoners with 15 guards. From the camp they found it impossible to discover what, if anything, had been done about the admiral's promise to send help to Kamilanisi. They might have convinced their rescuers, but they remained objects of some suspicion to the authorities in Alexandria and had to go through further lengthy interrogation to satisfy the British that they were not enemy seamen. Their Czech nationality finally established—and Ali having been sent home to neutral Turkey—they were transferred to a civilian hospital, where Lichtenfeld underwent no fewer than three major operations on his left ear.

"We watched over Imi day and night," Schalk later recalled. "The doctor said if he wasn't so strong he would surely have died."

In the spring of 1941, as soon as Lichtenfeld had recovered sufficiently, the four of them joined the Free Czech forces which were fighting alongside the British in North Africa. Although Palestine, their goal, was only a short train ride away from Alexandria, it would be a long time before any of them would reach it—and before they would discover the fate of the comrades they had left behind on Kamilanisi.

10

*C*itron remained outwardly buoyant, exuding a confidence in the certainty of rescue from Kamilanisi which, genuine or not, did a great deal for morale. Although he had scant grounds for such optimism and had no way of knowing whether Schalk had managed to raise the alarm, he "felt sure the world knew of our whereabouts and would come to our help."

Though infectious, his optimism was not universal.

Haim Laszlo, for example, one of the Betar rank-and-file, was "quite unafraid because I was very young and to me the whole thing seemed like a great adventure," while his friend and contemporary Turo Neumann, depressed and fearful, scratched his name and hometown on a rock beside his shelter "so that if we died, people would know who we were." Fellow Betari Aaron Hellinger also feared they were doomed to a slow death by starvation and thirst. He wrote a few lines to his parents, sealed them in a bottle and threw it into the sea.

Grete Ehrenfeld was so relieved to be free of the *Pentcho* that she was unable to feel anything but hope for the future.

In contrast, her fiancé, Karol Hoffmann, felt cast down by the death of the *Pentcho* because "it represented somehow our last link with the outside world and maybe we entertained some vague hope that the damage could be repaired and the ship would be afloat once more."

The eccentric sage of the *Pentcho*, Professor Heller, professed an optimism to match Citron's. "Never in history has it occurred that five hundred people were in danger and nobody came to their rescue," he assured his young companions-in-peril with a good deal more fervor than accuracy.

By his own admission, Daniel Hamburger was beyond either hope or fear: "I was not rational by this time. My feelings were those of an animal, intent only on surviving, day to day, hour to hour." He hid himself in a cave and refused to lift a finger to help himself. "If I don't exert myself, I'll last longer," he said.

The ever-resourceful Tibi Laufer was prepared for the worst. He drew his friend Oskar Salomon into a cave and showed him two empty oil drums and five planks which he had squirreled away to make into a raft. "We'd probably never reach safety," he conceded, "but I'm not going to stay here and die like a starving dog."

A few of the castaways seemed able to forget the perils and privations of their existence on Kamilanisi in contemplation of the scenery—the breakers rolling into the sweeping curve of the sandy bay and the majestic cloudscapes filling the lowering skies. "In spite of the danger of our situation, some of us were deeply stirred by the beauty of the island and the sea," Heskel Lillienthal would recall, while Grete Ehrenfeld found that "the water in the bay was so clean and crystalline, it was sheer joy to swim in."

Others found consolation in supernatural signs and portents. One of the religious zealots assured anyone who would listen that they would be rescued from the island on the feast of Simhat Torah, which occurs twelve days after Yom Kippur.

One of the Betar girls, Heidi Weiss, dreamed that she received a telegram, which read, "HOLD ON. HELP COMING. SCHALK." She clung to her dream like a frightened child clutching a bedtime toy, and as the castaways' reserves of food and water dwindled, she sat on a rocky promontory day after day watching the sea and sky, waiting for her dream to come true.

A hundred miles away, in the magnificent Crusader castle which he had made his headquarters and official residence, Count Cesare De Vecchi di Val Cismon, Governor-General of Rhodes and commander-in-chief of the Italian Aegean, learned with some irritation of the castaways' presence on the smallest and remotest of the islands over which he was absolute ruler. He had quite enough to concern him without this.

In the four months since his Duce and onetime friend, Benito Mussolini, had strode onto the balcony of the Palazzo Venezia in Rome to announce that Italy was joining the conflict on the side of Germany, De Vecchi had come to realize just how ill-prepared Italy was for war—and in particular, for war with the British in the Eastern Mediterranean. Mussolini might call it "Mare Nostrum" and "an Italian lake," but the facts of the situation proved otherwise.

With Germany in possession of Europe's Atlantic seaboard from Norway to Spain, the British might have their backs to the wall at home. But here in the Eastern Mediterranean Theater they deployed formidable naval strength, and it was the islands over which De Vecchi ruled as Mussolini's proconsul, long touted as "the advance guard of Italian power in the Middle East," that were under siege.

De Vecchi, an Old Guard "Fascist of the First Hour," had been Mussolini's Minister of Public Instruction before they fell out over some detail of policy and the Duce got rid of him by sending him to Rhodes in 1936. Although bitter at being banished from the center of power and influence in Rome, De Vecchi had found it a pleasant enough exile, in which he occupied himself with colorful if empty ceremonials, lavish entertainments and the refurbishment of the ruined Palace of the Grand Masters of the Knights of Rhodes, which was to become his palazzo and that of all future governors.

As Governor-General, he was absolute monarch of Rhodes and its satellite islands. When he drove through the city in his official car, the Rhodians were expected to come to attention and give the Fascist salute. Woe betide those drinkers at the sidewalk cafés of the Piazza Mandracchio who failed to do so.

But with the intrusion of war into his island idyll, Rhodes, raided and blockaded by air and sea, had become De Vecchi's bed of nails, and with each military setback he had grown increasingly out of sorts. Now there was this problem of a shipload of Jews, wrecked on one of his outlying islands.

Their presence had been reported to the International Red Cross by the British, who proposed sending a rescue party, provided the Italians guaranteed safe-conduct. Rome's answer had been a very definite "No." Though uninhabited, Kamilanisi was an Italian island; the British would set foot on it at their peril. If the Jews were to be rescued, the Italians would do it.

So the fate of the *Pentcho* people had been dumped onto the inlaid-mahogany desk of the Quadrumviro De Vecchi, who was forced to concede that under the circumstances, there was nothing for it but to send a naval vessel to take them off their desert island and bring them here to Rhodes.

This displeased De Vecchi, a man not noted for his love of mankind in general ("a living example of reactionary obtuseness," a postwar historian would call him) or of the Jews in particular. Where the majority of Italian officials and party functionaries regarded the Duce's anti-Jewish legislation with distaste and did their best to circumvent it, De Vecchi had enforced it with enthusiasm. He had made the Jews of Rhodes keep their shops and businesses open on the Sabbath and other holy days, looted a hundred of their marble tombstones to pave the courtyard of his palazzo and generally treated them with even greater contempt than he showed toward his Greek and Turkish subjects. By Nazi standards, he was a mild enough oppressor, perhaps, but Hezekiah Franco, the president of the Rhodes Jewish community, considered him "a truly terrible man."

It was with a certain degree of impatience, therefore, that De Vecchi gave the order for a naval transport to set out for Kamilanisi, and it was with a certain degree of satisfaction that he decided to pass on the problem of feeding his unwanted guests to their coreligionists. Rhodes was an island under severe blockade and food was tightly rationed, so it seemed to him only fitting that the Jews of Rhodes should have the responsibility of providing for their brethren.

Meanwhile, there might be some propaganda mileage to gain from the affair. Let the world know that Italy was a humane nation, that while others might let these unfortunates starve on a barren rock in the sea, not so the nation of Michelangelo, Dante, Garibaldi and Mussolini.

There was little to occupy the castaways once shelters had been made and the kitchens were functioning. Even the labor of drawing water by hand from the well had been obviated by the installation of a pump salvaged from the *Pentcho*.

A group of women got together and started fashioning a large fishing net out of string. Some of the men were trying to catch fish using bent pins as hooks but, not surprisingly, had little success. But at least, thought Karol Hoffmann, fishing gave one something to do and took one's mind off their desperate situation. The irrepressible Citron, viewing the anglers' negative results, cracked that "the fish around here must be anti-Semitic."

While unbelievers scoured the shore and rocks for shellfish to augment their meager diet of macaroni, rice and onions, the faithful condemned the very idea of consuming such unclean food and warned that God would punish those who defied Him by eating *treif*.

Citron tried to keep the Betarim as busy as possible. He had them parade in full uniform to mark Jabotinsky's birthday. He conducted a course on the principles and practice of *hadar*. He organized an evening of community singing on the Feast of Succot, four days after Yom Kippur. Relays of Betarim kept round-the-clock watch for ships and aircraft, with signal fires ready to be lit at various points on the island, blankets laid out in an SOS pattern and hand mirrors fixed to a big wooden board, ready to flash a distress signal.

A plane had flown over the island on Yom Kippur, but there had been low cloud and one could not be sure if it had spotted them. From time to time ships had been sighted far out at sea and the signal fires lit, but there had been no response. The weather remained bad, and Markeyevitch predicted that it would not improve for eight or nine days.

As stocks of drinking water dwindled and rations were progressively reduced, despair and privation began to whittle away at morale. *"People are getting more and more depressed,"* noted Karol Hoffmann. *"They look desperate with their emaciated faces and figures, clad in rags, the men all unshaven. People don't walk around too much in a bid to preserve their strength and some come out of their shelters only to line up for their daily meal."*

On their ninth day on the island, true to Markeyevitch's prediction, the sky began to clear. On the morning of the tenth day, an Italian reconnaissance aircraft flew over the island, and the mirror signal flashed a plea for rescue. The plane circled Kamilanisi three times before making off to the east.

Obviously, their whereabouts were now known: what remained to be seen was whether anyone would act on that knowledge.

The answer came late that night when Heidi Weiss, keeping vigil on her rocky lookout, spied a dark mass offshore and saw a small ship heading into the bay. "My dream was true," she shrieked excitedly, "my dream was true! Help is coming."

Others had seen the blacked-out Italian ship looming up out of the dark, and suddenly all three signal bonfires burst into flame. "Put those fires out, put those fires out!" came a shouted command through a loud-hailer. "Don't you know there's a war on?"

By the time the first of the ship's boats had grounded on the sand of the bay and an Italian officer had stepped ashore, scores of castaways were on the beach to greet him. "We've come on the orders of the Governor of the Aegean to rescue you," said the Italian. "Do you want to be taken to Rhodes?"

"Yes, yes!" came the reply. "*Viva Italia! Viva Mussolini!*"

Women were crying with relief; children were running up and down the beach, dancing with joy; men pressed forward to shake hands with the Italian seamen who stood in the surf, steadying the boats.

Amid the hubbub, Citron was able to confer briefly with the officer, who said he had not enough room to take everyone off at once. Women, children, the sick and the elderly would be taken first. He would return the next day for the men. And before long, the first of the women and children were being rowed out toward the waiting transport.

Among the Betarim there were mixed feelings about the arrival of the Italians. A hard core of determined optimists remained convinced that the British would be along soon and wanted to wait for them. They reasoned that if they went with the Italians they would find themselves on the wrong side of the war—and might even be handed over to the Germans.

Citron disagreed, and there was a lively discussion. He told them he considered the fact that the Italians had taken the risk to come for them to be a sign of their good faith and that he was sure they would be fairly treated. "But it's up to you," he said. "Those who want to stay behind and wait for the British are free to take their chances, but I'm for going to Rhodes with the Italians."

The next day, when the Italian ship returned, 20 men hid in a cave and were left behind.

On the 90-mile trip to Rhodes, the warship carrying Citron and his followers sailed into one of those sudden, violent storms for which the Aegean is notorious at that time of year. Enormous waves crashed over the vessel and virtually everyone was sick, including the captain. "One thing is sure," remarked Oskar Salomon; "the poor old *Pentcho* would never have survived that one."

Six days after the others had gone, leaving them with enough food and water for a couple of weeks, the 20 men who stayed on the island to wait for the British saw a vessel in the bay and a boat coming ashore. Thinking it must be the British this time, they went down to the beach, only to find that the Italian Navy had returned to collect the belongings the *Pentcho* people had left behind.

The holdouts were allowed no option but to go to Rhodes and join their comrades in whatever fate the Italians intended for them.

11

*T*he *Pentcho* people's euphoria at having been rescued evaporated rapidly once they got to Rhodes and were put into the hurriedly improvised tent camp that had been prepared for them in a soccer stadium. It was not that the Italians were hostile. There was none of the brutality the castaways might have expected had they fallen into German hands. But neither was there anything to eat.

The Jews of Rhodes—an ancient community much depleted in recent years by the departure of its young men to work abroad and impoverished by Mussolini's discriminatory legislation—protested that they lacked the resources to feed the newcomers. The civil authorities tried to shrug off responsibility by arguing that since the *Pentcho* people had been brought to the island by the navy, feeding them was a problem for the military. The military retorted that since these were not prisoners of war but civilian internees they must be the responsibility of the civil administration. And De Vecchi, it seemed, just did not want to be bothered any further by this minor but irksome matter.

As Citron saw it, "Nobody was willing to make the first move, for fear they would be committed to an obligation they couldn't sustain, so for three days we had nothing to eat."

While they went hungry, De Vecchi was getting his propaganda bonus. "In spite of the state of war," reported *Il Giornale d'Italia,* "the Governor did not hesitate to send help to the unfortunate travelers. . . . Rejected during their long voyage by all those countries which oppose the policies of the Axis, the story of these hundreds of unfortunates is a clear demonstration of certain governments' bad faith.

"Only in these Italian waters were these unfortunates able to find the help and human solidarity for which they searched in vain those five months."

At the stadium camp, the situation of the internees was becoming desperate. When there was no sign of a break in the deadlock by the morning of the fourth day, Emerich Dukas staged a melodramatic protest which brought temporary relief. Marching up to the Italian warrant officer in charge of camp security, he tore open his shirt, baring his chest as if inviting execution, and declared: *"Maresciallo,* I am a soldier. Give me food or give me a bullet!"

It was a gesture that might have come straight from grand opera, and it brought a manly tear to the Maresciallo's eye. Putting his hand into his pocket, he drew out a wad of his own money and sent an orderly into the town to buy whatever he could find. An hour or two later, the orderly returned with sacks of figs and olives—enough to give every internee a handful of each. It was the first time in his life that Citron had ever eaten an olive.

The next day, a truckload of cabbages and a sack of salt, paid for by the Jewish community, arrived at the camp. The *Pentcho* people lived on those cabbages for three weeks.

Food was not the only problem. Chill winds from the Turkish mountains and driving winter rains turned the stadium sports ground into a frigid mud bath. The old army tents the Italians had provided gave inadequate shelter from the wind and rain, and water lapped over the duckboards on which the internees tried to sleep. Sickness spread, and by the end of November they began to die.

Emerich Dukas was one of the first to succumb, his body weight reduced to a mere 90 pounds by pneumonia and dysentery. His tentmate, Turo Neumann carried him to a waiting ambulance, so wasted that he was able to pick him up like a child. The others stood in silence, watching, and as Neumann put him into the ambulance, Dukas raised enough strength to give the Betar salute and call out its slogan, *Tel Hai*—"Hill of Life," the name of the Jewish settlement in upper Galilee where Trumpledor was killed.

A couple of days later, his comrades learned that Dukas had died in the Italian military hospital. Thirty of them, headed by Citron, to whom he had shown such devotion, were allowed to go under escort to the Jewish cemetery for Dukas' funeral. At a memorial service, Citron called him a "symbol of loyalty."

As the death toll mounted, the local Jews became increasingly alarmed about the fate of their coreligionists and anxious at the prospect of having to continue to feed them out of their own slender resources. In the first week of December, Hezekiah Franco, the president of the community, sent an urgent appeal to the representative of the Jewish Agency in Geneva, with whom he had already been in contact on the subject.

Complaining that the 12,500 lire received so far from Jewish organizations abroad to help support the internees amounted to only six-tenths of one lira per person per day, Franco warned the Jewish Agency that "we are now at the end of our resources—I repeat, at the end of our resources," and begged them to provide the means to "enable these unfortunates to continue their voyage as soon as possible."

Quite apart from the "large amounts of money" that were needed to feed them, Franco entreated the Agency to give serious consideration to "the one solution that exists, TO SEND THEM A SHIP, A SAVIOR SHIP, which will take them to the country of their destination."

Evidently the Agency considered this proposal to be as excessive as the capital letters in which it was framed. It was not inclined to send refugee ships into battle zones, or to annoy the British, with whom it was cooperating closely at the time, and the suggestion was ignored.

Relief did eventually come in the form of a monthly subvention of 30,000 lire from Delasem, an Italian Jewish refugee-relief organization. This was enough to provide a daily ration sufficient to keep the internees alive. From then on nobody starved, but they were hungry all the time they were on Rhodes.

The children of the *Pentcho,* at least, were safe during the worst period before the Delasem money started coming. With the agreement of the authorities, they had been "adopted" by local families, with whom they were living in the Jewish quarter, close to the commercial port.

Karci Farkas and some of the others started a little contraband trading in bread and raisins, which they sold to buy the occasional luxury, such as an egg. Then they would go to the stadium, walk up to the wire, calling for their parents, and throw them whatever they had been able to scrounge.

Meanwhile, in the difficult circumstances of the stadium camp, morale among the internees plummeted, old grievances surfaced again and Citron was plagued by indiscipline, recrimination and backbiting. Things came to a head when, learning that some of the young women were according sexual favors to the guards in return for extra food, he banned all fraternization between the internees and Italian personnel. Some of the young women were openly defiant, and a male internee, notorious for his black-market activities, demanded, "Who are you to tell others what to do?" Infuriated, Citron felled him with a punch.

The atmosphere in general, and that incident in particular, so disturbed Citron that he called together all the leading personalities among the *Pentcho* people and delivered an ultimatum: Either he and his advisory committee were given full backing or an entirely new leadership would have to be elected. The meeting ended inconclusively, and Citron decided: That's that. I've quit.

Citron felt he had no further role to play, except as commander of his own Betar group. His job was over. The project had failed. He saw no reason why he should be "the scapegoat for a bunch of lazy good-for-nothings." The following morning, November 14, he noted in his diary: *"I am no longer the leader of this transport."*

A five-member committee of business and professional men—persons of experience and substance who it was thought would be better qualified than Citron to deal with the Italians and make their plight known to the world—was elected to replace him. It was to be only the first of several committees, one replacing another as discontent and dissension continued to dominate the affairs of the *Pentcho* people throughout their stay on Rhodes.

Often the bickering led to ugly scenes, as in an incident that occurred a couple of weeks after Citron's resignation. With the tools they had salvaged from the *Pentcho,* Oskar Salomon and his friends Steinmetz and Laufer had set themselves up in an improvised workshop where they manufactured pots and pans, stoves, kettles and a number of other essential items out of old tin cans left behind on a dump by the Italian troops. One evening, while joining the line for his daily cup of cabbage soup, Salomon noticed a member of the new governing committee returning for a second cup. "Hey," he protested, "how come he gets two cups while we get only one?"

Another member of the committee intervened. "He gets two cups because he works."

"I work too," Salomon retorted, "so if he gets two cups, I get two cups."

But the committee members were adamant. "Okay," said Salomon, "no soup, no work. We'll take our tools and close down the workshop."

Matters moved swiftly to a crisis. Members of the committee and their supporters tried to confiscate the tools, claiming them as community property. Salomon and company resisted. Tibi Laufer brandished a sledgehammer over his head, shouting, "I'll kill the first man that touches those tools."

One of the committee, a lawyer, defused the crisis by proposing that an independent "tribunal" decide the ownership of the tools. Eventually, they ruled that since Salomon and his friends had risked their lives to retrieve the tools, they rightly belonged to them.

Thus involved in trivial internal disputes, the governing committee was making no progress in getting the Italians to improve their living conditions. Many of the internees were seriously ill in their tents, five more had followed Dukas to the grave and, as Marcel Friedmann would recall, "if things had gone on like that, the winter would have killed off scores of us."

Although he was now out of office, Citron was not a man to sit back and let that happen. Calling together a group of his Betar loyalists, he asked for volunteers to break out of the camp and go direct to the Italian high command to dramatize their situation.

Feri Neumann was one of the volunteers. Getting over the wall was easy enough, he found, because security on the perimeter of the stadium was not too rigorous. The difficult part was getting to military headquarters undetected through the curfew. The Italians on Rhodes had invasion jitters and were liable to shoot on sight at any unauthorized group of men moving through the city after dark But Neumann and the other volunteers reached headquarters undetected and marched openly up to the main gate, where Neumann appointed himself spokesman on the basis of the smattering of Italian he had acquired. "We demand to see the *commandante*," he told a flabbergasted captain of the guard. "We're dying like flies in there. We won't go back alive. You can kill us if you like, but we won't go back."

The captain responded by locking them in the guardhouse overnight and sending them back under escort, in handcuffs and leg irons, the next morning. As they shuffled back to the stadium, Neumann and the others put on a show of defiance, singing Betar songs all the way.

At the camp they were told that court-martial charges were being prepared against them for breaking out. That evening, lining up for his daily bread ration. Neumann was summoned to the *Maresciallo*'s office. There the warrant officer clapped him on the shoulder, gave him an extra piece of bread and admonished, "Please don't do anything like that again." That was Neumann's court-martial. Feckless the Italians may have been; inhuman they were not.

A few days later, on Christmas Eve, a convoy of trucks arrived without warning and moved the *Pentcho* people and their meager belongings from the stadium to the comparative warmth and comfort of the San Giovanni Barracks, near the center of the town.

Whether it was the protest breakout, the Christmas spirit or orders from De Vecchi that caused the Italians to relent nobody knew.

At San Giovanni, the *Pentcho* people were quartered in three large basement garages where, although conditions were still far from ideal, they were at least warm and dry—and, as they soon realized, a good deal safer than the Italian troops on the upper floors during the almost nightly bombing raids by British planes based on Cyprus. On nights when the bombing was particularly heavy, Italian soldiers would come down and take shelter under the *Pentcho* people's bunks.

Air and ground crews of the German Luftwaffe, using Rhodes as a base for operations against British ships and shore positions, were also occasionally quartered in San Giovanni, to the understandable anxiety of the Jewish internees. But there were no incidents: the Italian authorities took care to see that there was no contact between the two groups. Once when the *Maresciallo* noticed a group of Luftwaffe men eyeing the Jewish prisoners curiously through the perimeter fence, he drove them off.

Complaisant guards allowed some individuals to leave the barracks to forage for food, and the internees set up both kosher and nonkosher kitchens. Olives, onions, figs and oranges were their main diet. Meat and eggs were virtually unknown, and so was fish because of the severe restrictions the Italians had imposed on the island's Greek fishermen when Italy went to war with Greece at the end of October.

For many of the *Pentcho* people, the meager rations available on the island were augmented by an occasional food parcel from home. The Final Solution had not yet been formulated and the Jews of Slovakia were still living a precariously "normal" existence, so that to the families they had left behind it seemed that the internees were the ones in need of aid and comfort.

Karol Hoffmann, for example, received a letter from home, dated January 10, 1941, saying that money was on the way to him. Meanwhile, the letter said, his father, Alfred, and older brother, Bela, were still working in the family grocery store. They expected that the business would soon be "Aryanized," but, said his father, *"we're getting used to the idea and re-signed to it."*

Hoffmann's parents were still living in their own apartment on fashionable Stefanikstrasse, and life was "quite comfortable." His brother Paul added a note, saying there had been good powder snow in the hills around Bratislava and *"I'm doing a lot of skiing."*

At about the same time, Oskar Salomon received a parcel from his parents which contained a book. Concealed inside its pages were small items like razor blades and lighter flints which could be bartered for food. Marcel Friedmann's father sent him money via a third party—one of the Gentile school friends who had given him a boisterous send-off that last night in Bratislava. Friedmann also received a food parcel from relatives in Chile, while others received cash and food from relatives in the United States, which was still neutral.

Citron, whose family were in New York, was sent something a good deal more valuable than razor blades, lighter flints, food or money: the chance of freedom. A letter from his brother in March 1941 told him that he had been accepted as a student by Boston University. An affidavit certifying this had been sent to the American Embassy in Rome. All Citron had to do was make contact with the consulate and his passage to the States would be arranged.

Jabotinsky's son Eri, also writing from New York, enclosed a note from Peter Bergson, head of the American Friends for a Jewish Palestine, urging Citron to accept the offer, saying he could help the Jewish cause more from America than from an internment camp on Rhodes.

But Citron "never considered it seriously." His bond with Shosha and the Betarim was very strong and he did not believe he could do anything to help them in America, which he was sure would soon be at war with the Axis powers.

One internee who did leave Rhodes at about this time was an Austrian named Heinz Wisla. Having acquired a Portuguese visa, he was allowed to leave for Lisbon via Rome. Before he left, the governing committee drew up a petition which he promised he would try to present to the Pope.

In a letter to Rhodes from Lisbon some weeks later, Wisla reported that he had taken the petition to the Vatican, where he was granted an audience with Pius XII. Waiting ahead of him to receive the pontifical blessing was a large group of German soldiers. *"I was scared stiff, but they didn't realize who or what I was,"* Wisla wrote, *"and after the Pope had blessed them I was able to present the petition. He promised to do what he could."*

By the spring of 1941, Grete Ehrenfeld and Karol Hoffmann decided that their engagement had been a mistake and broke it off by mutual agreement, Grete returning his ring and the jewelry his mother had given her.

The break was made with regrets but without rancor. The months of squalor and privation aboard ship and in the camps had stripped the patina of romance from their relationship, exposing the bare wood of incompatible personalities. As Karol would recall later, "When you're under those kinds of pressures, you tend to become selfish. She had her parents, and perhaps I felt I could manage better if I had only myself to think about."

Besides, there was Antonio. The ever-romantic Grete had fallen wildly in love with one of the camp guards, a member of the black-shirted Fascist Militia. She found him "dazzlingly handsome" with his dark, curly hair and fine Roman features. No less irresistible were his splendid tenor voice and the food he brought for her and her parents when he came courting.

"He used to serenade me with operatic arias," she would recall. "His favorite—and mine—was '*O dolce bacci, languide carrezze*' from *Tosca*. He used to sit with me and my parents, all very respectable. We kissed when we were alone together, but we never made love."

The idyll came to an end when Antonio innocently asked his commanding officer for permission to marry *la bella internata*. Although prepared to turn a blind eye to fraternization, the Fascist authorities could hardly give it their official stamp of approval by sanctioning a marriage between a guard and a prisoner. Antonio was banished to Lindos, at the other end of the island.

Grete was heartbroken. Every other weekend, when he got leave, Antonio would come to San Giovanni and murmur passionate endearments to her through the chain-link perimeter fence while his ex-comrades of the camp guard detail obligingly looked the other way.

It was hopeless, of course; and if the affair was reminiscent of Puccini at his most florid—the handsome guard, the beautiful prisoner, the arias at the window, the cruel separation—it has been observed that life among the Italians *is* often indistinguishable from grand opera.

The *Pentcho*'s crew had long since been repatriated, but for the stateless Captain Markeyevitch and his wife there was no easy exit. They were obliged to share their passengers' internment, and as their stocks of morphine dwindled, so—almost visibly—did their hold on life.

Since the wreck of the *Pentcho*, Markeyevitch had seemed an utterly broken man. It was as if the loss of his ship had snapped the last threads of his self-respect, and the old émigré withdrew deeper into the private torment which consumed him, growing daily gaunter and more spectral.

The old couple had fixed up a corner of one of the basements as living space and curtained it off with a blanket, behind which they dragged out their shared misery. The Betarim kept a respectful distance; the best they could do for the Markeyevitches was see that they got their share of the food and were spared any heavy chores.

Salomon remained the attentive orderly. Whenever they needed something, Ludmilla Markeyevitch would call peremptorily for him—"*Salomon, kommst du her!*"

In the summer of 1941, the captain's condition became so poor that the camp authorities decided he must be removed to a hospital. Citron and a handful of his Betarim watched as Italian medics took him away on a stretcher. Having seen Emerich Dukas and others leave the same way, they hardly expected to see Markeyevitch again.

The recollection of Markeyevitch's drugged stupors aboard the *Pentcho* and of his total collapse on the night of the shipwreck remained, but they could still feel a pang of regret for the strange and tortured old mariner whose dogged skills had brought them a good deal closer to their goal than anyone might have expected.

Old Ludmilla tried to follow her husband to the ambulance and was gently restrained by the medics. Two Betarim led her back to her bed space, where she immediately retired behind the curtain, whimpering wordlessly for the mate who had been taken from her.

From time to time, word reached camp from the hospital that Markeyevitch still clung to life, and occasionally the Italians would take Ludmilla for a brief bedside visit. Between visits, she would remain behind her curtain, speaking to no one but Salomon, who continued to place himself at her beck and call.

"Salomon, come here," she would call, imperious as ever. "Coming, Madame Kapitän!" he would answer, dropping whatever he was doing to go to her assistance.

12

Toward the end of 1941, after the Germans' capture of Crete had made the shipping lanes between Italy and Rhodes more secure for the Axis, the Italian authorities decided to relieve the island of the burden of its hungry "guests" by transferring the *Pentcho* people to a camp in Italy.

News of the impending move caused some concern among the internees. Although they had been treated humanely enough, after the privations of their first few weeks, by the Italians on Rhodes, they didn't know what to expect of the authorities in Italy itself. They were uneasy, too, at the idea of returning to the Nazi-dominated European mainland after having got so close to their destination. But of course, they had no choice in the matter and they resigned themselves to the prospect of leaving.

Not so the *Pentcho*'s dentist, Ladislav Kurti. He had become obsessed with the idea of escaping to neutral Turkey, whose Taurus Mountains beckoned so invitingly from across the 10 miles of water separating Rhodes from the Anatolian mainland. He had no intention of allowing himself to be shipped off to Italy—a resolve that had been triggered by a letter from his father in Bratislava saying that his sisters, Gisella and Elisabeth, were being held in the Patronka transit camp with several hundred other young Jewish women before being shipped off to Poland to work in a Nazi war factory.

His father, steeped as he was in German culture—"It was like a religion, a rock, to him," Kurti would recall—couldn't believe anything very terrible would happen to the girls. But Kurti guessed that they were destined for something far worse than mere factory work, and became frantic with worry for them.

As he looked out the window of his makeshift clinic in the San Giovanni Barracks, Kurti could see the Turkish mainland just across the straits, appearing in the hard Mediterranean light to be so close that he could reach out and touch it, and he conceived "this crazy idea that if I could somehow get to Turkey I could get visas for them and that somehow their release could be arranged."

Kurti's assistant, a pugnacious seventeen-year-old named Anchi Antmann, also felt the lure of the Turkish coast, though for somewhat different reasons. His idea was that if he could get to the mainland he would make his way on foot to Palestine. And from Kurti's clinic, a former army brothel which backed onto a donkey track skirting the barracks, both men were well placed to scout out the possibilities of escape and make their preparations in secret.

On unauthorized trips into town they had spotted what looked like a suitable getaway vehicle, a fisherman's boat lying high and dry on a slipway at the edge of the commercial harbor. It had no oars or rowlocks, but Kurti and Antmann remedied this deficiency by ripping up clinic floorboards to make paddles.

Once these preparations were completed, they chose the

next moonless night to make their break, joined by four other Betar men. The fact that the chosen night was Friday the 13th of February did not deter them.

At about 11 P.M., Kurti and Antmann removed a number of stones they had loosened in the outside wall of the clinic and one by one the escapees dropped down onto the donkey track below, Antmann handing down the paddles before joining his comrades on the outside.

Their first problem was to reach the harbor without being spotted. Antmann had the idea that if they shouldered their paddles like rifles and marched noisily through the town they would be taken in the dark for a detachment of Italian soldiers going on guard duty and thus pass unchallenged. The ruse worked perfectly.

Once at the harbor, they had to manhandle the heavy 18-foot boat down the slipway and into the water without attracting attention. Once again luck was with them. It was a stormy night and the roar of the sea covered whatever noise they made as they got the boat into the water.

Five of them got into the boat, but the sixth—a nonswimmer named Ossie Kunstler—lost his nerve at the last minute and backed out with a mumbled excuse. Undeterred, the others struck out into the dark.

Inside the harbor the water was calm, but as they passed out between the twin columns flanking the harbor entrance and crossed the harbor bar, they encountered heavy seas, and within a minute or two they realized to their horror that the boat was shipping water fast. They tried to put about and make it back to the harbor, but wind and waves were driving them farther out to sea, even as their boat began to settle lower into the churning water.

Frantic attempts to bail were useless: the water was coming in faster than they could throw it out. Then a bigger-than-usual wave hit the boat, and the next thing Antmann knew he was "in the sea, swimming for my life."

In the water with him were Kurti and a third man, Oskar Elbert. The other two—Alexander Rosenberg and Itzhak Mittelmann, both of them poor swimmers—were still in the boat, now almost up to their waists in water and crying, "Don't leave us, don't leave us!"

Kurti clung to the side of the boat with one hand while he tried to remove his boots with the other, noticing incongruously as he struggled to do so that there were lightning bugs in the water—"millions of them, looking like little departed souls."

Antmann, observing that the boat, though awash, remained afloat, swam back toward it, hoping to hang on. It seemed less risky than trying to swim to shore through the heavy seas. "But just then a big wave hit the boat and it vanished into the dark.

"I thought this must be the end, and I began saying the prayer my father had taught me—'Sh'ma Yisrael.' He had always told me that when everything seemed to be lost I should throw myself on God's mercy—and believe it or not, I had no sooner said the prayer when like a miracle, I saw a life preserver floating in the water near me and I was able to grab it."

Antmann got into the life belt, which had apparently been put into the boat by Ossie Kunstler before he lost his nerve and backed out of the venture, and began to strike out toward the harbor. At first, he could see and hear nothing of his comrades. Then, from about 500 feet away, he heard a voice calling and swam toward it. It was Oskar Elbert, who was shouting, "Come this way—I can feel the bottom."

Meanwhile, Kurti too had been praying for deliverance, stripping off his clothes as he did so until all he had on was his shirt. "I was terribly tired," he would recall, "and I must have passed out, because the next thing I remember is slamming into something hard and realizing that a wave had thrown me against a rock. I tried to hold on to it, but when the water went down I went down with it, and I realized the top of the rock was as high as a house. I had enough sense to wait for the next wave to take me up again, and this time I just managed to hang on. I was so exhausted I could scarcely move my limbs, but I was able to throw one leg over a projection and hold on."

Kurti was at the end of a massive stone breakwater. Slowly and painfully he crawled over it until he could see calm water on the other side and realized he had reached the safety of the harbor. Gratefully, he slipped into it and swam two or three hundred yards to a sandy beach.

Scrambling to safety up another section of the same breakwater, Antmann and Elbert were beginning to feel the lash of the night wind. Within seconds they were shivering uncontrollably. "Where are the others?" Antmann asked Elbert. Elbert shook his head. He had a cigarette lighter, wrapped in oilcloth, in one pocket He removed it and after several attempts got it to light, cupping the flame against the wind.

Immediately they heard a voice in the darkness, calling out, "Who goes there?" Within seconds the two would-be escapees were surrounded by bayonets. Sabotage teams of British frogmen had raided other islands of the Italian Dodecanese group in recent weeks, and clearly the Italians thought this was another attempt in progress.

Antmann and Elbert were taken to a guardroom, where an Italian officer began interrogating them with the help of his leather-bound swagger stick. "It wasn't so bad, that beating," Antmann would recall with a laugh. "It helped to restore our circulation."

Not far away, Kurti was receiving similar treatment. He had been surrounded by soldiers as he waded ashore inside the harbor and, like the others, questioned none too gently about his presumed membership in a British sabotage team.

Antmann and Elbert kept trying to tell the Italians that they were Jewish internees, not members of a British commando team, and that two of their comrades were still in the sea; but they spoke little Italian, while their captors seemed not to understand German, so little progress was being made. Kurti, however, did speak Italian fluently by now and was able to persuade his captors to put a boat out into the raging seas to search for Rosenberg and Mittelmann. Neither was ever found.

Toward dawn the three shivering survivors were reunited, bundled into a van and driven off to the city jail, where they joined a number of Greek prisoners accused of sabotage and other activities against the Italians. After a week in the lockup, they were returned under close guard to San Giovanni Barracks.

Ten days after that, the other male internees left on the troopship *Vesta* for Italy—the women, children and old people having preceded them on an earlier vessel—leaving Kurti, Antmann and Elbert behind to face a military tribunal.

It was during their trial, several weeks later, that they discovered why their stolen escape boat had proved so disastrously unseaworthy. Its Greek owner testified that in accordance with emergency regulations he had drilled a hole in the hull so that the boat could not be put to unauthorized use. "Didn't they know about this regulation?" he asked incredulously.

To Antmann the trial seemed almost theatrical. "We were marched through the town to face the military tribunal, and a lot of people just tagged along to watch. The court was crowded with civilian spectators and Italian officers in splendid full-dress uniforms. It was like a scene from an opera."

The list of charges was daunting—escaping from captivity, larceny, damaging Italian Government property, spreading enemy propaganda and the military catchall: conduct prejudicial to the maintenance of good order and discipline. For such offenses in wartime the penalty was death.

The evidence against them was incontrovertible; they had

done all the things alleged, except to spread enemy propaganda, and it was left to the lawyer appointed by the court to defend them to plead justification and extenuating circumstances. Prisoners of war had an inherent right to attempt to escape, he argued. The defendants had not been motivated by ill will toward Italy. The Jewish people had suffered greatly and deserved mercy. The local Jewish community would gladly pay for the boat. And so forth.

The members of the tribunal adjourned and after an hour returned to deliver their verdict: Guilty as charged. Antmann, who knew little Italian, failed to realize that they were facing execution. Kurti, however, was well aware that their lives were at stake as the public defender rose to make a final plea for clemency.

"*Questi miserabili,*" the attorney declared melodramatically with a sweeping gesture toward the three defendants—"these miserable men—have they not suffered enough? Do they really deserve to go before a firing squad for so slight an offense? Are we Italians so insensitive that we cannot temper justice with mercy? Surely it would be more humane, and more practical, to send them to a prison camp where they can be put to work in behalf of the war effort?"

The spectators seemed to hold their breath, while the officers of the tribunal conferred. So did the defendants. Then the chairman, a colonel in the Italian Judge Advocate General's Department, pronounced sentence: execution would be commuted to indefinite detention in a prisoner-of-war camp recently opened at Appolona, on the other side of the island.

The courtroom spectators rose to their feet and cheered "as though applauding a tremendous operatic performance," said Antmann. "People were shouting '*Bravo, bravo,*' crowding around us, shaking our hands, crowding around the officers of the tribunal, shaking their hands, embracing them, kissing them."

Antmann and his two comrades spent seven months in the camp at Appolona, a cluster of tents laid out in a clearing in a dense forest, much of the time in the company of British, Australian and South African servicemen captured during the fighting in North Africa.

Kurti was befriended by one of the Italian officers, a young nobleman who, when Kurti complained of having nothing to read, gave him his own copy of *The Divine Comedy*. Finding that Dante's allegory gave him spiritual sustenance when he most needed it, Kurti committed whole passages to memory. He was especially struck by the opening lines of Canto One, which seemed so appropriate to his situation: *"Nel mezzo del cammino di nostra vita / Mi trovai per una selva oscura / Che la diritta via era smarrita"*— "Midway through the journey of our life / I found myself within a darkling wood / Wherein the way ahead could not be seen."

And when Dante described the gates of Hell, Kurti was chillingly reminded of the deportation of his sisters to a destination he rightly suspected would be truly infernal—*"Per mi si va nella città dolente / Per mi si va nell'eterno dolore / Per mi si va tra la perduta gente"*—"Through me lies the way to the city of suffering / Through me lies the way to eternal pain / Through me lies the way to the land of the lost."

As Kurti was to learn much later, the Nazis had put a less poetic inscription on the gateway to Auschwitz, the hell to which his sisters had been consigned. "ARBEIT MACHT FREI," it read—"Work makes you free."

The sudden appearance, toward the end of his time in the Appolona camp, of Captain Markeyevitch provided Kurti with the powerful memory of another kind of tormented soul. Despite his critical condition when the Italians had moved him to a hospital from the San Giovanni Barracks, Markeyevitch had survived and recovered sufficiently for the authorities to decide he should be sent to the prison camp in the woods.

But he was in a bad way, and desperate for drugs. Kurti saw him in his tent one night, eerily lit by a kerosene lamp as he dissolved a pain-killing tablet in a spoon held over a lighted candle, before carefully pouring the solution into a filthy syringe and injecting it into his arm.

Antmann's final memory of the doomed captain before he and Kurti were sent to join their colleagues in Italy in October 1941 was, if anything, even more macabre—"He went crazy toward the end, jabbing at his arm with a fork as if trying to give himself an injection."

The prisoners in Appolona were not the only *Pentcho* people to remain behind on Rhodes when the others left for Italy. The brothers Sidney and Rudolf Fahn and Sidney's bride, Regina, stayed too—and under considerably more comfortable circumstances, with permits to reside and work on the island issued on the personal instructions of none less than the Governor-General.

The Fahns owed their good fortune to the Governor's skill as a hunter, for if nothing else De Vecchi was a fine marksman. During a hunting expedition in the mountains overlooking the city of Rhodes in the spring of 1941, he had bagged a pair of martens, shot cleanly through the back of the neck to do minimum damage to the pelts. His intention was to have them made into a stole to adorn the fine shoulders of his Contessa, and he was considerably irritated when he learned that among the 20,000 civilian inhabitants of Rhodes—Greeks, Italians, Turks and Jews—there was not one with the technical expertise to prepare the pelts.

When he complained about this shortcoming to Captain Arnoldo Pellegrini, commander of the island's Carabinieri detachment, Pellegrini suddenly thought of the internees in the San Giovanni Barracks. Surely, he surmised, there must be at least one furrier among a group of 500 Jews from Central Europe.

His assumption proved correct. When he inquired at the barracks the next day, the Fahn brothers stepped forward. Their family had been tanners and furriers for six generations. Their father was the well-to-do proprietor of a tannery in Brezova—or had been until the business was "Aryanized"—and they had both been brought up in the business. How could they be of service? they asked.

As Pellegrini described the Governor-General's problem, the Fahn boys exchanged winks. This could be the start of something good.

The following morning a Carabinieri sergeant named Giovanni—a German-speaker from Bolzano, in the Italian Tyrol—arrived at the camp to take them to De Vecchi's *palazzo*. Dressed in smart sports jackets, borrowed from comrades whose wardrobes had survived the journey better than their own, the brothers followed him through the city streets, past the massive 30-foot-thick walls of Fort San Niccolo, to the Palace of the Grand Master of the Knights of Rhodes, from which De Vecchi exercised his absolute rule over the Dodecanese.

They passed by sentries in ceremonial uniform, through a magnificent arched doorway, into an interior courtyard decorated with classical statuary and paved with the looted gravestones of their Rhodian coreligionists, then up a staircase of richly veined black marble to an anteroom where they waited a few minutes, fidgeting nervously, until they were ushered into the presence of the Quadrumviro.

De Vecchi—a large, floridly handsome man in his late forties—was sitting behind his desk in full uniform, the pelts in front of him. With scarcely a glance at the Fahns, he called the sergeant forward, handed him the pelts and told him to take the brothers to see all the tanneries in the city so that they could choose which one to work in. Then with an imperious wave of the hand, he gestured at them to leave. Sergeant Giovanni sprang to attention and gave the Fascist salute. The interview was over.

As they left the palace, Sidney caught a glimpse, through a classical archway, of a sumptuous garden containing royal palms, hibiscus and cascades of multicolored bougainvillea, and couldn't help comparing the splendor and luxury in which the *Quadrumviro* lived with the misery and squalor of life in the camp at San Giovanni. The thought made him more than ever determined to find some way to work his passage out of detention.

Working from a typewritten list, Giovanni took them to see the tanneries of Rhodes—most of them crude affairs, little more than open sheds with a concrete channel for water running down one side. Only one, bearing the name Fratelli Vittorio, seemed adequate, and they chose that. Then the sergeant took them to lunch at a restaurant on a pier overlooking the sea, where he told the proprietor: "You must feed these men on the orders of the Governor. I'll bring ration cards tomorrow."

Scarcely believing their good fortune, the Fahn brothers tucked into their first square meal since leaving Bratislava almost a year before—mountains of steaming pasta awash in a rich cheese sauce, and helped down with a bottle of rough Rhodian wine, a combination that left them replete and reeling. With the ration cards that would be issued to them they would be able to take their lunch daily at administration expense at the same restaurant, Giovanni told them with a friendly wink as he escorted them back to barracks. He was to be their liaison officer, he said, and would monitor the progress of their work.

The following morning the Fahn brothers started work on

the two pelts at the Fratelli Vittorio tannery. It was a job which they could have completed in two weeks. They were determined to spin it out a good deal longer than that.

First they washed the skins thoroughly and scraped away the remnants of flesh with tanners' knives. Then they soaked them for half a day in water, before preparing a porridgelike mixture of bran and water in which they were soaked for three days more. For the next stage in the process, they told Giovanni, they would need two dozen eggs. They actually required only two and took the rest back that night to the barracks, where they shared them with Sidney's fiancée, Regina Sonnenfeld, and her brother Desider.

At the tannery the two pelts soaked in an egg mixture for a further three days, before being squeezed out, washed again, rubbed in a new bran mixture and then pinned to boards to dry. From time to time, Giovanni would stop by, inquire how the work was going, pass the time of day, drink some wine and saunter off. He seemed to be enjoying the assignment almost as much as the Fahns were.

But there was serious business to be done. The job could not be spun out indefinitely, and if they wished to continue their privileged life-style the Fahns knew they would have to parlay their skills into permanent employment at the tannery.

They had learned that the island was suffering from a chronic leather shortage. The local tanneries were unable to produce anything other than tough leather for soles and heels. Anything supple enough for uppers or coats had to be imported, at considerable expense and with a good deal of uncertainty, owing to the blockade. The Fahns went to Signor Vittorio with a proposition: they would produce leather suitable for making uppers, using locally available materials, if he would give them full-time work once they handed in the marten furs.

Vittorio jumped at the offer and gave them the facilities

for a series of experiments in a hut he owned in a nearby orange grove. There, in a 100-liter vat, the brothers began preparing a mixture of dog and chicken excrement and wine vinegar in varying proportions in an attempt to find a formula that would soften the raw hides they would have to work with. Rudi, a brilliant chemist, was the mastermind.

The barrel was clamped to a revolving table, turned by a steam engine. The mixture had to be spun for eight hours nonstop to achieve the required chemical reaction between the vile ingredients of the Fahn brothers' witches' brew. Once the engine broke down, and to save losing the whole barrelful, they kept the vat turning by hand.

It took them four months to get the mixture right. Vittorio used to visit the foul-smelling hut daily to see how they were getting on, and his workers used to mutter to each other that the *ebreos tedescos*—German Jews, as they called the Fahns, to distinguish them from the local variety—were magicians.

When the Fahns announced that they were ready to go into production, Vittorio threw a party, serving roast pheasant which he had shot himself. Then the Fahns finished the Governor's furs, combing them to a lustrous softness before notifying Sergeant Giovanni that they were ready. Captain Pellegrini came to the barracks the next day to escort them personally to the palazzo with the precious furs.

This time they were met at the top of the marble staircase by the Governor, clad in a black uniform and a long flowing cape which, Sidney thought, made him look "like a cross between a cardinal and a doorman," and the Contessa De Vecchi di Val Cismon. The furs were to be a surprise, and the brothers bore them up the stairs at arm's length like vassals bearing tribute to an empress.

She was ecstatic, and seeing her delight, the Governor glowed with self-satisfaction. When the Contessa had finished cooing over the furs, she asked the Fahns, in German, where they were from. When they replied "Pressburg"—the German name for Bratislava—she exclaimed that she had an aunt, the Gräfin So-and-So, living there.

"Yes," Sidney was able to reply with perfect aplomb, "I know her by sight," explaining that he and his parents had lived on the same street, Venturgasse, in the "best" part of the old city.

Not only was their work superb: it seemed that the Fahns were almost socially acceptable, too. "What can I do for you in return?" asked De Vecchi. "Nothing," Sidney answered with a self-deprecating smile. "Perhaps a few bars of soap will do."

The Governor appreciated the jest. "No, no," he said. "I insist. What can I do for you?"

So the Fahns modestly outlined their plan to revive the island's leather industry and respectfully requested work and residence permits. The following day Rudolf, Sidney and Regina, whom he had married a month previously, moved out of the San Giovanni Barracks to lodgings in the town as free residents of Rhodes—or as free as it was possible to be in a Fascist colony under siege.

The Fahn brothers' fame spread rapidly among the Italian governing and military elite of the island, as well as among the townsfolk and the peasantry from whom Sidney purchased the ox, goat and sheep skins for the revitalized Vittorio tannery. Marshal Mutti, commander of the Italian Air Force in the Aegean, came to see if the fabled "German Jews" could produce leather coats fine enough to serve as presents for his many lady friends on the islands. The Fahns told him they would need various chemicals, oils and dyes obtainable only on the mainland. Within three days he had had flown in what they asked for.

Meanwhile, Sidney and Regina—a lively, dark-haired beauty to whom he had been engaged since 1938—had a second wedding to conform with Italian law, this time a civil ceremony in the capital's ornate town hall. The ceremony was performed by the *Podestà*, the government-appointed mayor; Captain Pellegrini gave away the bride and Rudi was the best man. Vittorio and Sergeant Giovanni were witnesses, and after the ceremony Vittorio laid on a wedding breakfast in one of the town hall's banqueting rooms.

Sidney felt almost guilty to be enjoying such luxury while his former shipmates suffered the privations of life under internment. He could not imagine the price he, his brother, his wife and their as yet unborn child would eventually have to pay for their privileges.

13

*N*ot long after the women and children from the *Pentcho* left Rhodes on January 12, 1942, on a troopship bound for Italy, Walti Ehrlich's mother went into labor. With a characteristically Italian regard for the institution of motherhood, the officer in command of the troopship ordered the captain to put into the Aegean island of Calino, and there, in the military hospital overlooking the harbor, she gave birth to a healthy 7-pound boy whom, in sincere if muddled tribute to Mussolini, she named Benito.

It was the Italian people as a whole who were deserving of a Jewish mother's gratitude rather than their preposterous Duce, who had flown in the face of their best traditions and even contradicted his own previous policies by introducing anti-Jewish legislation, modeled on Germany's Nuremberg Laws, in 1938.

Italy's tiny Jewish minority—fewer than 50,000 out of a population of 50 million—had been thoroughly integrated since the unification of the country, and Mussolini's sudden decision to bring his domestic policies into line with those of his Nazi allies had been greeted with astonishment and shame by most Italians, from King Victor Emmanuel down. Even those responsible for enforcing the Duce's unpopular race laws—the police, the provincial prefects, the functionaries of the Interior Ministry—were reluctant to do so, not only with regard to Italy's own Jews but also with regard to the thousands of German, Austrian, Polish and other Jews who had found refuge in their country.

The result was that though they were objects of legal discrimination, the Italian Jews were not persecuted, ostracized or terrorized, and that foreign Jews, though given six months to quit the country, were actually able to stay and lead comparatively normal lives until Italy's entry into the war. After that they were interned, but under conditions no harsher than those under which, for example, the U S. Government was to confine its citizens of Japanese descent or the British Government its "enemy aliens."

The same pattern pertained in the territories where the Italians were an occupying power—Yugoslavia and later Greece and the South of France. In all those countries, Italian soldiers, administrators and diplomats went to considerable lengths, in fact, to protect Jews from the deportation and extermination policies of their Nazi allies and pro-Nazi satellites.

The *Pentcho* people had been among the beneficiaries of this splendid paradox. On Rhodes they might not have been pampered, but in Italian custody they certainly had been secure. To that extent, the unworldly Bella Ehrlich's instinct had been accurate. She had merely failed to note the gulf that yawned between the humanity of the Italian people and the cynicism of their Duce.

Two days after giving birth to baby Benito, she began to worry that the troopship might continue on to Italy without her, so she sent little Walti out to make sure it had not left. When he reported back that it was still lying in the harbor, she decided to discharge herself, and sweeping aside the objections of the nursing staff, she gathered up her belongings and her baby and returned to the ship. There she was given a cabin to herself for the rest of the journey to Bari, and there, eight days after his birth, baby Benito was circumcised according to Mosaic law while a handful of invited Italian officers watched with considerable interest.

Mrs. Ehrlich was amused to hear the Italians' appreciative comments about the deftness of the operation and the speculation of a ship's doctor that male circumcision might be the reason for the low incidence of cervical cancer among Jewish women—a theory that has since come to command a good deal of support in medical circles.

With a certain amount of girlish embarrassment she heard another officer express the opinion that circumcision might also have something to do with the supposed sexual prowess of Jewish men.

The ceremonial removal of baby Benito's foreskin turned out to be the most dramatic event of the voyage from Rhodes to Bari. Despite disquieting word that British submarines were active along their route, which meant that the ship was blacked out and they wore life jackets all the time, the voyage passed without incident. When the men of the *Pentcho* followed the same route seven weeks later in the *Vesta,* they had a similarly uneventful journey.

Immediately after their ship docked at Bari, however, the men had a revealing introduction to Italian mainland attitudes. In accordance with regulations, they were handcuffed before they disembarked, and as a detachment of Carabinieri marched them from the docks to an unannounced destination, crowds gathered to watch. The mood of the populace seemed ugly; they began shaking fists and shouting insults at the prisoners. The men in the marching column grew alarmed. Here, it seemed, was the Jew-hatred they had not so far encountered among the Italians, but which they had always half-expected.

The crowd grew more menacing, and the Carabinieri escort drew protectively close. It looked as though the mob might attack at any moment. Then the reason for the hostility became clear: Bari had been heavily bombed by the British, with considerable loss of civilian life, and the vengeful locals thought the handcuffed Jews were British prisoners of war.

The officer in charge of the escort hastily put them right. Halting the column, he turned to face the crowd. "These men are not our enemies," he declared. "They are not British; they are Jewish refugees."

At once the mood of the crowd changed. The jeers, threats and insults stopped and instead the Italians became sympathetic. Some of them even stepped forward to offer the prisoners cigarettes and pieces of bread.

The prisoners' march through Bari had an equally happy denouement: their destination turned out to be the municipal Turkish baths, where they were able to get themselves thoroughly and luxuriously clean for the first time since leaving Bratislava, a year and ten months before.

After their bath, they were marched to the main railroad station, where they were put aboard a train heading south to an unknown destination in Calabria, the bleak and mountainous toe of the Italian boot.

The wording on the big signboard that stood beside the camp gate at Ferramonti di Tarsia—"Campo di Concentramente"—was scarcely reassuring. By 1942, the phrase had acquired connotations of such unmitigated evil that the good impression created among the men of the *Pentcho* by their reception at Bari evaporated at the sight of it.

But as they were very soon to learn from the prisoners already there, and from the women and children of the

Pentcho who had arrived ahead of them from Rhodes, this was far from being a concentration camp in the Nazi sense of the term.

Ferramonti was the oldest and largest of a dozen camps set up after Italy's entry into the war to house "enemy aliens" and foreign Jews who had entered the country to escape from Mussolini's Nazi allies. Although conditions were somewhat primitive in these camps, which had been thrown up in a hurry on often unsuitable sites, they had absolutely no punitive purpose, and in all of them the inmates were treated humanely.

Nowhere was this more true than at Ferramonti, where at the time of the *Pentcho* people's arrival a population of about 1,500—1,200 of them Jews and the remainder Gentile Yugoslavs, Greeks, Corsicans and Chinese—was living under the benign rule of Commendatore Paolo Salvatore, the camp director. Major Salvatore of the Pubblica Sicurezza was a man with a swashbuckling past. He had been with Gabriele D'Annunzio when the flamboyant soldier-poet led his army of superpatriots into the disputed territory of Fiume in 1919; he had been one of the "Fascists of the First Hour" whose 1922 March on Rome had propelled Mussolini into power; he had slaughtered Somalis, Eritreans and Ethiopians in pursuit of Mussolini's mad dream of Empire. But somehow he had never quite lost his fundamental humanity.

In short, he was one of those Fascist romantics whose essential decency transcended the brutal ideology of force and domination they professed.

To find himself, as a result of wounds received in the invasion of Abyssinia, the director of a civilian internment camp rather than leading men into battle must have ravaged the soul of Paolo Salvatore. But he never allowed his frustration to affect his behavior toward his prisoners.

Maurice Hoffmann, a German Jew who was sent to the

newly opened Ferramonti camp in the winter of 1940, was struck by a speech of welcome given by Salvatore when he arrived with the first batch of prisoners from Milan. "My dear friends," said the camp director, "please do not be upset at finding yourselves confined here. Regard yourselves as my guests and me as your friend. What I am telling you is not merely my personal inclination but represents the guidelines laid down by the Ministry of the Interior and the Duce himself. We don't regard you Jews as our enemies, but we have to keep you isolated for reasons of security, due to wartime conditions. So, as I say, please do not feel upset but consider yourselves the guests of the Italian Government."

As a practical expression of his government's concern, Salvatore added that they would receive a ration allowance of 80 lire every ten days, and that while the bread ration for Italian civilians was 150 grams a day, the internees would be entitled to 200 grams "because you will not have access to the black market."

Hoffmann, who had been living in Milan since 1933, knew the Italians well enough to recognize that Salvatore's expressions of goodwill, though theatrically profuse, were probably sincere. In the almost three years he spent at Ferramonti he never had cause to reverse or revise that opinion.

After three months, women internees began arriving at the camp. Among the first were Emmy Weiss, her mother and her two teenage daughters. Salvatore—"a good-looking man in his forties, very Italianate, very charming," as Mrs. Weiss would recall—drove to the local train station in his white Lancia to meet them.

When he learned that she had been a physical-training instructor in Prague, Salvatore encouraged Emmy Weiss to organize daily gym sessions for the women internees. "He was a great ladies' man," she remembered. "He came every day to watch us work out, but there was absolutely nothing offensive about it. He remained the perfect gentleman and never tried to force his attentions on me or, so far as I know, any of the other women."

An old-fashioned gallantry toward women seemed to pervade the camp administration from the top down. Morning roll call, among the female prisoners, was taken by two policemen in civilian clothes who would go from hut to hut counting heads. It was scarcely an intimidating experience; when they came to the hut occupied by the four Weiss women, it was their custom to sing a fragment from a Calabrian folk song about four beautiful sisters—*"Quattro sorelle, proprie belle."*

Despite the easygoing regime, Ferramonti was no pleasure resort, if only for reasons of climate and topography. It had been built on a partially drained malarial swamp, covering an area of about 5 acres in a depression in the Calabrian mountains, some 20 miles from the city of Cosenza—unbearably hot in summer and bone-chillingly damp during the winter rains, when the entire site lay under 4 to 6 inches of water. The strawboard huts, arranged in pairs with connecting washrooms and toilets, provided little insulation from the extremes of heat and cold. But Johnny Weissmann, a refugee from Berlin, would recall that "the worst thing about the camp was that there were no doors on the toilets."

By the time the *Pentcho* people arrived at this very untypical concentration camp in the spring of 1942, a sharply defined social system had evolved, dominated by a comparatively well-to-do upper crust, composed of foreign Jews who had been living comfortably enough in Italy at the time of Mussolini's entry into the war, and Jewish refugees from Yugoslavia who had been allowed in by the Italians with whatever wealth they could carry. Italian Jews were not being interned.

The newcomers from Rhodes, having long since disposed

of whatever money or valuables they had, found themselves at the bottom of this social pyramid, and the more enterprising among them set out to rectify this as quickly as possible.

Salomon and his friends Laufer and Steinmetz, for example, quickly set themselves up as artisans, using the tools they had salvaged from the *Pentcho* and kept from the clutches of the governing committee. The Maresciallo responsible for internal security gave them an empty hut to use as a workshop, where they were soon plying multifariously as mechanics, tinsmiths, carpenters and shoemakers.

The syndicate's first enterprise was to build an oven, in which people could cook for themselves in return for a fee. This did not prove altogether successful: they located the oven too close to one of the huts, which caught fire and burned to the ground. Then they hit on the idea of making a boiler, so that they were able to offer their customers hot showers for a small charge. But the biggest money-spinner was a line of wooden sandals, which they made from waste lumber.

Many of the women internees laundered, sewed or performed cleaning chores for the better off. Gisella Farkas, for one, worked from early morning to seven or eight at night, cleaning for comparatively well-to-do families from Yugoslavia. She earned 5 lire an hour, with which she bought extra food for Karci and paid for him to have private English lessons and religious instruction.

Although she wasn't much of a seamstress, Grete Ehrenfeld also sewed to earn extra money, and it was this which brought her into embarrassingly intimate contact with the gallant Commendatore Salvatore. His roving eye had first alighted on her pertly attractive figure when she refused to return his stiff-arm Fascist salute at *Appel*. Stepping down into the ranks, Salvatore confronted her. "Why don't you salute?" he asked with a smile that registered a mixture of amusement and menace.

"Because I'm a Jew and I don't admire your Duce," she replied.

Salvatore's smile hardened perceptibly. "You will salute, young lady, or I'll have you put in jail."

Grete felt her resolve weaken. She had not yet learned that Salvatore's tough talk concealed a soft heart. "No, I won't do it," she said, though this time with less conviction.

Sensing her irresolution, Salvatore gave her one more chance. "Come on, now, salute or you go to jail," he insisted.

Despite the smile which accompanied the threat, Grete had no doubt he would carry it out. Suddenly, the principle didn't seem all that important. Meekly, she put out her right arm, looking off into the distance over Salvatore's shoulder to avoid his eyes. A week or so later he stopped her as she was exercising on the parade ground and asked her name and what kind of work she was doing. When she said she was sewing, he commissioned her to make him some shirts.

It was when she delivered the shirts to his quarters that Salvatore made his move—"He put his arm around me and tried to kiss me. When I resisted, he said, 'Don't be scared; I'm not going to rape you.' I wasn't really afraid of him; he was too much of a gentleman, and when I continued to resist, he didn't try to force himself on me."

Despite the rebuff, Salvatore kept up the pursuit. When Grete began going steady with Edmondo Verstandig, a fellow internee, the camp director showed signs of jealousy. "You spend too much time with that fellow," he complained one day. "If he gets in my way I'll put him in jail."

But Grete was not to be intimidated, and Salvatore apparently overcame his jealousy—so much so that when Grete married Verstandig, a Roman Catholic convert, in the village church at nearby Tarsia, Salvatore assigned them a small self-contained apartment of their own and sent them a demijohn of olive oil and two kilos of sugar as a wedding present—a munificent gift in those days of stringent rationing.

The catch came a couple of weeks later, when Salvatore entered Grete's apartment while her husband was working at the other end of the camp. "Now you're not a virgin anymore we can sleep together," he said as he lunged for her.

"When I said no this time, he didn't take it as well as he had before," Grete would recall. "He had us put out of our apartment, and we had to go and live in one room with my parents. After that he just ignored me, though he never took any other reprisals."

Two words—one Italian, one Yiddish—would sum up the personality of Paolo Salvatore as far as Grete was concerned: "He was a *mascalzone*"—a scoundrel—"and also a *mensch*"—a real human being.

Among the many aspects of life at Ferramonti that made it, in Citron's words, "a paradise compared with Rhodes" was the variety of food available, as well as the quantity. "You could choose the kitchen you wanted to eat from—kosher, Chinese, Italian or Slavic—and your ration money would be assigned to it," Marcel Friedmann would recall, "or you could collect your ration money and spend it at a free-lance restaurant that had been set up by a guy named Arnstein. The guards used to let him slip out every day to shop."

Black-market food was smuggled in regularly by the men who went out during the day to perform voluntary paid labor to supplement their meager 8-lire daily ration allowance. The *Maresciallo* knew this was going on, but gave instructions to his men not to search the returning internees.

Though generally good-natured, the *Maresciallo* was a man of variable mood. Frustrated by the tedium and purposelessness of life at Ferramonti, he drank heavily and would occasionally give vent to his feelings by shouting and cursing at the internees. But they noted that he always seemed to be full of remorse after one of these bouts.

On one occasion when he shouted at a small boy whom he found off limits, the child burst into tears. The *Maresciallo* relented immediately. Maurice Hoffmann saw him bend down and embrace the child, saying, "Don't cry, *bambino*. I didn't mean to be angry." Then he took the child to his quarters and gave him a whole loaf of bread.

Like the *Maresciallo,* Salvatore turned a determinedly blind eye to the illicit trade—including even the smuggling in of livestock for the unofficial camp butcher's shop—which he knew very well was going on. He sent one internee who kept trying to inform on his fellows to live in the hut occupied by Citron, Salomon and some of the other Betar bachelors. "Salvatore was afraid that if this guy made an official complaint he might have to do something about it," Salomon recalled, "so he sent him to us, hoping we'd shut him up. We did."

In general, then, the robust norms of Western capitalist society combined with a characteristic Italian tolerance quite free of the racism that was so much a feature of the time set the tone of life inside Ferramonti. If there was exploitation, theft, racketeering, prostitution and for many a degree of privation and hardship, there was also honest enterprise, selfless endeavor, community spirit and a modicum of compassion.

Even among the poorest internees, without the means or the skills to enable them to buy the occasional luxury, conditions were tolerable, if harsh. Like most of the children, Karci Farkas had little to wear. He ran barefoot in summer and played soccer with a bundle of rags for a ball. But "It seems to me we always had just about enough to eat, and I'd say that all in all, I had a very good childhood in that camp. The guards were always friendly, especially to us kids. All that I can honestly say I was deprived of as a child was chocolates and candy—and that by the time I came out of the camp at fourteen I'd never been to the movies."

* * *

Despite the generally primitive conditions, the harsh climate, the psychological stresses of being cooped up and the fact that the camp had been built on a malarial swamp, the health of the internees was surprisingly good.

Apart from the Italian camp doctor, Enzo Continelli—"a Good Samaritan if ever there was one," according to Adolf Kellner, the camp interpreter—there were a number of physicians and surgeons among the internees. Dr. Erwin Freundlich, an internee from Zagreb, found it impressive that during his eight months at Ferramonti there was not a single death from any cause. "Food was short," he would recall, "but there were no malnutrition diseases, and although there was a good deal of malaria, it was not of a virulent type. The medical facilities were adequate, although, as throughout Italy, there weren't sufficient drugs."

Drugs and medicines may indeed have been scarce at Ferramonti, but the internees appear to have been better supplied than the surrounding civilian population. Karol Hoffmann, for one, was able to lay his hands on enough Atabrine antimalarial pills to trade them with the local peasants for food.

The camp's cultural life was thriving. It owed a great deal to Professor Lav Mirsky, formerly musical director of the Belgrade Opera. Among the internees he found a number of singers and instrumentalists of the first rank, and under his direction symphony concerts, operas, oratorios and chamber-music recitals became frequent.

There were also theater groups, a weekly newspaper and a debating society which met at the camp's busy coffee shop. The better-off internees would gather there daily to drink an ersatz brew made from acorns and to gossip, reminisce and talk politics, just as they had done in the old days in Vienna, Warsaw, Prague or Belgrade.

Citron and his Betarim dominated the athletics of the camp, particularly soccer. The renown of Ferramonti's soccer players spread beyond the camp, inspiring the general commanding an Italian Army base in the region to put up a purse of 3,000 lire for the winners of a match between his players and Ferramonti's best. When the Ferramonti eleven won, with Citron playing a dashing game at right wing, the soccer-mad Paolo Salvatore arranged a banquet in their honor.

"He was a very decent man, scrupulously fair," Citron would recall, "and although he liked to talk tough, he really had a heart of gold."

Not surprisingly, in this benign if austere atmosphere, some of the Betarim began to lose the ideological fervor with which they had set out. But Citron never for a moment lost sight of the purpose behind their voyage from Bratislava: getting to Palestine with his young pioneers so they could play their part in the creation of a Jewish state remained his prime objective.

With the other Zionist ideologues of Ferramonti, he organized Hebrew classes, study groups and a rudimentary agricultural training school alongside the barbed-wire perimeter of the camp to help would-be settlers prepare themselves for life in "the Land of Israel." They had little idea how the war was going and no grounds for believing it would be over soon. But a blind faith that somehow, someday, they would reach their destination kept their hopes alive.

14

In the late autumn of 1942, the arrival of three gaunt and wasted Jewish escapees from Nazi-occupied Poland sent a shiver of apprehension through the Ferramonti camp. They brought with them firsthand accounts of Nazi atrocities which were so horrifying that at first they were scarcely credited.

The three newcomers—Kawe Herzl, Moshe Liverant and Zvi Nelkenbaum—had been among 500 young Jews from Siedlice who were held in a forced-labor camp about halfway between Warsaw and the Russian border after the 18,000 women, children and old men of their town were shipped off to the extermination camp at Treblinka. Put to work on railroad maintenance under Polish guards, supervised by the SS, Herzl and his companions soon came to realize that once hunger, physical abuse and exhaustion made them too weak to continue laboring on the tracks they would follow their families to the gas chambers.

Their daily routine was fifteen hours' work with pick and shovel on the roadbed, then the march back to camp—where they subsisted on a starvation diet, where their sleep was constantly interrupted by meaningless roll calls and savage beatings, and where the slightest infraction of the often illogical and incomprehensible rules was punishable by death. Execution by hanging for the most trivial offense was a matter of routine at morning *Appel* on the camp parade ground. Day by day the dwindling number of survivors felt themselves growing weaker and more desperate.

For two weeks before their escape, Herzl, Liverant and Nelkenbaum had observed Italian troop trains, on their way back from the Russian front, as they clanked slowly through the marshaling yard where they were working. For two weeks a sympathetic Polish engineer had been urging them to make a run for it—"Get away; get away while you still have the chance."

At last, in the late afternoon of October 26, 1942, as two trains traveling in opposite directions approached the spot where they were working, they saw their chance. On a signal from Herzl, the three of them dropped their tools and ran alongside a slow-moving Italian train, identifiable by its red-white-and-green tricolor flag, and managed to scramble aboard. They found themselves inside an empty car with rows of wooden benches inside and a stove at either end.

Herzl had hidden a hunk of stale bread and a small medicine bottle full of vodka under his shirt. As the train gathered speed and they cleared the freight yard, he drew out the bottle and the three of them drank a tremulous toast to freedom. They still hardly dared to believe that they would make a clean getaway.

Three days later they were at the Italian frontier, at the Brenner Pass, but they were not out of danger yet. The station was under joint Italian-German control, with a Gestapo office at one end of the platform and a Carabinieri post at the other. But it was the Carabinieri, not the Gestapo who discovered them when the car was opened for inspection.

After a brief and sympathetic interrogation by the commander of the Carabinieri detachment, the three Jews were locked in a back room. Two hours later they were taken out, put into a van and driven to prison at Vipitano, about 20 miles away, where they were held while their case was referred to the authorities in Rome. A few more days and they were put on a train to Ferramonti. Their ordeal was over.

Soon after their arrival, Herzl, Liverant and Nelkenbaum went before the camp committee to describe what they knew of the Nazis' systematic extermination of the Jews of Poland. "At first we thought they must be exaggerating or touched in the head," Citron recalled. "Despite all that we knew about the Nazis, it just didn't seem possible that even they could be so inhuman. Only gradually did we come to accept that what we were hearing was the truth."

With that acceptance came the numbing realization for many of the young people from the *Pentcho* that they would almost certainly never see their families again. Karol Hoffmann, for one, was aware that his father, mother and two brothers had been deported to Poland; now he had to come to terms with the knowledge of what that implied.

Letters from home, their full meaning not comprehended until now, had spelled out the step-by-step process by which the fate ordained by the Nazis and their Slovak accomplices had closed in on his family—the family which had tried so hard to persuade him to abandon the "foolish idea" of going on the *Pentcho* to Palestine.

In a letter dated December 20, 1941, Hoffmann's father had reported that although Karol's two older brothers, Bela and Paul, had been sent to work on the construction of new living quarters at the Patronka transit camp, they were not themselves being kept there. *"As you know,"* he wrote in an obvious reference to pending deportations, *"many people are departing from here. We hope we will still be able to stay and will advise you immediately in the event of any change."*

Ever the generous father, Hoffmann senior said he hoped some money he had recently sent had arrived. Nor was he too preoccupied with his own problems to comment approvingly on the news that Karol was studying English.

Karol's mother added a note to inform her son that she was suffering from diabetes, for which she blamed herself: she had not paid sufficient attention to her diet, she said. Apparently believing that the Italians might yet repatriate the *Pentcho* internees, she appealed: *"Write to me, my child, if there is any chance of your returning here. Seeing you would make me well again."*

In a letter dated March 30, 1942, Hoffmann's father noted with pleasure his son's improved circumstances at Ferramonti, adding that Bela and Paul were now in separate labor camps in Slovakia, from which *"they will presumably be sent to Poland."* Enclosed in the letter was a note from Bela in the Vajnory camp, near Bratislava. *"Some of the people in this camp have already been deported,"* he told his brother, *"and I expect it will be my turn soon. At least, now I'll see a little bit of the world. As the poet says, 'Whom God wishes to reward He sends out into the wide world.' The only thing is, I'm not quite sure how wide it will be for me."*

On June 1, Alfred Hoffmann wrote to tell his son that while Paul was still in the labor camp at Szered, Bela had been sent away, and so far he had not heard from him. *"He and several thousand other youngsters who were deported at the same time are not allowed to write from their new place of residence for the first two months. We don't know why this is so. . . . It's a trial for the spirit."*

The letter added: *"Now they are starting to deport the Jews from Bratislava, but so far we've been able to stay put because of a medical certificate your mother obtained from a police physician who examined her."*

By the time Alfred Hoffmann wrote again, on July 23, he and his wife had been evicted from their apartment in the fashionable part of the city and assigned to a building on Judengasse, in the ancient ghetto quarter. He had still not heard from Bela or from Paul, who by now had also been deported. *"Unfortunately,"* he wrote, *"continual deportations are now taking place and no one knows when it will be his turn. . . . We have to muster all our strength to face this situation."*

He still had sufficient spirit to attempt a little paternal pleasantry. He was glad, he said, to hear that Karol was working in the kitchen at Ferramonti, which *"will be good for both your physique and your stomach."*

The last message from Hoffmann's father came on a postcard dated July 30, in the handwriting of Karol's aunt Gisi, to whom it had obviously been dictated. *"Dear Karli,"* it read. *"I regret to advise you that the police picked us up yesterday at our apartment and we will be transported by the end of the week to Poland. Your dear mother and I wish you all the best. Your Father."*

A week later Hoffmann's aunt wrote to say: *"You must not take it too tragically, because your father was very courageous and your mother was also composed. We hope that somehow things will be tolerable where they are going. They promised to be strong in order to survive and see their children again someday."*

They never did. Alfred, Berta, Paul and Bela Hoffmann all died in Auschwitz. "My father was an optimist to the bitter end," said Karol. "He just refused to accept what was happening."

The process that had sent the Hoffmann family, and thousands more like them, to their deaths was set in motion at the July 1940 meeting in Salzburg between Hitler, Father Josef Tiso and the other leaders of the Slovak Republic. After that meeting, Slovakia openly proclaimed itself to be a National Socialist state, the only Nazi satellite to make such a claim, and instigated a series of anti-Jewish measures the Nazis themselves could scarcely have improved upon.

While Hlinka Guardsmen and their ethnic German colleagues of the Freiwilliger Schutzstaffel beat up and kidnapped Jews at random, looting their homes, shops and businesses, the state began drafting the regulations that would make such banditry "lawful." Stirred up by official propaganda and enticed by thoughts of the "return" of the wealth which they were told the Jews had "stolen" from them, the majority of Slovaks gave their approval. A few courageous voices were raised in protest, but these were ignored. As happens so often, a people who had themselves been downtrodden for centuries were all too ready to assume the role of the oppressor.

At police headquarters in Bratislava, Eichmann's chief assistant, Wisliceny, was encouraging the security services to purge themselves of elements, like Schalk's friend Police Commissioner Yakouboczy, who had shown themselves to be "soft" on the Jewish question, while Wisliceny's colleague Viktor Nageler was attempting to turn the ragtag Hlinka Guard into an imitation SS.

By this time the loss of the eastern provinces, emigration and escape had reduced the Jewish population of Slovakia to fewer than 90,000. At about 3 percent of the total population they were scarcely a significant minority, but the puppet rulers of Slovakia set about legislating against them as if the life of the republic depended on it. Law followed law, depriving the Jews of basic civil rights, strictly limiting their freedom of movement, barring them from access to public places, forbidding them contact with Gentiles and proscribing their right to assemble so that they could not even make a quorum for religious services.

Parallel with these measures, the state deprived the Jews of their stocks and bonds, furs, jewelry and other valuables, even their clothes, as well as their shops, businesses and other enterprises. By the end of 1941, the value of Jewish property that had been "Aryanized" was officially estimated at more than 3 billion crowns.

A law enacted in September of that year redefined the term "Jew" on the principle of "race" rather than religion, so that converts to Catholicism and their descendants were now included. The yellow star was introduced, and all Jews between sixteen and sixty were liable to be drafted for forced labor, while 10,000 of Bratislava's 15,000 Jews were evicted from their homes.

The next step was deportation. It began with a request from the Germans in early 1942 for 20,000 able-bodied Jews between the ages of sixteen and thirty-five to work in their war factories. The demand was met with indecent alacrity. Despite pleas by a handful of public figures and churchmen, and a protest note from the Vatican, the first transport—carrying 1,000 young women, including Ladislav Kurti's two sisters—left for Auschwitz at the end of March.

After the rest of the 20,000 youngsters had gone the same route, the Slovaks decided—"in the spirit of Christianity," as President Tiso put it—to send their elders after them, "so that families could be reunited." Since the older Jews would have considerably less economic value than the sixteen-to-thirty-five-year-olds, the Nazis demanded payment of 500 Reichsmarks for each one they took. In a protocol dated June 23, 1942, the Tiso government agreed to this, provided the Germans guaranteed that none of the deportees would be sent back and waived all claims to their property.

The Nazis took their payment in timber and other raw materials—a transaction that had disastrous effects on Slovakia's economy, to say nothing of its image. The Nazis' other Central European allies, such as Admiral Horthy of Hungary and General Antonescu of Rumania—not to mention the Italians, to whom such behavior would have been unthinkable—recoiled in horror at so blatant a traffic in human lives.

Even Eichmann appeared to be contemptuous. "Slovakian officials offered their Jews to us like someone throwing away sour beer," he commented.

Transport followed transport until the end of July, when they were suspended. A census held the following month showed that the Jewish population of the puppet republic had been reduced to 25,000. Shortly afterward, Tiso said in a public speech that it was a Christian duty for Slovakia to rid itself of its "pests," and in September and October there were three more transports, bringing the total number deported to just under 68,000, according to official documents, or two-thirds of the Jewish population. The vast majority of these died in the gas chambers of Auschwitz and Maidanek or from starvation and disease while at forced labor in the Lublin area of Nazi-occupied Poland.

Then, for a variety of reasons, including the intervention of the Vatican and the start of ransom negotiations between the SS and Jewish representatives in Switzerland, the deportations were halted again. Those who had been lucky enough to survive so far were given a temporary reprieve.

15

On January 1, 1943, Paolo Salvatore called together the hut leaders at Ferramonti to toast the New Year in the harsh wine of the region. In an informal speech he told them, "Today I'm the director and you're the prisoners, but this time next year it may be the other way around, so drink up and enjoy yourselves."

It was prophetic enough, even though at that point the *Pentcho* people and their fellow internees could see little reason to celebrate. Despite what they had heard of Allied military successes in North Africa, it did not appear likely that they would be relieved anytime soon from the tedium, frustration and futility of life in internment. Nor did the accounts they had heard of conditions for Jews in Nazi-occupied Poland help to allay their fears for their families.

Just the same, some of them were able to persuade themselves that perhaps the situation was not too bad in Slovakia. After all, Marcel Friedmann's parents did not forget to send him a telegram wishing him "HEARTIEST CONGRATULATIONS" on his twenty-third birthday at the end of February 1943, while Oskar Salomon received another parcel from home containing a book with razor blades and lighter flints concealed within its pages. Others received letters which, though cryptic and strained—for they had to pass through censorship—carried the message that life went on.

Then a rumor swept Ferramonti that the Italians were going to transfer them all to a camp in northern Italy, prior to handing them over to the Germans. Greatly alarmed, the camp committee sent an urgent plea to the Vatican, begging for the Pope's intervention.

At the instructions of Pius XII, the Papal Nuncio, Cardinal Borgongini Duca, traveled to Calabria to reassure the internees. The children of Ferramonti lined up to greet him with a song of welcome composed by Professor Mirsky, and the Cardinal told them that so far as the Holy See was aware no such move was intended. If it were, he promised, the Pope would vigorously oppose any attempt to have them moved. He concluded by quoting the 137th Psalm—"By the waters of Babylon, we sat down and wept when we remembered thee, O Zion"—and predicting "God willing, you will return to the Promised Land one day."

Their fears allayed, the *Pentcho* people were able to contemplate a gray but not entirely hopeless future, thankful that things were not a good deal worse and occupying themselves with the daily minutiae of camp existence, until mid-May brought the stunning news, which even the official Fascist radio could not suppress, of the surrender of all Axis forces in North Africa.

Other dramatic events followed pell-mell—the Allied occupation of a handful of small islands off the Italian south coast in mid-June, the invasion of Sicily in early July and little more than two weeks later the most sensational news of all: the overthrow and arrest of Mussolini and the appointment of Marshal Pietro Badoglio to head a government still notionally allied with Nazi Germany, but hardly likely to remain in the war any longer than it had to.

For the internees at Ferramonti, the first tangible result of the Duce's downfall was the sudden disappearance of the affable Salvatore and the overnight transformation of the militiamen guarding the perimeter from Blackshirts to Greenshirts as the Fascist Party and its uniforms were abolished. Whether Salvatore was moved in a purge of Mussolini loyalists or whether the new regime simply transferred him to a post more suited to his talents remains a mystery. He left without time to offer either farewells or explanations, and his place was taken by a less flamboyant official named Giovanni Fraticelli who, happily for the inmates, turned out to be equally humane.

Fraticelli brought his wife, three children and elderly father to the camp with him. Marcel Friedmann, who became a paid member of his household staff and a firm friend, found him to be "a well-educated, highly intelligent man, always very concerned about the welfare of the camp inmates." It was not long before that concern was to be demonstrated in the most practical way.

As that hectic summer wore on and hopes of release burgeoned, the life of the camp took on an almost febrile intensity. In a period of eight weeks between July and September, no fewer than 30 couples were married, among them Citron and Shosha Spiegel.

Although they had been informally engaged for seven years, the journey and the almost three years of captivity that followed it had imposed peculiar strains on their relationship, and Shosha was unexpectedly hesitant when Citron proposed that they wait no longer to marry.

Idealism, prudishness perhaps, a sense of the responsibilities of leadership and the lack of privacy aboard ship and in the camps had persuaded them since embarking on the *Pentcho* to set an example to the Betar rank-and-file and avoid close physical contact. A kiss, an embrace, any intimacy beyond the holding of hands or a peck on the cheek had been out of bounds. And Shosha had perhaps acquired the habit of abstinence. It was familiar, comfortable, safe. Now that Citron's proposal faced her with the prospect of breaking the habit and unleashing the emotions she had suppressed for so long, she seemed afraid.

Citron pressed her. To wait longer was pointless. They had done their duty, set an example, seen their followers through the worst. Although prisoners, they were free now in a way they had not been before—free to think about themselves and each other. At last, still hesitant, Shosha agreed. Citron wrote to her parents and received their blessings. The Spiegels had so far escaped deportation.

Two days before the wedding, Citron's Betarim threw a bachelor party and presented him with a wedding ring they had bought outside the camp. Because Jewish tradition requires the bridegroom to pay for the ring, Citron gave them a token payment of 11 lire for it.

Though still disdaining religion, Citron could not avoid the Jewish wedding ritual, both for nationalistic reasons and because no civil ceremony was possible in the camp. However, he told the Yugoslavian rabbi who would officiate that he had no intention of fulfilling the obligation of going to the synagogue the day before the wedding to read a portion of the *Torah*. Faced with Citron's threat to "make a scandal" if he insisted, the rabbi agreed to dispense with that part of the proceedings. It was a repetition of Citron's boyish *Bar Mitzvah* rebellion.

By contrast, Shosha remained true to her upbringing and insisted on going through the preliminaries, including the *mikvah,* or ritual bath, which all Orthodox Jewish brides are supposed to take before their wedding. *"Mamouka"* Farkas was chosen to administer this ritual, and with other women from the camp she made a pool for the bath by damming a stream that ran past the perimeter wire.

There were 150 guests at the wedding. Citron had sold his wristwatch to buy the food, but without his knowledge the Betarim took up a collection to buy it back and presented it to him at the feast. He was also presented with a bottle of champagne, donated by one of the wealthy refugees from Yugoslavia, but decided to save it for the liberation.

The Citrons' wedding night was interrupted by the war. British bombers flew over a nearby power plant and knocked it out, cutting off all electricity to the camp. Four days later, on August 27, the war came a good deal closer than that when two Allied fighter-bombers, ranging the skies over Calabria in search of targets of opportunity, roared in at rooftop level and sprayed the camp with machine-gun and cannon fire, obviously thinking it an enemy military installation.

The attack came suddenly, totally without warning, and was over in less than a minute. Karol Hoffmann, who was walking across the parade ground, threw himself flat and saw a line of machine-gun bullets stitch themselves into the ground inches in front of him.

As the two warplanes climbed steeply, before turning and diving to make a second low-level pass, the internees who were out in the open dashed for cover. But the thin strawboard walls of their huts afforded no protection.

Aviva Weiss, one of the *Pentcho* girls who had been married only a few days before, was mortally wounded as she cowered under her bunk. Erwin Guen, another of the *Pentcho* people, was killed outright. So were two other male internees, sheltering in the hut next to Citron's. Ironically, these were the only violent deaths to occur in the three-year history of the Ferramonti camp.

Later Citron held Aviva Weiss s hand for a few moments as she lay dying of her wounds in the camp infirmary. She did not realize how badly injured she was, or even what had happened. "I've such a pain in my stomach," she complained.

On September 3, six days after the raid on the camp, a division of the British Eighth Army crossed the Straits of Messina from Sicily and landed on the toe of Italy, near Reggio di Calabria, about 100 miles south of Ferramonti.

The battle for Calabria was not to be one of the more notable engagements of the war. The landings at Reggio were a feint, designed to lure German reinforcements into the foot of Italy while the real assault was made on the ankle at Salerno. But the Nazi commander, Field Marshal Albert von Kesselring, wasn't fooled, ordering his forces to offer only moderate resistance and to withdraw in an orderly fashion to more defensible positions. Calabria was to be surrendered, if not exactly without a fight, then without inordinate blood-letting.

As the front line moved steadily toward Ferramonti, fearful speculation rippled through the camp that Kesselring's troops might carry out a vengeful pogrom as they pulled back. Fraticelli, the new camp director, shared that apprehension and tried to contact Rome to consult on how best to protect the internees under his charge. But telecommunications with the capital had been knocked out by Allied bombing, and on September 6 he left for the capital to seek instructions in person, taking two members of the camp committee with him.

Before leaving, he gave orders to the *Maresciallo* to open the gates and let all the prisoners out if the camp appeared to be in the path of the withdrawing German troops. A couple of days later, learning that the Hermann Goering panzer division was moving north on the main road which passed the camp, the *Maresciallo* carried out Fraticelli's instructions. All but about 50 of the 2,000 internees headed for the hills in small groups and dispersed. Citron went with Shosha and his young brother-in-law Poldi to a farmhouse about three miles from the camp and remained there.

Those who stayed in camp were mainly the old and sick, plus a group of younger men—led by Mischa Bauer, a former officer in the Yugoslav partisans—who remained behind to protect them. Hoping to deter the German troops from entering the camp, they ran up the black-and-yellow cholera flag at the entrance. And as a desperate expedient, in case the cholera bluff did not work, they set up a sandbagged position and mounted a machine gun taken from the armory of the militia guards, who had fled days before. Two rifles and three pistols completed their arsenal as the vanguard of the Hermann Goering Division rumbled past the main gate.

A panzer division on the move, even one in retreat, is an awesome sight; and this was no exception, despite the mauling it had received in the battle for Sicily. A seemingly endless succession of tank transporters, armored personnel carriers, field guns, supply trucks and staff cars, with dispatch riders roaring up and down alongside on their motorcycles, trundled by nonstop for two days, paying the pitiful little band of would-be defenders no more attention than a herd of migrating elephants might give to a handful of gnats.

On the third day two Wehrmacht motorcyclists, each with a light machine gunner in his sidecar, pulled up at the gate, followed by a Mercedes staff car. A general officer emerged with a young aide-de-camp and, covered by the two machine gunners, walked up to where Bauer stood with half a dozen of his men.

"Who are you?" he demanded.

"Civilian internees, Herr General."

"And what are those weapons for?"

"There are women and children in the camp, Herr General. We must protect them from bandits and looters."

The general grunted. "And that flag? You have sickness inside?"

"Yes, Herr General, five cases of cholera."

The general pondered for a moment, then withdrew to confer with two medical officers, who came racing up alongside the halted column. The little band of defenders waited nervously, "hardly daring to believe that such a transparent bluff would work," as Adolf Kellner, the camp interpreter, recalled.

But the Hermann Goering Division had pressing business to attend to and neither the time nor the inclination to find out if the story was true. With an order to his aide that none of his men was to enter the camp, the general returned to his Mercedes and drove off. The tail end of the Hermann Goering Division followed him. More Wehrmacht stragglers would pass the camp gates, heading north, in the next few days, but none showed any inclination to disobey orders and enter.

The danger past, Bauer and his band split up and headed south to link up with the advancing British. Kellner was taken on as interpreter for a British field intelligence unit.

Meanwhile, in the hill villages surrounding Ferramonti, the internees who fled the camp had been experiencing the simple humanity of the Italian peasant. Calabria was a desperately poor region and its people had little enough for themselves. "But whatever they had they shared with us," Citron remembered. "I never heard of any internee who was refused food or shelter until the Germans had passed and it was safe to return to the camp."

Many of the internees had not yet come back from the hills when, at about eight o'clock on the morning of September 14, an Eighth Army tank clattered up the main road leading north from Cosenza. The cholera flag had been removed, and the tank nosed its way in through the open gates of Ferramonti, swinging its gun turret quizzically left to right a few times, before stopping in the middle of the open square of administration huts. A few seconds passed before the tank's hatch was lifted and the head of a young British officer wearing a rakish black beret and a flamboyant mustache popped up.

The camp appeared deserted, and after a minute or two of surveillance the officer pulled himself up through the hatch, swung over the side of the turret and dropped lightly down to the ground, to be followed by two other members of the tank crew, Sten guns at the ready.

From inside the camp director's abandoned office Marcel Friedmann observed the intruders long enough to make sure of their nationality before showing himself in the open doorway and moving out into the hard Calabrian sunlight, hands high above his head, clutching a broomstick with a white cloth tied to its end. As he crossed the dusty parade ground toward the tank and the muzzles of the soldiers' leveled submachine guns, other figures emerged hesitantly from the line of huts stretching back toward the barbed-wire perimeter. "Friends. We are friends," Friedmann called out in English, "not Germans—civilians. Civilian internees."

The officer looked him over, then nodded. "All right. You can put your hands down."

Friedmann lowered the white flag, turned around and beckoned reassuringly with it to the other prisoners. "Come," he called, lapsing into German, the internees' *lingua franca.* "Come. The British are here."

Thus occurred the liberation of the first Axis concentration camp to be overrun by Allied forces. It rated no more than passing mention in a unit commander's routine report to Brigade HQ and was completely overlooked in news dispatches from the front. There was, after all, little about Ferramonti to justify the frightful associations that went with the phrase "concentration camp" and nothing to prepare the world for the horrors that would be encountered later in the war as American, British and Russian forces stumbled across the SS murder mills of Eastern and Central Europe.

As the fugitive internees began to drift back to Ferramonti, a small team of support troops and civilians from AMGOT—Allied Military Government in Occupied Territories—arrived to take over the running of the camp. After them came men in British Army uniforms with the word "PALESTINE" on their shoulder flashes. They were soldiers of the Jewish Brigade who, hearing that there were several hundred of their coreligionists at Ferramonti, had come to give help and encouragement. One of them was Reuven Franco, the Bulgarian-born Revisionist agent who had given his nickname to the *Pentcho*. Meeting these men, and hearing about life in Palestine, Citron felt certain that they were at last near the end of their journey.

On September 26, his twenty-fifth birthday, he opened the bottle of champagne he had saved from his wedding, and he and Shosha toasted each other and the future: *"L'chaim—to life."*

16

From the balcony of the rented house that was now his home in Rhodes, Sidney Fahn looked out across the Piazza Mandracchio to the ancient harbor beyond and, as had become his habit, contemplated how irony and paradox ruled the lives of men. They had certainly dictated the course and texture of his.

In the piazza below, the waiters were putting out the tables after a rainy night which had left the island fresh-washed. The breeze blowing down from the hills behind the city brought with it the scent of orange blossoms and the distant clanking of goat bells. From the next room he could hear Regina singing to herself—softly, so as not to wake their month-old son, Alexander—as she tidied up.

Strange, Sidney thought, that he could have achieved such contentment living under the rule of the Nazis, who had ousted the Italians and now controlled the island.

If life had followed any kind of logical pattern, he would never have been here in the first place. His father had emigrated to America at the turn of the century to avoid the grim servitude of conscription into the Austro-Hungarian Army, and Sidney had been born in Chicago. But Arnold Fahn had brought his wife and his two-year-old son home for a visit in 1914 and had been trapped there by the outbreak of World War I. After the war he had made the fateful decision not to return to America—an unusual choice for any Central European immigrant, especially a Jew; but to Arnold Fahn, as to many others, the collapse of the Hapsburg Empire and the birth of the Czechoslovak Republic had seemed like the beginning of a bright new era.

Despite his family's return to Slovakia, Sidney retained the U.S. citizenship to which his birth in Chicago entitled him— or so he believed. It was only when he became engaged to Regina in 1937 and decided to return with her to America that he discovered he had forfeited his birthright by allowing himself to be conscripted into the Czechoslovak Army on reaching the age of eighteen. At the U.S. Embassy in Prague, where he went to have his long-expired American passport renewed, he was told by a consular officer—with some show of officious satisfaction, Sidney thought—that it was being confiscated and invalidated. By obeying his ancestral country's compulsory call to arms, he had lost his U.S. citizenship and with it his best means of escape with his fiancée from a Europe increasingly threatened by the Nazis.

Eventually, the *Pentcho* had offered another way out, although that had ended in shipwreck and detention. Then, here on Rhodes, a further twist of fate had opened yet another door, and thanks to his and his brother's skills and quick wits, the hunger and privation of internment had been exchanged for a life of relative freedom and comfort.

For the next two years the luck of the Fahns had seemed almost too good for belief. While their comrades had been shipped off to an uncertain fate in Italy, they had continued to enjoy privileged status on Rhodes, hobnobbing with top civilian and military officials while they ran the tannery, which was proving to be such an economic asset to the block-aded island.

While most of the civilian population of Rhodes suffered from the effects of stringent food rationing—it was not unknown for people to faint in the street from hunger—the Fahns usually had enough to eat. Their dealings with the peasant farmers from whom they bought hides for the tannery meant that it was always possible to obtain some eggs, meat or vegetables on the side.

Then had come the sudden surrender of the Italians to the Allies, and with it another twist of fate that seemed likely to create a dramatic reversal of the Fahns' fortunes.

Determined to prevent the loss of so important a strategic base as Rhodes, Nazi military headquarters in Berlin sent urgent instructions to its 7,000-man force there to seize control of the island at all costs. Supported by Stuka dive-bombers from Crete, the German troops moved swiftly and decisively against an irresolute Italian garrison five times as numerous, and within a few days Rhodes was theirs.

Thus, at the very moment when their comrades were being liberated by the British Eighth Army in Italy, the Fahns—and the 1,700 indigenous Jews of Rhodes—were passing from the relatively benign rule of the Italians into the power of the regime they had good reason to fear the most.

And yet things had not worked out badly. Here it was, the end of 1943, more than three months into the period of Nazi rule, and life went on very much as before. The Wehrmacht did not discriminate between the Jews and the other inhabitants of the island, and to the Fahns the only thing that had changed was that now it was German rather than Italian officers who came to them to buy soft, supple skins to be made into leather coats or comfortable boots.

The Wehrmacht officers invariably behaved correctly, and Sidney was by now a frequent visitor to military headquarters at the Albergo della Rosa, where the German commander-in-chief, Lieutenant General Ulrich Kleemann, was one of his customers. When Kleemann wanted a new pair of riding boots made, or some saddlery for his horses, he would send for Fahn. And when, at the beginning of December, Sidney had applied urgently for a curfew pass so that he could rush his wife to a hospital through the blackout for the birth of their first child, Kleemann had seen that he got it.

Armed with the pass, Sidney had driven Regina in a horse-drawn cart through a heavy British air raid to the hospital, where, despite the bombs and the blackout, she had delivered a strong and lusty baby boy after a relatively easy labor. Now, hearing Regina cooing over the child in the next room, Sidney was reminded that General Kleemann had promised him another personal favor—to use official channels to send Sidney's mother in Slovakia a photograph of her first grandchild.

No, it was certainly not what he had expected when the Germans took over the island, and as he reflected on the twists and turns that had brought him here and on his current status on Rhodes as a "German Jew"—a term identifying him with the occupying power and, as such, a man to be treated with deference by the Greek and Turkish islanders— Sidney Fahn told himself that, surely, fate was a supreme ironist.

For Citron, a man given more to action and less to reflection than Sidney Fahn, the euphoria of liberation had been followed by frustration and disappointment as Palestine remained a distant dream and his hitherto tightly knit Betar group began to break up under the novel stresses of freedom. Although allowed to come and go and enjoying improved material conditions, the former internees were still living in the Ferramonti camp and seemed likely to remain there as long as the war lasted. But for the young men there was a quick way out.

On the heels of the Eighth Army's forward troops had come representatives of the Free Czech Army, the Free Polish Army and Marshal Tito's partisans, looking for recruits among the internees at Ferramonti, and Citron realized that for young men eager to even scores with the Nazis and desperate to find out what had happened to the families they had left behind, the temptation to join up was strong.

His own priority remained to get to Palestine with his original group intact. He feared that once they split up and were absorbed again into the Diaspora, many of them might be lost to the Zionist cause for good. To prevent this, he proposed that they volunteer *en masse* to join the British forces, provided they could serve together in the Palestine Brigade.

Citron put the proposal in writing and passed it to the British military authorities through a senior officer in the Allied Military Government (AMGOT), which now administered the camp. He received no answer. At that time the British, with an eye perhaps to postwar problems with the Arabs over resumed Jewish immigration, were allowing only Jews already resident in the Mandate to wear the "Palestine" flash.

When Citron began to make waves, the British offered to take the *Pentcho* group into the army as a unit of the Pioneer Corps, under Citron's command but not as Palestinians. Citron rejected the offer angrily. As Pioneer Corpsmen their role would have been to dig trenches and latrines, fill sandbags and throw up earthworks, as if they were still unwilling conscripts of the Slovakian Army's Labor Corps.

The Betarim approved of his decision, but this did nothing for his attempts to keep the group intact. To remain indefinitely in Ferramonti, clinging to a remote ideal when they were free to leave, was too much for many of them, and despite Citron's lectures on steadfastness and loyalty to the Zionist cause, the young men began to drift away one by one—Marcel Friedmann to the Free Czechs, Oskar Salomon to the Americans in North Africa, Ladislav Kurti to Tito's partisans, Karol Hoffmann to the British as a civilian interpreter. And so on. By the time the process of erosion had ended, Citron had lost between 70 and 80 of his Betar men.

The older people of the *Pentcho* group too drifted off where they could—some to civilian jobs with AMGOT and relief agencies that were setting up shop in the liberated areas of Italy and some to a large displaced persons' camp south of Naples, from which eventually 1,000 Jewish refugees would be shipped direct to the United States to sit out the war in a camp at Oswego in New York State.

Meanwhile, Citron and the loyalists who remained with him at Ferramonti continued doggedly, with the help of Zionists in the Jewish Brigade of the British occupation forces, to prepare themselves for *Aliyah,* the "going up" into Israel, by studying Hebrew and the agricultural techniques developed by the pioneers who had preceded them. Eventually their persistence was rewarded. The Jewish Agency— the government-in-embryo of the future Jewish state—had set up an office in Bari, headed by Enzo Sereni, the Italian Zionist who would die later on a parachute mission for the Allies into Nazi-occupied northern Italy. Through Sereni, Citron applied for certificates of entry into Palestine for the group of 350 ex-internees—*Pentcho* people and others—who had coalesced around him and were waiting patiently at Ferramonti.

Sereni forwarded the application to the Jewish Agency in London, where after lengthy negotiations the British Government agreed: the five-year quota set in the prewar White Paper had not been filled, and Citron and his people would be able to enter Palestine as legal immigrants as soon as shipping was available to take them there.

At first, Citron could scarcely believe it. Despite the outward show of unwavering optimism he had maintained all along, even he had had the occasional moment of doubt.

Now the last obstacle had fallen and journey's end was in sight.

Shosha cried a little and embraced him when he came back to Ferramonti from Bari with the good news Citron's mood was more triumphant than tearful. "We'll finish our journey openly," he exulted, "not sneaking in like criminals."

In a British Army camp in East Anglia, Zoltan Schalk too had been living through a period of boredom and frustration.

As an infantryman in the Free Czech Army, he had been through the seesawing desert campaign with Montgomery's "Desert Rats," taking part in the grim siege of Tobruk, the decisive onslaught at El Alamein and a dozen lesser engagements before the final defeat of the Afrika Korps under Rommel. Along the way, his little group had split up, Lanes and Hercz being posted to different units of the Czech forces while Imi Lichtenfeld, still suffering the aftereffects of his three operations, had been given a medical discharge in Palestine.

After the victory in North Africa, Schalk's unit had returned to Egypt before sailing on the troopship *Mauretania* from Port Tewfiq to Southampton to join men of all the Allied nations in Britain as they prepared for the assault on Hitler's Fortress Europe.

And a long and tedious preparation it had been in the drab atmosphere of wartime Britain—month after month of boredom and "bull" in a succession of dismal military camps, punctuated by periods of intensive training for no one knew precisely what, enlivened only by an occasional weekend leave in London and recurring rumors about the start of the long-promised invasion.

The experience of war changes men's outlooks, and by the beginning of 1944, Schalk realized that his priorities had altered again. All he really wanted now was to survive the war so that he could see the Nazis defeated, get home to

Bratislava to find out what had happened to his widowed mother and then take off to savor the good life in comfortable and civilized surroundings.

Zoltan Schalk, onetime convert to radical Jewish nationalism, admitted to himself that, quite frankly, he no longer hungered for Zion.

17

On May 28, 1944, Citron with his group of 350 ex-internees embarked from Taranto on the liner *Batory*, bound for Palestine. On June 7, 1944, Schalk boarded a trooper at Southampton with several hundred other men of the Independent Czech Brigade to join in the battle for Normandy. On July 23, 1944, Sidney, Regina, Alexander and Rudolf Fahn were herded onto a coal barge to begin the long and agonizing journey by sea and rail to Auschwitz, together with most of the 1,700 indigenous Jews of Rhodes.

Hitler's insane vendetta against the Jewish people had suddenly and without warning overtaken the handful who lived in Rhodes. It was the farthest-flung outpost of the Nazi empire, almost 2,000 miles from the murder mills of Auschwitz. Germany was in retreat on all fronts, shipping and rail transport were crucially short, but the war against the Jews had to be prosecuted until every last one was exterminated.

Almost overnight, the fragile world the Fahns had built for themselves in exile collapsed around them; it seemed to

Sidney that the fate whose workings had so preoccupied his imagination was now demanding that he, his wife, his child and his brother should pay the price of their past privileges. It was their destiny to be the surrogates for the 500 Jews who had escaped the Nazis aboard the *Pentcho*.

The SS "special action group" who had been sent to the island from Greece to organize and carry out the deportations had completed their preparatory work with quiet efficiency, and at first the civilian population was quite unaware of their presence. The Jews went about their daily lives as before, fearing not so much the Germans, who had so far bothered them little, as the persistent Allied air raids which were taking an almost daily toll of life and property—especially in the Jewish quarter, which lay close to the port, and in which earlier that year 22 Jews had been killed in one raid alone.

Then on July 18, posters appeared all over the city of Rhodes ordering all Jewish males between sixteen and sixty to present themselves at the air-force barracks on the following day, bringing their identity cards and work permits, to register for forced labor. Given the correct behavior of the Wehrmacht up to that point, the Jews were not unduly alarmed and obeyed the command. Even when they were lined up on the parade ground of the air-force barracks and an SS major appeared on the scene no one took fright. Isolated as they were from mainland Europe, they did not know what the black uniform and the death's-head badge portended. They had heard rumors of the deportation and destruction of the large Jewish community of Salonika, on the Greek mainland, but had dismissed these as Allied propaganda.

"Wer spricht Deutsch?"—"Who speaks German?" demanded the SS officer. There was no response at first. The Sephardic Jews of Rhodes spoke Ladino, an antique form of Spanish, among themselves, and Italian, Greek or French

to outsiders, and the Fahns prudently kept silent. Then a man behind them spoke up: "Go on, Signor Sidney—you speak German."

The SS man called Sidney out. "Why didn't you speak up?" he demanded.

"I didn't hear you," replied Fahn.

The major snorted, but his tone remained mild. "Tell your coreligionists," he said, "that they must go home now, leaving behind their ID cards and work permits, and return tomorrow morning with their women and children and all their money, jewelry and other valuables, plus food for four days. Then they will be sent to work on a neighboring island."

Sidney translated the order. Then the major added: "Tell them also that those who obey will come to no harm but that for every one who fails to report ten others will be shot. And remember, there is no escape on this island."

Even after a threat as cold-blooded as that, Sidney Fahn did not fully comprehend the Nazis' intentions. The threat was probably an exercise in hyperbole, designed to ensure obedience, he told himself. After all, Rhodes was not Vienna or Cracow, and Kleemann, the Wehrmacht commander, had proved himself a decent enough fellow. Surely, he wouldn't sanction anything like a full-scale pogrom.

No, the Germans might be harsh, but they would behave correctly. Had they not explained that the women and children were being sent along to avoid separating the men from their families, and had they not explained that all the money and valuables taken from them would be in safekeeping pending their return from the labor assignment? Obviously it was no holiday camp they were being sent to, but at least they would be out of the way of the British air raids, which were beginning to make life on Rhodes unbearable.

Despite such sensible rationalizations, the Fahn brothers left the air-force barracks determined to pull whatever strings they could to get themselves removed from the compulsory-labor detail. At the very least, it would be unpleasant to have to uproot themselves in order to perform manual labor in the heat of a Mediterranean July.

Sidney was the one with the personal contacts, so it was agreed that he should go to Wehrmacht HQ and ask for some kind of exemption. Kleemann and his officers had been helpful before and there was no reason to suppose they wouldn't be again. After all, who would run the tannery if they were sent away to do forced labor?

But when Sidney presented himself at the reception area inside the Albergo della Rosa, the atmosphere was less cordial than it had been on previous visits, when Kleemann or one of the other staff officers had sent for him. His request to be allowed to send a message in to Kleemann's adjutant was curtly refused by the sergeant on duty at the front desk. "Who sent for you?" he demanded. "What business do you have here?"

When Sidney was unable to give a satisfactory reply, the sergeant ordered him to leave. "Get out before I throw you out," he shouted, "and don't come back without a summons!" On a signal, a sentry took Sidney by the arm and marched him briskly to the door.

The next day, when the Jews of Rhodes reported to the air-force barracks with their women and children, the Fahn brothers were among them with Regina and little Shani. Once again the SS major called Sidney out and set him to work as interpreter.

A desk was set up on the parade ground and the Jews were ordered to line up and file past it, handing over their money, watches, jewelry and other valuables. All items and sums surrendered were meticulously noted down in a ledger. Their property would be returned to them, they were assured again, when they had completed their period of compulsory labor.

Despite the occasional meek protest, the looting proceeded

in a quiet and orderly fashion until one teenage girl refused to part with a gold chain with a Shield of David pendant. Without a word, the SS major stepped forward, ripped the chain from around her neck, felled her with a blow and kicked her as she lay on the ground at his feet. At that moment, Sidney Fahn began to realize what the Nazis were capable of.

For the next three days they were held, under guard, on the parade ground, forced to stand without shade or water under the blistering July sun with their faces to the barrack walls. When General Kleemann heard that some of his troops were muttering about having to stand guard on women and children who were being treated in this fashion, he issued an order banning all discussion of the matter. "From their narrow point of view," he declared, they were not qualified to pass judgment.

Thirty-nine of the captive Jews had Turkish citizenship, and the Turkish consul intervened vigorously on their behalf. After protracted arguing, the Nazis agreed to let them go. For the others there was no one to intercede. Protests by local civic and religious leaders were brushed aside with contempt.

On Sunday morning, the Jews were ordered to form ranks, pick up their baggage and prepare to move off. Sirens were sounded as they left the barracks—a signal to the civilian population to stay indoors and keep away from their windows on pain of shooting—and 1,673 Jewish men, women and children, of whom the youngest was little Shani Fahn, were marched off.

Sidney Fahn would never forget the scene as they went through the deserted streets toward the ancient port, "like slaves being marched into Egypt," flanked by guards with rifles and bayonets and under orders to keep their heads bowed and not to look around them on pain of being shot on the spot. Sidney carried Shani on one arm, with a valise in his other hand and a rucksack on his back. On one side walked his wife, silent, bewildered and terrified; on the other, his brother Rudolf.

At the port, three open motorized coal barges were waiting for them and they were crammed into the holds, 800 to each vessel. The loading completed, they headed out to sea, due north through the chain of islands skirting the Turkish coast.

Conditions inside the iron holds were atrocious under the broiling July sun. Women, children and old men fainted from heat and thirst. From time to time the SS guards assigned to the barges would hose them down with seawater. There was just enough bread and drinking water to keep them alive, with the result that there were only five deaths en route.

After four days the convoy reached the island of Leros, where it was joined by a fourth barge, bringing 94 more Jews from the island of Cos. Then they headed north for Samos and west for Piraeus, reaching the Athens port on July 31.

On the quayside at Piraeus, the deportees were herded into cattle trucks and driven to the Haidar prison camp on the outskirts of Athens, where they were to remain for four days. It was thirty-six hours before they were given anything to eat, and that only by grace of the Red Cross.

Then the men were separated from the women, who were strip-searched by the SS for hidden valuables with the utmost brutality. Any woman who tried to resist the prying fingers delving into anus and vagina was smashed in the face with a rifle butt; any husband, father or fiancé who dared to protest was whipped or beaten mercilessly.

During the daylight hours, the prisoners were forced to stand out in the sun without shade or water. At one point, Sidney Fahn, his baby in his arms, begged an SS guard for water for the child. Addressed in flawless German by a man who did not look at all like the olive-skinned Rhodian Jews, the guard asked in astonishment, "How do you come to be here with *these* people?" He let Fahn take some water from a pig trough to give to the baby.

The rest were not so fortunate. One group of prisoners, appealing for water, were told by the SS that they could line up at a fountain in a neighboring yard and help themselves. The guards obligingly unlocked a gate to allow access to the fountain, but when the prisoners rushed for it, they drove them back at bayonet point. This game so amused the SS men that they repeated it several times, forcing the frantic prisoners back from the fountain with bloodied bayonets, regardless of sex or age.

At night the men were separated from the women and crowded 20 at a time into cells intended for three or four at most. There was so little air that the men were in danger of suffocating. Sidney Fahn opened up the ends of his leather belt and poked it through the bars of the cell as a breathing tube, taking turns with his brother and others close to him to suck in air from the corridor outside.

During their four days at Haidar, a dozen more people died. Already, those not fit enough to withstand the rigors of forced labor were being weeded out. Then, on August 3, they were taken in trucks to a freight yard where they were loaded onto a train, 65 people to a car, for the start of a twenty-eight-day journey to Auschwitz.

The Fahns, unlike some families who were split up, were fortunate enough to be put into a car together. Sidney would remember the journey as a seemingly endless nightmare as the train crawled fitfully through Greece, Bulgaria, Yugoslavia and Hungary to Slovakia, reversing to a large extent the journey they had made by river on the *Pentcho* four years previously. Every so often, the SS guards would open the doors to allow the prisoners to refill their water barrels, sweep out the ordure that fouled the floors and remove the dead, who would be buried in shallow graves beside the track. Twenty-two women, children and old men died en route.

They had been traveling twenty-four days when the train stopped on a siding alongside an open transit camp for Jews who were waiting to be deported at Szered, not far from Bratislava. Peering through the cracks in the car, Sidney Fahn saw a man he had known before the war and called out to him. Realizing that the train would pass close to Ruzomberok, in the Tatra Mountains, where his parents were living, Sidney asked the man to telephone his father and tell him they were on a train that was heading his way.

That Arnold Fahn could still be contacted by telephone at a time when most of his coreligionists had long since had theirs confiscated, and either had been deported or were about to be, was a measure of the talent for survival which he appeared to have handed down to his sons. He could not have known that his decision to remain in his homeland after the first war would have such disastrous consequences for his family, yet he had shown a remarkable ability to ride the storm of Slovak nationalism with its anti-Semitic excesses.

Although his thriving tannery at Bresova had been "Aryanized" under the discriminatory legislation that followed the birth of the puppet Slovak republic, his skills had been considered too valuable for him to be harmed. So while it would hardly have been "proper" for him to stay on and manage the factory that had once belonged to him, the expropriator—a brother of the president of the Slovakian Senate—had felt it fitting to send Fahn to run a tannery in Ruzomberok which he had filched from another Jew.

Accompanied by his wife, Berta, Arnold Fahn had thus been able to enjoy a life which, by comparison with the wretchedly precarious existence of most Slovakian Jews, was both comfortable and secure. So when the phone call from Szered came through to his office in the tannery at Ruzomberok, he did not even have to ask anyone's permission to leave and drive to the freight yard at Jilina, where he learned that the train carrying his sons, his daughter-in-law and his grandson to Poland was scheduled to stop to take on a new engineer.

There, a few hours later, a last encounter between the Fahn brothers and their father occurred. Through the cracks in their car, as the train stood at rest, they could see the old man searching frantically for them. They called out to him—"Here, Papa, here." The old man ran forward. "The child," he cried—"let me see the child!"

An SS man jumped down onto the track. "Get back," he shouted. "Keep away from the train." Frantic to see his sons and grandson, the old man found the courage to ignore him. Pressed close to the car he had time—before the SS drove him off at gunpoint—to get his longed-for glimpse of Shani, held in the arms of his mother, and time to tell Sidney and Rudolf that he had bribed the relief engineer to slow down and give them a chance to jump from the train at a spot some miles up the track.

But Arnold Fahn had wasted his money. The train did not slow down, and even if it had, there was no way the prisoners could have got out of the sealed cattle car.

The next time the train stopped was at Auschwitz, and it was on the platform there that Sidney Fahn saw the last of his wife and baby. As they staggered from the car, drained and exhausted by the nightmarish journey, faint with hunger, bewildered and terrified by the shouted commands and the baying of the SS guard dogs, they were subjected to the infamous selection process.

An SS medical officer in a hospital coat, whom Fahn would later claim was the notorious Dr. Josef Mengele, gave the prisoners a cursory inspection as they filed past him, pointing with his riding crop to the right or the left—"*rechts, links, rechts, links*"—as though he were in charge of a fast-moving production line. Sidney had no way of knowing it, but women with babies in arms were automatically sent to the left, the line that led straight to the gas chambers.

It happened so quickly that Sidney scarcely realized what had occurred. One moment they were side by side; the next they were forking off in different directions, he and Rudolf to the right, Regina and the baby to the left. He called out to her, and she turned eyes wide with uncomprehending fear on him before being swallowed up in the crowd of prisoners, *kapos** and SS guards.

It would be two or three days, by which time he had absorbed some of the grim lore of camp life and the brutal rules for survival, before Sidney realized that he would never see his wife and child again—that they had already, in the jargon of the death camps, "gone up the chimney."

As he recalled it: "I happened to see a girl named Olga whom I had known in Bratislava and I gave her my wife and child's photographs and documents and asked her to look out for them. But she just shook her head and said, 'They won't need these anymore.' She'd been there two years and knew all there was to know about Auschwitz, but still I didn't realize what she meant. Then I was put into a barrack hut just 100 meters from the crematorium in Block Four and I could see the smoke rising all day and all night, and still I couldn't believe it. Finally, after two more days, I believed it."

Tattooed with the number B-7310 on the inside of his left forearm, Sidney was sent with his brother to the neighboring Birkenau camp to carry out the exhausting and seemingly pointless labor of moving rocks weighing up to 50 pounds by hand from an excavation site. They remained at this back-breaking work until Yom Kippur, when they were sent to the coal mines at Rydultau, near the Polish city of Czestochowa, one of the thirty-eight hellish labor camps affiliated with the Auschwitz-Birkenau industrial complex.

The mine adjoined the Hermann Goering Works, a syn-

* Trusties appointed by the SS to maintain discipline over their fellow prisoners.

thetics factory run by the giant Buna concern, where margarine was made from coal. More than 1,200 feet belowground, in corridors leading off from the main shaft, the Fahns joined hundreds of other Jews—most of them doctors, teachers, lawyers and businessmen—in hewing coal from the exposed seams. Conditions were so brutal that two bank clerks from Bratislava threw themselves down the mine shaft during the Fahns' first week there.

The brothers were on the night shift, hewing coal nonstop for ten hours. During the day, their guards would not allow them to sleep, waking them constantly with roll calls and searches. Coming off shift, many of the slave laborers were too exhausted even to shower off the coal dust with which they were encrusted. But an elderly SS man gave the Fahns some whispered advice: "If you want to survive, be sure to wash the dust off when you come up. Don't miss this. It will save your life." The brothers heeded his advice.

Somewhat to his surprise, Sidney—medium-sized and slenderly built—found himself standing up to this brutally harsh regime rather better than his brother, who was taller, stronger and six years younger. Weakened by a diet of sugar-beet soup and crusts of hard bread Rudolf began to develop terrible sores and other infections from the coal dust and had to go to the infirmary. This was always hazardous, for if one did not make a prompt recovery one was likely to be taken off to the gas chambers as unfit to work.

Down in the mine, Sidney had struck up a friendship of sorts with a Polish engineer who was in charge of his zone. Although violently anti-Semitic, the Pole appeared to have taken a fancy to Sidney, whom he knew as the interpreter for the Greek- and Ladino-speaking Jews from Greece and Rhodes. Although it was punishable by death to give food to the prisoners, he brought Sidney a piece of bread smeared with pork fat and a clove of garlic every day. The garlic had no nutritive value, but labor-camp prisoners had learned that it induced a sense of fullness, blunting the debilitating pangs of constant hunger.

Every day, when he came up from the coal seam, Sidney would take half the bread and half the garlic to his brother in the infirmary. After eight days, Rudolf had recovered sufficiently to be able to return to work.

The Fahns had been in the mine for four months, outliving scores who had arrived there at the same time, when word spread through the camp that the Red Army was advancing rapidly on Czestochowa. It was mid-January 1945, and Himmler issued the order that those prisoners fit to leave were to be cleared from the camps and the others killed before the Russians arrived. "The liberation of prisoners or Jews by the Red Army or the Polish underground is to be avoided," said a directive from SS headquarters in Berlin. "Under no circumstances are they to be allowed to fall into the enemy's hands alive."

So, in the depth of winter, clad only in their flimsy prisoner's clothes, without socks and wearing only wooden clogs on their feet, the Fahns and the rest of the Rydaltau slave laborers who were able to walk began the long march west, driven by the whips, dogs and rifle butts of their guards.

For Sidney Fahn, the experience would blur into a nightmare recollection of pain and privation. A Polish priest who witnessed part of such a march provided an onlooker's account: "They marched . . . while insane shrieks, the sound of shots and the barking of dogs urged them on. . . . They marched, ravaged by hunger and cold, the frozen earth resounding with the clattering of their wooden shoes. They marched . . . and on the way the slumbering earth gave forth the terrible echoes of five years of pain and torment in the camps."

The Fahns' march lasted three days and three nights, until they came to a camp named Grossrosen, inside Germany, and rested one full day. Scores had died en route, those who fell being shot where they lay by their guards. The Fahn brothers had survived because, as Sidney said, "I am a careful capitalist—I always keep some little thing to fall back on." In this instance it was the heel of a loaf, which he kept hidden under his shirt, and a little marmalade which Rudi had managed to steal from the infirmary. Sharing what they had, the brothers retained sufficient strength to keep going.

After their rest at Grossrosen, they were herded into the open cars of a freight train to begin the journey west to the concentration camp at Mauthausen. The temperature was below freezing and it was snowing heavily as they left, lying on top of each other for warmth. During the two-day journey to Mauthausen, a fifteen-year-old boy lying close to Sidney went mad, raving and screaming for hours, before dying of cold and hunger.

At Mauthausen, SS guards stripped them of the flimsy clothing they had on and forced them to spend the night outdoors, naked. In the morning they let those who had survived the night have a hot shower, gave them clothes and put them into a barrack hut, without bunks or blankets, where they had to sleep on the floor. More died there.

After a day at Mauthausen, the survivors were shipped to one of its satellite labor camps at Ebensee, set on the shore of Lake Traun in the idyllically beautiful Salzkammergut region of Upper Austria. The Fahns were not able to appreciate the loveliness of their surroundings. They soon discovered that compared with Ebensee, conditions at Auschwitz had been good.

Ebensee was the site of one of Hitler's last desperate gambles as his empire collapsed around him—a vast underground mine gallery system in which he planned to build a bomb-proof factory for the construction of his vaunted "secret weapon," the V-2 rocket which had already brought death and destruction to London and southeast England. The project had been started in greatest secrecy, and Nazi scientists and technicians were rushing to complete it by Hitler's deadline of October 1945. The slave laborers who were employed on its construction were being driven to the limits of endurance and beyond by the Mauthausen guards, who were noted for a degree of sadism remarkable even by SS standards.

The penalty for even the most trivial of offenses was invariably death. A prisoner who slipped a discarded piece of cement sack under his shirt to help keep out the cold risked execution by hanging. Likewise anyone who dared to slip a piece of rubber waste into his shoes to keep his feet dry. Such executions were carried out daily at *Appel* "in the name of the German people."

By mid-April, knowing the end was near and that the Third Reich would never last long enough for the V-2 factory to be completed, the camp guards had become totally profligate of the lives of their work force, constantly inventing new offenses punishable by death, which was generally meted out on the spot, either by the guards themselves or by the *kapos*—the sweepings of the German prison system—who helped to maintain "discipline."

On April 29, Rudi Fahn fell victim to one of these. Finding a scrap of cloth, he took it into a washroom to dry himself with, in violation of one of the insane new rules. Seeing him commit this offense, a *kapo* beat him to death on the spot. But for that lapse, Rudi might conceivably have survived, as Sidney did. Ten days later, U.S. troops liberated the camp.

When the Americans came, Sidney Fahn's weight was 80 pounds. A nurse at the improvised U.S. Army hospital in the Hotel Post at Bad Ischl, to which he was taken, was able to lift him like a baby to give him a bath.

Well-meaning GIs who visited the hospital with gifts of food for the ex-prisoners literally killed some of them with kindness. They brought chocolate, jam, canned meats and other comestibles which the camp survivors' digestive systems, ravaged by starvation and sickness, could not possibly cope with. Sidney was too weak to get out of bed to claim his share of the lethal gifts—"and so again I survived; again my fate intervened."

He was not sure how long it was after the day of his liberation, but Sidney would remember distinctly "the day I came back to life." It was a bright summer morning, and looking out the window of his room at the Hotel Post he "heard the birds, saw the flowers blooming and smelled their scent—and suddenly I realized that there was no more forced labor, no more SS, that I was free and that I was going to live."

18

They reached journey's end via Egypt. The Polish cruise liner *Batory*, conscripted for the Allied war effort as a troopship, put into Alexandria on the afternoon of Thursday, June 1, 1944, and discharged its cargo of servicemen and refugees, among them Citron's group of 350 men, women and children from Ferramonti. From the bustling dockside, loud with the cries of Egyptian vendors and British NCOs, they were bused to a nearby railway siding to board the train that would take them across the Nile Delta to El Qantarah, then due east along the Sinai coast to Palestine.

Citron felt a curious mixture of triumph and anticlimax as the train clattered through a desert night, feebly lit by a dying moon. Unable to sleep, he watched the ghostly shapes of sand dunes and the occasional clump of palms slip past the grimy window of his carriage. Shosha, now seven months pregnant, slept fitfully in the opposite corner seat, her brother Poldi's head against her shoulder.

So many years of planning and hoping, striving and waiting. And now that it was all over, he felt—well, not quite the wild elation he had often imagined.

Maybe it had something to do with the realization that now that he had accomplished his mission and fulfilled the dream which had obsessed him for so many years, nothing else—not even the struggle for statehood which lay ahead—might ever matter quite so much. There was the more mundane consideration, too, that, aged nearly twenty-seven and without any occupational skills, he must for the first time think about supporting not only himself but also a wife, a child and a young brother-in-law. There could be no question of his resuming his medical studies; it was too late for that. He would have to find whatever work he could.

The sun was coming up over the desert when they entered the Palestine Mandate at Rafiah and Shosha awoke. Citron leaned forward to take her hands. Others in the car, and up and down the train, were weeping and gesticulating, singing and laughing, suddenly overwhelmed by the realization that they were at last within the boundaries of Biblical Israel.

Like Citron, Shosha was not given to displays of emotion, and when he squeezed her hands and said quietly, "We're here; we made it," she simply smiled, still heavy with sleep and the child within her, and returned the pressure. They were "home."

The Jews of Palestine made much of the arrival of the refugee train, the first substantial group to reach the country legally since the outbreak of war. Moshe Shertok, head of the Jewish Agency's Political Department, who would later become Israel's first Foreign Minister, delivered an address of welcome as the train steamed into the station at Lydda, en route to the reception center at Athlit, on the coast near Haifa. But the rhetoric of politicians of Shertok's stamp did not greatly impress Citron. Shertok was a leading member of the Labor-Zionist establishment who, as the Revisionists saw it, had been rather more concerned about cooperating with the British than about getting Jews out of Europe and breaking the immigration quota.

These were the people who were likely to hold the levers of power and patronage in the future Jewish state, a fact of which Citron was reminded when Jewish Agency officials came onto the train with clipboards and pencils to begin conducting an informal census of the newcomers—name, country of origin, date of birth, occupation, political affiliation.

The questioning irritated Citron and others in his car. One woman began berating her interrogator. "We've just arrived," she shouted. "We've been on our way four years and you come on with these political questions. Why don't you ask us if we're happy to be here? Why don't you ask us if we think the country is beautiful?" With that, Citron and the others put the Agency official off the train.

They spent a week at Athlit, a drab collection of huts reminiscent of Ferramonti, formerly used as a detention center for captured "illegals," before dispersing throughout Palestine. As Citron had feared, times were hard indeed: there was no housing for new immigrants and jobs were scarce. He, Shosha and Poldi found themselves in the raw, new seaside settlement of Natanya, living in the garage of a relative's house. Citron went to work as a laborer in a diamond factory. Out of his first fortnightly wage packet of £5—about $20—he had to buy an icebox to keep their food fresh in the steamy heat of a Mediterranean summer.

But even before moving into the spartan accommodation and taking up the menial work forced on him by the harsh circumstances of life in wartime Palestine, Citron performed two acts that confirmed his commitment to the struggle which, for him, still lay ahead: he adopted the Hebrew name Yehoshua Halevi and he joined the Irgun, which was preparing for a prolonged terror campaign against British rule.

For a man of Citron's temperament, it seemed, the journey would never really end.

While Citron was playing his part in the battle to drive the British out of Palestine, Schalk was helping those same British and their allies drive the Germans out of France. The Independent Czech Brigade, having landed at Arromanches on D-Day plus Two as part of the British Second Army, took part in the fierce battles for Caen and the Falaise Gap before breaking through into the plains of central France.

Later, after France had been cleared of the Nazis and the Wehrmacht forced back across the Rhine, Schalk and the Free Czechs linked up with the American Third Army in its drive eastward through southern Germany and into Czechoslovakia. Their advance ended on May 7, 1945, at a line just east of Pilsen, where they met the Russians, and at that point, Schalk obtained leave to find out what had happened to his aged mother.

At the wheel of an Opel car which he had "liberated" from its German owner, he crossed into the Soviet Occupation Zone and drove to Bratislava. There he learned that in the five years he had been away more than 80 percent of Slovakia's Jewish population had been exterminated.

In the final phase of murder and deportation from October 1944 to the end of March 1945—following an abortive uprising against the puppet regime of Monsignor Josef Tiso, in which many Jews had taken part—2,000 to 3,000 had been shot on the spot. Another 13,500 had been deported, the last trainload leaving as late as March 30, 1945, for Theresienstadt, while about 5,000 more, hiding out under false papers as Aryans, had escaped. Those who returned, haggard and broken, from the camps brought the immediate postwar Jewish population of Slovakia to about 15,000. Seventy-five thousand Jews had perished.

But at least the survivors, and the returnees like Schalk who had come back with the Free Czech forces, had the satisfaction of knowing that Tiso and his cabinet would pay for their crimes. Already a national tribunal, set up by the interim postwar government of a reunified Czechoslovakia, was preparing to put them on trial for their lives. None of them would escape the gallows.

To his enormous relief, Schalk discovered that his mother had been one of the Holocaust survivors—another consequence of his extraordinary talent for making useful friendships. A Hlinka Guard officer in charge of a detachment that went to a nursing home to take her and seven other sick and elderly Jewish women away for deportation had recognized the name and spared her because of his onetime friendship.

After finding his mother alive and well cared for in the house of friends, Schalk's next concern was for the onetime Police Commissioner Yakouboczy, who had been liberated by American troops from Mauthausen, where he had been sent as punishment for his stubbornly sympathetic attitude toward the Jews.

Schalk found him at home in bed, recovering from typhus and the other horrors of concentration-camp existence, his once burly frame reduced to a mere 70 pounds. A priest who was present said later that he had never witnessed such an emotional reunion. Afterward, Schalk drove to the nearest American forces' PX store in the adjoining occupation zone and filled his car with chocolate, jam, soap, dried milk and canned goods for his friend.

With the performance of that small but heartfelt act of appreciation, Schalk felt that he had no further business in Bratislava. Before leaving, he walked down to the Danube and stood for a while on the quayside of the winter port where, almost exactly five years before, on another morning in May, the *Pentcho* had slipped its moorings and sailed off downstream at the start of its unlikely journey.

By now he had learned at first hand the fate of the comrades he had left behind on Kamilanisi. His brother Tibor, one of the group who had gone to Palestine with Citron, had written to tell him of their years in internment in Rhodes and Italy. And others, having joined the Free Czech forces after their liberation from Ferramonti, had crossed his path in the later stages of the war. Four of them, to his knowledge, had lost their lives in the battle for France.

Some, like Yosef Hercz, one of his companions on the desperate lifeboat journey from Kamilanisi, had returned to Czechoslovakia, intending to stay. Others had come back just long enough to find out the fate of their families before moving on, either to Diaspora countries with less painful memories or to Palestine.

Schalk himself, having given up thoughts of Palestine, decided he would take up the option to become a transport driver with the United Nations Relief and Works Agency, ferrying urgently needed supplies and industrial equipment across the Continent from the French coast to Czechoslovakia. As he shuttled to and fro between Le Havre and Pilsen, he debated in his mind the relative merits of America and Australia. He'd had enough of struggle and hardship and yearned for a quieter and more comfortable life than Palestine, already sliding into the bitter struggle for an independent Jewish state, could provide.

But an unexpected meeting in Paris with his older brother Eugen, who had gone to Palestine as a legal immigrant before the war, changed his mind. Eugen, by now the proprietor of a thriving business in Haifa, was on his way to Bratislava to see their mother. He offered Schalk a well-paid job and assured him that he could find the good life he sought in the Jewish homeland. After three days in his brother's company Schalk was won over.

The British had initiated a scheme whereby Jewish ex-soldiers who had joined the Allied forces in the Middle East could receive entry certificates to Palestine, and Schalk linked up with a group of former Free Czech Army men traveling from Pilsen to Naples for onward shipment to Alexandria. On June 20, 1946, he arrived in Palestine, just over two years behind Citron.

A few more of those who had sailed with them from Bratislava would follow, among them the Auschwitz survivor Sidney Fahn; but Schalk's arrival—however different in spirit from Citron's—was essentially the end of the odyssey of the *Pentcho*.

For Schalk, as for the others, it had been as much a voyage of discovery as a flight from persecution. And inevitably, what those who took part in that voyage had discovered—about themselves as individuals and about the world and the Jews' place in it—was not always the same.

For some, existing beliefs had solidified into unshakable convictions; for others, ideological fervor had given way to considered pragmatism. For some, the Nazi terror would forever be the criterion of Gentile hostility; for others, the basic humanity of the Italians would seem a more appropriate measure. For some, a nation-state—either as a refuge in which to hide or as a secure base from which to venture—was the only answer to the Jewish situation; for others, the Diaspora—with or without assimilation—would remain a desirable habitat.

In short, some of the passengers of the *Pentcho* had been tempered by the fire from which they had escaped, while others were merely singed. But none remained unaffected—and none would ever forget.

But the rest of the world, both Jewish and Gentile, did forget—if indeed they ever knew. For in the immediate postwar years, shipload after shipload of "illegal" immigrants would follow the *Pentcho* people to Palestine from the ruins of Nazi Europe in a well-financed, brilliantly organized and expertly led campaign by the mainstream Zionists. Amid the glare of sympathetic world publicity which was to surround that massive "ingathering," nobody would remember the handful of men and women who had boarded a derelict riverboat and, unobserved and virtually unsupported, had blazed the trail while Hitler was at the peak of his power.

Epilogue

In the summer of 1983, the *Pentcho* people held a reunion
to mark the fortieth anniversary of their liberation from the
camp at Ferramonti. Of the 514 men, women and children
who had been cast away on Kamilanisi, about 200 were still
living, and since two-thirds of these were residents or citizens
of the State of Israel—the rest being scattered across the globe,
from America to Australia—the reunion was in Tel Aviv.

It took place at a particularly anguished moment in the
thirty-five-year history of the Jewish state. Life there had always been marked by anxiety and tension, for Israel's existence had been established and its security maintained only
at enormous and continuing cost. But now, in the aftermath
of the Lebanese invasion, which had so damaged the country's reputation abroad, political, religious and social con-
flicts were tearing at the national consensus, and it had become clear that despite the peace treaty with Egypt, the grim
cycle of war with the Arab world had not been broken.

The country was in a bitter, defensive mood which, inevitably, had its effect on the modest *Pentcho* reunion. Yet the

occasion was able to evoke a powerful sense of the hope and idealism which had attended the birth of the state and of the strength and courage which had sustained it.

The bonds of affection—love, perhaps—that exist between these elderly men and women who had shared an indelible experience all those years ago were palpable. To witness the unaffected pleasure with which they greeted and embraced each other was a warming experience. "We're a family," explained Willi Klopfer. "We look after each other. It's a very close relationship."

The ambience and the babel of languages—German, Hungarian and Slovak intermixed with Hebrew—were considerably more Central European than Middle Eastern, and it took no great flight of the imagination to picture the *Pentcho* people as they had been that May morning in 1940 when the old sidewheeler churned away from the winter port at Bratislava.

There was Imi Lichtenfeld, still unmistakably the athlete despite his seventy-three years, his face permanently twisted and scarred by the three operations he had undergone in Alexandria to remove infected bone and tissue from around his left ear; especially for a handsome man, proud of his looks, that was no small disfigurement. But his body retains the stealthy grace of a panther, and one can sense that if called upon it could still respond with the speed and accuracy of an assassin's knife.

For more than twenty years following independence, he was the Israeli armed forces' chief instructor in unarmed combat, teaching a system which he developed and refined himself to generations of instructors who in turn taught it to the commandos, paratroopers and other special forces who have given Israel an almost legendary preeminence in their particular brand of warfare.

The system, called Krav Marga, is so lethal that unlike the other martial arts, it is never practiced as a competitive sport.

Yet Lichtenfeld gives the impression of an essentially unassertive, peaceable man, unwilling to speak ill, or to hear ill, of anyone. Although long retired from the army, he is still instructing at a government sports and physical-training center, and despite his years is trying to raise the capital to open a center of his own in Natanya.

There was the nimble-witted Oskar (now Yehezkel) Salomon, another whom the years have treated kindly, intense and wiry as he was when young, now a resident of Israel after more than thirty years in America.

After serving as a civilian interpreter with the U.S. Army in North Africa and then joining the Free Czech Army for the liberation of Europe, he had found his way after the war first to Cuba and then to America, arriving in New York in 1947 without money or a trade—endowed with nothing, in fact, but his native energy and enormous *chutzpah*.

On Manhattan's 47th Street, he persuaded the proprietor of a diamond-cutting establishment—a breed with eyes as hard as the stones they deal in—to give him a job. The fact that he had absolutely no experience in this demanding craft seems to have held no terrors for him.

One error at the workbench can ruin a stone worth thousands, and no one guilty of such an offense would ever get a second chance in the close-knit diamond trade. But somehow Oskar managed to survive in the sweatshops of 47th Street, learning as he went, until eventually he graduated as a full-fledged craftsman to a well-paid and secure post as a stone setter at Tiffany's, the Fifth Avenue jewelers, so far removed in style if not in distance from the gemstone jungle a few blocks away.

After some years with Tiffany's he started up his own business before retiring in 1981, when he came to live in Israel with his American wife, Rose, making his home in Natanya, where many other veterans of the *Pentcho* live.

There was Berta Ehrlich, well into her eighties, and refreshingly bright and vigorous for her age—the mother of Walti Ehrlich, who renamed himself Avram Orly, and of the baby boy, born on the way from Rhodes to Italy, whom she named Benito but who is better known as Benny, which sounds rather less exotic to Israeli ears.

She was in mourning for her older son, who had died of natural causes the year before. Orly had risen to national distinction as a major general in the Israeli Army, his last post before retirement having been as "Coordinator" of the territories occupied by the Israelis in the 1967 Six-Day War, a *supremo* to whom the military governors of the West Bank, Gaza and the Golan Heights were responsible.

If anyone had predicted, when the *Pentcho* people were escaping down the Danube in their decrepit old sidewheeler, or when they were huddled together on Kamilanisi facing starvation and death, that one of the youngest among them would someday rule over a subject people in territory occupied by a Jewish army, he would surely have been laughed to derision.

Another amazingly durable *Pentcho* veteran, Gisella Farkas—widowed these twenty years, but spry and vivacious at eighty-three—was present too, still known to all as "Mamouka." Accompanying her was Karci, now gray-haired and a grandfather, but still quick and boyish, so that one can well imagine that to her he remains the bright, inquisitive child she took aboard the *Pentcho* all those years ago.

Karci (more formally, Haim) Farkas, an importer of marble, granite and similar construction materials, is the unofficial secretary and recording angel of the *Pentcho* people, keeping track of their whereabouts, notifying them of forthcoming reunions—which are to continue until 1990, the fiftieth anniversary of their departure from Bratislava—and removing their names from his active file when, one by one, they drop from the tree of life.

Looking back on the days when she did menial work in

the camp at Ferramonti to pay for his English and *Torah* lessons, his mother deplores, laughing mischievously, that he is neither particularly fluent in English nor especially attentive to his religious obligations.

And there was Sidney Fahn, the Auschwitz survivor.

If one had been asked to pick out the one man from among the 150 people present at the reunion who looked as though he had been through the hell of Hitler's camps, Fahn is perhaps the last person one would have chosen. A bulky seventy-one-year-old, with a genial, bearlike manner and the remains of the powerful physique that had enabled him to endure the savage hardships of life in the *Lagers,* he quite lacks the desiccated, haunted look so many concentration-camp survivors carry with them to the grave like the numbers tattooed on their forearms. Sidney Fahn wears his scars where they cannot be seen.

He came to Israel from Bratislava in 1949 with his second wife, Lili, and his mother. His father's talent for survival had finally failed him at the end of 1944 when he was shot in a final pogrom in which even "protected" Jews were engulfed. But Berta Fahn was sent to the "model" concentration camp at Theresienstadt, where conditions were less harsh than elsewhere, and she survived.

Among the belongings she took to the camp with her were the treasured photographs of Sidney and his doomed bride, taken on their wedding day in Rhodes, and of their baby son, Shani, which she had received by courtesy of the Wehrmacht commander, General Kleemann. In later years she used to say that those pictures—reminders of a life beyond the misery and torment of her existence in Theresienstadt—had sustained her and made her survival possible. Evidently, she also had unusual physical strength, for she lived on in Israel until 1982, when she died peacefully, aged one hundred.

As for Sidney himself, he had opened a tannery shortly

after his arrival and had prospered over the years. He is retired now and likes to travel abroad with his wife. "We go to Europe every year," he says, "but never to Germany, never to Austria. Although I don't usually talk of it, I carry the memories of the camps with me always. They will stay with me till I die."

A handful of the many former comrades who chose to make their lives in the postwar Diaspora attended the reunion, among them Ferdinand Lanes, who now lives in Venezuela, Louis Hofstadter from California, Alex Goldberger from Brooklyn and others. But for most, the trip to Israel was too long or too costly, or else the timing was not convenient.

Marcel Friedmann, a travel agent in Cleveland, Ohio, was one of the "absent friends." Of those not living in Israel, he seems to be the most nostalgic about the *Pentcho* experience. He lived for a while in the Jewish state, in the years immediately after independence, but emigrated to the United States in the 1950s because, as he frankly admits, "life was too difficult in Israel."

To those Israelis who resist the temptation, or do not get the opportunity, to return to the Diaspora, those who do are known as *yordim*—a faintly pejorative term implying a "going down." A desire to compensate and make the point that he has not broken faith with the ideals of his youth perhaps accounts for Marcel's enthusiasm and punctiliousness about keeping in touch with his old comrades.

Over the years, he has maintained contacts not just with ex-shipmates in Israel and the United States, but also with the handful who went back to Czechoslovakia after the war and stayed there, among them Yosef Hercz, who rose in the medical profession to become chief surgeon at one of Prague's biggest hospitals. Marcel even went to the trouble to seek out

Zalan Petnehazy, the Hungarian naval officer who wrote the article recalling how he piloted the *Pentcho* across the frontier into Yugoslavia from Hungary.

Untypically, Marcel admits to a deep nostalgia for his native land, despite the death of his parents in the Holocaust. Perhaps, having been a country boy brought up on his father's farm, he had a closer relationship to the soil of Slovakia than was possible for his largely city-bred fellow travelers.

In New York City, the *Pentcho*'s dentist, Ladislav Kurti, now Dr. Leslie Curtis, a psychiatrist, looks back on his experiences aboard the *Pentcho,* and later as an *internato di guerra* and a partisan with Tito's forces, with an air of bemusement, as though he cannot quite believe it happened to him. Nonetheless, his recall is acute and precise, and his recollections studded with sharp images.

One of those Jews who straddle Israel and America, he follows his occupation and makes his home in New York, while maintaining an apartment in Jerusalem.

Although his parents died in the Holocaust, his two sisters, Gisella and Elisabeth—news of whose deportation had spurred him to make his ill-fated attempt to escape from Rhodes— survived more than two years in Auschwitz. Because of their bookkeeping and secretarial skills they had the good fortune to be assigned to the camp administration, which meant that they were housed in the block occupied by SS women guards. There, although they had to sleep in the cellar and were constantly abused and ill-treated, they were able to keep themselves adequately fed and meticulously clean, thus warding off infection and disease.

The romantic Grete Ehrenfeld also lives in New York City with Adolf Kellner, the Ferramonti camp interpreter, whom she married in Italy after the war, following the breakup of her first marriage to the Roman Catholic convert Edmondo Verstandig.

Grete's parents went to Palestine with Citron's group in 1944. Grete and Kellner—an actor, singer and comedian better known by his stage name, John Garson—followed them there in 1949. But after four years, unable to make a living on the stage in Israel, the Kellners moved to the United States, where they have lived ever since, except for eleven years in Italy.

Grete recalls that in Bari, shortly after the war, she again met Antonio Ariano, the dashing camp guard with whom she had fallen so madly in love on Rhodes. On later acquaintance, and out of uniform, he seemed a good deal less compelling. "He wore loud, flashy clothes and seemed barely literate," says Grete, now a handsome sixty-two-year-old.

"I could see what a disaster it would have been if I had married him. Thank goodness they wouldn't let him do it."

In another part of New York—although they had not seen each other for thirty years—lives her erstwhile fiancé, Karol (now Charles) Hoffmann. He has never married, living alone in a high-rise apartment block, surrounded by his collection of paintings and mementos of his peripatetic life as a travel agent.

Like virtually all the young men who broke away from Citron's group after the liberation of Ferramonti and attached themselves to the Allied forces, he found the lure of the Western Diaspora stronger than the attractions of Israel, and when the chance came to emigrate to America after the war, he seized it.

After a second romance which ended unhappily he gave up thoughts of marriage. His work provided him plenty of movement, color and variety. But now that he is retired and alone, "there's not much left but memories."

Also living a solitary existence in America, aged eighty-three, is Daniel Hamburger, the refugee from Germany who managed to buy himself a place on the *Pentcho*. Another life-long bachelor, he makes his home in a kosher rooming house in Cleveland.

Although maintaining the outward observances of his religion and nearing the end of his life, he professes no more interest now than he did in 1940 in going to Israel. He considers himself fortunate to have had the opportunity to spend the second half of his life in America as a result of President Roosevelt's decision in 1944 to admit 1,000 Jewish refugees to the United States from a displaced persons' camp near Naples.

"I was never a Zionist," he says, "so why should I think to go to Palestine when the door was open to the United States?"

Hamburger has no nostalgic feelings whatsoever about the voyage of the *Pentcho* and little regard for the men who ran it. "Not Schalk, not Citron had anything to do with our survival," he says. "It was sheer luck."

And so to the antagonistic coleaders of the *Pentcho* expedition.

On arrival in Palestine, Schalk had felt no obligation to get involved in the struggle for independence. Although he had no doubt that the Jews must build a state of their own on their ancestral soil, he was, after all, almost forty years old. He'd had his fill of fighting, all the way from North Africa to southern Germany, and anyway, "my experience with the *Pentcho* transport had disillusioned me."

Also, he had grown to like and respect the British, with whom he had served, and whatever his views on their unwanted presence in Palestine, he had no relish for the idea of taking British lives. Barely a month after his arrival, Irgun terrorists under the overall command of Menachem Begin, the onetime Polish Betar leader, blew up the King David Hotel in Jerusalem, which housed British military headquarters. Ninety-one people died in the blast, including 41 Arabs, 28 Britons and 17 Jews.

That incident drove the last nail into the coffin of Schalk's militancy, deciding him finally to take no part in the underground war against the British. "I was passive, absolutely passive," he recalls quite candidly.

Schalk married and settled down in Nahariyah, a northern coastal resort founded by prewar refugees from Hitler's Germany, and after two years working for his brother's firm he joined the Israel Asbestos Corporation, rising to become its export manager.

Today, the once-raffish "Zolli" lives a life of suburban rectitude in a geometrically neat villa, surrounded by a meticulously clipped lawn—an environment reflecting the Teutonic values of the German Jews, among them his wife, who still dominate the life of Nahariyah.

At seventy-eight he has hardly a single gray hair and is without any obvious physical disabilities, although, of course, the years have slowed him down. Now that he is retired, his great interest in life seems to be his two grandchildren—"my best friends," he calls them.

Despite the bitterness and disillusion he claims still to feel about the whole *Pentcho* episode, he never misses a reunion, and he moved easily among the crowd at the Writers' House in Tel Aviv, greeting old comrades with obvious pleasure.

Between him and Citron, though, some of the old tensions obviously persist. "He's a very good boy," murmurs Schalk, with a wry smile and the lofty condescension of a seventy-eight-year-old man of the world toward an unseasoned youth of sixty-six. As he sat at the head table during the reunion ceremonies, Schalk calmly opened a magazine and began to read while Citron made his speech.

It was a speech full of fire and passion, interlarded with old Betar slogans and the shibboleths of the Zionist faith on which Citron grew up and which, as he says, is still his "only religion." Yehoshua Halevi, as he now is, remains the single-minded, unswerving radical-nationalist he was in his youth. And despite Schalk's pointed demonstration, it was plain that for the survivors of the *Pentcho*, "Citi" (for that is what they still call him) has retained much of the old charisma: he is still the hero of the *Pentcho* odyssey.

But life, in its treatment of heroes, tends to be somewhat less than indulgent, and Citron, who brought so much in the way of zeal, youth, energy and leadership to the country of his dreams, never achieved the prominence there that might have been expected for him.

It has not been due to any lack of fervor, for Citron is nothing if not a patriot. True, when he joined the Irgun, aged almost twenty-seven, he was felt to be a little elderly for active service, but he played an energetic staff role in planning and intelligence, earning himself a place on the British "wanted" list. With a price on his head, he spent much of the next four years living underground, moving from one safe house to another, often in disguise, and toward the end of the Mandate traveling abroad on arms-procurement and illegal-immigration missions.

It was an especially difficult time for Shosha, who bore two children in those years while still living, in conditions of considerable hardship, in the converted garage in Natanya. But she too found time to devote to the cause, carrying messages for the Irgun and nursing young fighters wounded in action against the British security forces.

Israel's declaration of independence and the Arab invasion of May 1948 found Citron-Halevi on an Irgun mission in Munich. He dropped what he was doing and hurried home to join the fledgling Israeli Army. "I didn't want to have to tell my grandchildren that I sat out the War of Independence in Germany," he says.

After the war he might have remained in the army and had a brilliant military career, but for his bitterness over an internecine incident in the summer of 1948. During a lull in the war with the Arabs, old hostilities between the Labor establishment and the Revisionists had erupted in a pitched battle between the Irgun and the army over the contents of an Irgun arms ship called the *Altalena*. Sixteen Irgun men were killed and dozens wounded, including two of Citron's men from the *Pentcho,* Feri and Turo Neumann.

Outraged by this affair, Citron vowed that he would never make his career in an army whose commanders would order their men to fire upon fellow Jews.

In politics, too, Citron found his way barred by principles on which he would not yield. For a while after the War of Independence, he was an official of Herut, Begin's right-wing opposition party, which offered him a "realistic" place on its electoral list, meaning that he would stand a good chance of becoming a member of the Knesset. But Citron understood what all politicians in Israel come to realize—that it is impossible to form a government without the support of one or more of the religious parties—and opposed as ever to rabbinical interference in secular affairs, he felt unable to make the compromises this would involve and declined the offer. Today more than ever he is disturbed by the stranglehold the religious parties—"blackmailers," as he calls them—have on Israeli life.

As a member of an outsider group, in the formative years of the Jewish state, he could not hope for any kind of government appointment. So to support his growing family, Citron took a job with the Bank Ben Leumi in 1956 and rose to become manager of one of its branches. Now officially retired, he works part time as a welfare officer for the same institution, attending to the problems of widows and fellow pensioners.

He lives alone in the modest apartment in Rishon-le-Zion where Shosha died of a stroke in December 1981. "She didn't have an easy life with me," he admits.

Like Citron himself, Shosha clearly mellowed little with the years, leaving behind the impression of a "woman of courage" in the Biblical mold—energetic, busy with her charities and her grandchildren, though racked by chronic migraines, and as strong, stubborn and unbending as her husband. Perhaps more so.

"She couldn't bear injustice or dishonesty," Citron recalls, "and would never hesitate to show her outrage in public whenever she came across instances of either. I was much easier and more tolerant of people's weaknesses. Sometimes"—and here he laughs ruefully—"I was a little afraid of her myself."

In his compact, still energetic frame Citron embodies much of the rocklike strength that characterizes the country in whose creation he played his part—and many of its inner contradictions. He remains an unblushing hard-liner, believing that any hint of territorial or political compromise with Palestinian nationalism is tantamount to treason, equating PLO terrorism with Nazi persecution of the Jews.

And although he cannot, as an atheist, believe that the Land of Israel belongs to the Jews by Divine gift, he is adamant that their right to the land is beyond dispute and that Zionism cannot be equated with the desire of another dispossessed people for a state of their own on their ancestral soil. "It's not just nationalism," he says. "There's a difference not simply of degree, but of kind, because the Jews have suffered longer and more deeply than any other people and because they have made such unusual contributions to the rest of mankind."

If Citron, the ideologue, is totally committed to the embattled nation he helped to create, he seems nevertheless dismayed by its internal divisions. By contrast, Schalk, the pragmatist, appears able to accept fractiousness as a regrettable but not necessarily fatal national character trait.

With just a hint of a sardonic smile, he says, "No one knows the Jewish mentality better than I do, as a result of my experience with the *Pentcho;* if you have three Jews, you have five opinions. So to me the State of Israel is a source of both pride and wonder. That such an unruly people could have achieved all this is the greatest miracle of the past two thousand years."

A Note on Sources

The foregoing account of the voyage of the *Pentcho,* the events leading up to it and its aftermath, is based largely on the personal recollections of those involved, a large number of whom are fortunately still alive and in possession of all their faculties—most importantly from the author's point of view, their memories.

As any journalist, policeman, sociologist or mere student of human nature can attest, no two people will give exactly the same account of an incident that has occurred as recently as a week or two previously, let alone of something that happened more than forty years ago, and the author has had to take this *"Rashomon"* factor into account in sorting through his notes and tape recordings of the dozens of interviews he has conducted with *Pentcho* survivors.

Inevitably, there were discrepancies in the different accounts, but rarely did these concern important matters, where invariably there was a reassuring unanimity. On points of detail, where recollections did sometimes diverge, the author has chosen the version that seemed to him most consistent with the known facts or, in the absence of inferential support, the one on which the majority of witnesses agreed. Whatever inconsistencies there may appear to be in the narrative can be ascribed to the ambiguities of real life rather than lapses of memory or intent to deceive or embellish.

Wherever documents have existed—diaries, logbooks, letters to and from home, ship's orders, unpublished memoirs and the like—these have, of course, been consulted and, where appropriate, quoted. The result is that this is not a work of "faction"—the fictionalized re-creation of an actual event or series of events—but a true work of nonfiction.

One of the things on which all sources for this book were

agreed was the humanity and basic decency of the Italians, including officials of Mussolini's Fascist regime, in their dealings with the *Pentcho* people and with Jewish refugees and internees in general.

Necessarily, the *Pentcho* story gives only a very fleeting glimpse of this little-known aspect of Holocaust history. Suffice it to say here that despite the anti-Semitic laws foisted upon them by Mussolini, the Italian people, with few exceptions, never allowed themselves to be infected by the virus of racialism that ran rampant through Europe before and during World War II. Not only did they refuse to go along with their ally Hitler's plans for solving the "Jewish Question" by extermination: they actively opposed those plans at all levels and in all areas of Europe where they held sway as an occupying power. That is another story which deserves to be told in full elsewhere.

As far as the *Pentcho* people are concerned, they are all well aware that had they fallen into the hands of the Nazis, or of any of Nazi Germany's other allies or puppets, their fate would have been very different, and at their regular reunions, they never omit to make reference to this.

The author wishes to thank all those quoted in the text for allowing him to delve into their memories, sometimes of deeply personal and painful matters. Although many of them also offered treasured snapshots, the author is particularly grateful to Willi Klopfer, Haim Laszlo, Marcel Friedmann and Charles Hoffmann for allowing him to plunder their albums.

Thanks are due also to Professor Livia Rothkirchen, whose collection of Nazi and Slovak government documents published in *The Destruction of Slovak Jewry* (Jerusalem: Yad Vashem, 1968) tells the grim and little-known story of what happened to the Jews who remained in the puppet Slovakian Republic between 1940 and 1945.

The author would also like to acknowledge Dr. Willi Perl's permission to draw briefly from his memoir *The Four Front War* (New York: Crown Publishers, 1978) and also to thank Eliyahu Galazer and Hillel Kook, a.k.a. Peter Bergson, for their guidance on matters pertaining to clandestine emigration from

Europe to Palestine before and during World War II, and Ethel Broido and Regina Kaspitsky for their help in translation.

Among the institutions that have been helpful are the Wiener Oral History Library in New York, in whose archives the author first stumbled across the story of the *Pentcho;* the Jabotinsky Institute in Tel Aviv, where he found "orders of the day" and other documents salvaged from the *Pentcho,* and the Yad Vashem library in Jerusalem, where he found firsthand accounts of the deportation and destruction of the tiny Jewish community of Rhodes which provided invaluable corroboration for Sidney Fahn's otherwise unsupported account.

Finally, thanks are also due to Gloria Loomis, my agent, for her unflagging enthusiasm and encouragement, and Fred Hills, my editor, for his sharp eye and cool judgment.

New York
March 1984